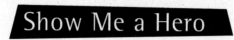

Show Me a Hero

Show Me a Hero

A Tale of
Murder,
Suicide,
Race,
and
Redemption

Lisa Belkin

LITTLE, BROWN AND COMPANY
Boston New York London

First Edition

Library of Congress Cataloging-in-Publication Data
Belkin, Lisa
Show me a hero : a tale of murder, suicide, race, and redemption / by Lisa Belkin.

p.   cm.
ISBN 0-316-08805-6 (hc)
1. Yonkers (N.Y.)—Race relations.   2. Yonkers (N.Y.)—Social conditions.
3. Yonkers (N.Y.)—Politics and government.   4. Afro-Americans—
New York (State)—Yonkers—Social conditions.   5. Poor—New York (State)—
Yonkers—Social conditions.   6. Public housing—New York (State)—Yonkers—
History—20th century.   7. Social conflict—New York (State)—Yonkers—
History—20th Century.
I. Title
F129.Y5B45   1999
305.8'009747277—dc21   98-41822

10 9 8 7 6 5 4 3 2 1

MV-NY

Book design by Unju Sim Goetemann

Printed in the United States of America

To my guys,
Alex, Evan, *and* Bruce,
who make our house a home

Also by Lisa Belkin : First, Do No Harm

Show me a hero, and I will write you a tragedy. . . .

—*F. Scott Fitzgerald*

CONTENTS

Foreword

The townhouses at the center of this tale are ten minutes from my house—a quick trip down the Saw Mill River Parkway, then a few more miles east. It is a short distance, which is why their story caught my interest in the first place. And, at the same time, it is a long way, an instructive, compelling journey between two worlds.

I am sitting in my house right now, gazing out at the nearby woods, as is my habit when I write. It is a calming, cozy view, and I am struck full force, as I have been so often while working on this book, by the primal power of home. I was a first-time homeowner and a protective new parent back in 1992, when I read a small notice in my local newspaper about a public housing lottery. I knew just a little about the townhouses at the time—that they were ordered into existence by a federal judge so that poor, minority public-housing residents could live on the white, middle-class side of town. I had been living back in Texas while the city of Yonkers fiercely fought that order, but even fifteen hundred miles away I had memories of the nightly reports on the national news, of the hundreds of people, chanting and screaming, faces contorted with hate. Now the housing was built. And it was near me.

The lottery would be held to determine which families would be allowed to move into the new townhouses. Out of curiosity—partly fear for my own life's investment, partly a reporter's sense that this might make a good story—I went. At the front of the room was an ancient bingo drum, filled with the names of the hopeful. I sat in the middle of the electric crowd, watching that fateful drum spin.

I met Alma Febles that night, a magnetic young mother, the

same age as myself, and one of the women whose stories fill this book. I was moved as she talked of wanting a bedroom all her own, a place for her children, a haven, a sanctuary, a home. Her yearning, the yearning so palpable throughout the School Street gym that night, was familiar because it mirrored my own. I had felt an exquisite completeness when I moved my family into our house. Everywhere I looked, I saw not only the present, but also the future: the driveway where my son, still an infant, would someday ride his bike. The single sunny patch of yard where my husband would grow our vegetable garden. The porch where we would barbecue, the basement where we would assemble toy trains, the nearby woods—those sheltering, welcoming woods— where we would take long walks.

Touched by Alma's dreams, I found myself rooting for her, fiercely. As the bingo drum grew emptier, and her name had not been called, I worried for her. Even as I did, however, I recognized the muddled impurity of my concern. I believed in the right of this woman to have her home. But what if bulldozers were to clear a site for that home in the trees so close to my own house?

It was this clash of dreams that I took home that night. I have carried it with me during five years of research and writing. During those years I have described the Yonkers housing experiment countless times to friends and acquaintances. Nearly every listener has asked the same question: Did it work?

It is, I have learned, a deceptively straightforward question with meanings that vary with the questioner. Did it work? Did the neighborhood fall to pieces? Did the lives of the tenants improve on the east side of town? Did property values fall? Did crime rates increase? Did the homeowners learn to accept the tenants? Did the tenants befriend the homeowners? Did the judge come to understand that he had done the wrong thing? Did the city come to understand that he had done the right thing? Were the results worth ten years and $42 million? Is Yonkers a model for the rest of the country? Or is it an example of good intentions gone wrong? Did it work?

Faced with this spectrum of questions, I had to answer a core question of my own: What did *I* mean by "Did it work?" Where would I look when deciding whether this broad-stroke experiment was a failure or a success? One luxury of journalism is distance—the ability to observe, record, judge, then move on. But the sense of home that led me to the lottery in the first place has also limited that freedom and made me wonder what my conclusion would be if I could not walk away.

Over time, I came to see the question as a single thought composed of two opposite but intertwined strands: Did it work for the people who moved in? And did it work for those who were already there?

"It's all about home," I answered. "If the tenants can find the comfort of a real home. If the homeowners don't lose the sanctity of theirs. Then, it worked."

That was the measure that guided my reporting, a measure I think of often as I look through my window and out into the trees. Did it work? Did it grant Alma a place to plant her dreams, and did it do so without trampling on other, equally passionate dreams that had already taken root? Did it allow the newcomers a chance to leave the past behind, while, at the same time, allowing the neighbors to keep it close at hand? Did it give a lucky few a safe spot in the world? And did it do so—is it possible to do so—without sacrificing the insulating, isolating woods?

Westchester, New York
September 1998

Show Me a Hero

Prologue, 1992

The pipe bomb was small as pipe bombs go, but the explosion could be heard from several blocks away—a sharp bang as rows of factory-fresh ceramic tiles shattered into a pile of razor-edged rubble. Neighbors who were drifting off to sleep sat upright, awake. Family members who were preparing for bed looked at each other first with questions, then with certainty that they had the answer. "I guess somebody is trying to blow up the new housing," one man joked to his wife. But it wasn't a joke. That's exactly what someone was trying to do.

Everyone heard the bang, but only one person called the police. The dispatcher decided it was an electrical transformer problem, so there were no sirens, no searches in the night. The next morning, crews of workmen arrived at the sprawling site, which had once been the overgrown ball fields of an abandoned school, and which now held the nearly finished shells of forty-eight cream- and lemon-colored townhouses. Seeing the damage, they, too, called the police, who quickly rimmed the area in yellow and black tape, and searched the wounded building for clues.

Soon the FBI was there, and the Federal Marshal's Office. The Bureau of Alcohol, Tobacco and Firearms. The Westchester County Bomb Squad. The director of the Yonkers Municipal Housing Authority. Assorted politicians who came to say "I told you so." The roads at the site were not yet paved, so each arriving official had to walk through the deep red mud to what, on the architect's models, was intended to be a tiny front lawn. They stood in the dirt outside Apartment 120, relieved to see the townhouse was still standing.

The pipe bomb had been placed on the outer windowsill of a

3

ground-floor bathroom, where the final grouting had been laid only days before. The window was blown out, the sill was charred and destroyed, the tiles on the floors and walls were shattered, and a mirrored door of the medicine cabinet was knocked from its hinges. Parts of the bomb were found a hundred feet away. Most chilling, however, was not the damage done, but the damage that could have been. Less than four feet from the windowsill was an open gas line. It was not working. But there was no way for the bomber to know that.

The crowd grew, as it always does in Yonkers. Some of the onlookers were nearby homeowners who had heard the explosion the night before. Others were just curious, drawn by the flashing emergency lights. They hadn't wanted these buildings from the start—hadn't wanted to be part of this court-concocted experiment in social history. A few were, not so secretly, glad about the bomb. Maybe it would do what their years of protests couldn't and cause the housing literally to crumble. And yet, it was hope all but extinguished by fear. Any impulse to gloat was stemmed by the stark reality of a bomb, just blocks away from their homes.

Eventually, the work crews took a break for lunch. But everyone else stayed for most of the day. The authorities, searching. The politicians, talking. And the neighbors standing, staring, from behind the double-height security fence.

Part One

The Explosion

1988 – 1991

1988

The Youngest Mayor in America

Nicholas Wasicsko had always wanted to be mayor of Yonkers. Growing up in a two-family house on the west side—the wrong side—of the Saw Mill River Parkway, he was not one of those who set his sights on escape to the east. Instead, he looked even farther west, to the Beaux Arts spires of City Hall. Bright, brash, and confident, Nick let other kids in his lower-middle-class Yonkers neighborhood have dreams. Nick had plans.

Both he and his younger brother, Michael, stopped growing at about 5'6", but that did not keep them from spending the afternoons of their teenage years on the basketball courts of a nearby schoolyard. During one pickup game, Nick mentioned casually that he would run the city one day. For months after that, his on-court nickname was "The Mayor." Over time, the joke wore thin and was eventually forgotten—by everyone but Nick.

He sensed early on that he had a knack, something that he didn't understand that made things go his way. At age ten, he talked the other paperboys in his neighborhood into letting him take over their routes, and when he had gained control of a large chunk of territory, he hired even younger boys to actually deliver the papers, pocketing the difference. By the age of thirteen, he had his own checking account, but because he was underage it had to be cosigned by his mother, who was a teacher's aide, and his father, who was a factory worker.

He paid for four years at Manhattan College by working at a Carvel plant near the river. When he started, he was driving a refrigerated delivery rig, but soon he had talked his way up the ladder and sat in a chair behind a microphone telling other workers what to load into which truck. He saved for New York University

Law School by working as a Westchester County police officer. Fighting bad guys did not pay as much as freighting ice cream, and he needed tens of thousands of dollars in loans to make up the difference, but the pictures of him in uniform in front of a squad car, he reasoned, could certainly help his political career.

That career began in force in 1985, when he won a seat on the City Council using the deliberately vague campaign slogan "Don't get mad, get a new councilman." He was twenty-six years old, with a baby face that he tried to mature with a slash of black mustache, but he still looked years younger than he was. He had not yet finished law school when he was elected, and, adding to the kid-goes-to-City-Hall image, he was still living with his mother.

He didn't do much as a councilman, mostly watched, listened, learned, and planned. Then, two years later, just five days after he passed the New York State bar exam, he stood on the traffic bridge over the Saw Mill and announced that he was not seeking reelection to the council. He was running for mayor, instead.

It was not, on the face of it, a rational decision—less the choice of a twenty-eight-year-old man than of that ten-year-old boy who had always wanted to be mayor. For one thing, the mayor of Yonkers was a largely symbolic position back in 1987, a bully pulpit with no real administrative power, a hot seat that received a lot of attention and an equal amount of blame. It was the city manager who hired and fired, who drew up the budget and signed the checks. The mayor was technically just the first among equals on the City Council. He had one vote, like everyone else, but he got to hold the gavel.

At $35,914 a year, it was considered a part-time job, one usually sought by more established men, successful in business, who were looking for a prestigious cap to their careers. Nick's opponent, Angelo Martinelli, was just such a man—a millionaire publisher who had held the mayor's office for twelve of the previous fourteen years. When Nick announced he was going to challenge all that money and history, no one in town took him seriously. Although Martinelli was a Republican, he got along just fine with the entrenched and powerful Democratic leader, so even Nick's own party was barely behind his candidacy. Both Nick and Martinelli

Show Me a Hero

had similar voting records, with one exception, one very important exception, but neither man would realize its importance until well into the campaign.

First Nick tried to portray the race as a referendum on Youth versus Age. But fifty-nine-year-old Martinelli, though twice as old as Nick, was hardly ancient, and the attempt fell flat. Then Nick tried to paint Martinelli as explosive and confrontational, but in Yonkers those qualities are not necessarily seen as negatives, so that didn't work, either. Soon, the local newspaper began to refer to Nick's "naive enthusiasm." He was a candidate in need of an issue.

Summer came and Nick had raised $5,170 in contributions. Martinelli had raised $67,388. The Wasicsko campaign organization was streamlined to the point of invisibility, consisting of Nick, Michael, and Jim Surdoval, a young political consultant who had helped out with Nick's first council race. The group was all generals and no troops. They did everything themselves.

"Isn't the candidate supposed to be telling *other* people to do this stuff?" Michael asked at two o'clock one morning as they drank coffee in an all-night copying center, where they were photocopying and folding thousands of brochures.

"*We* the people," Nick said, swatting his brother with a "Wasicsko for Mayor" flier.

The days were just as lonely. Everyone at City Hall thought Nick's political career was soon to be over, so they kept their distance, and he often felt as if no one in the building spoke to him at all. The only person who was consistently friendly was one of the secretaries, Nay Noe, a young Ecuadorian woman with a Filipina name. At the age of twenty, Nay was one of the few people at City Hall younger than Nick, and she was uncomfortable about being there. She had little interest in politics, but wound up with her very political job because, back then, she was still going to St. Peter's Church every Sunday. When Harry Oxman, the vice-mayor of the council, asked Father Duffell to find him a bilingual secretary, the priest thought of Nay.

She started her job as secretary to the council just after Nick started his mayoral campaign, and, at first, she saw his isolation as arrogance. Over time, she came to feel sorry for him. She saw how hard he was working in his dreary cubicle, returning all his constituents' phone calls, and, unlike some *other* members of the council, writing all his letters himself rather than expecting the secretaries to do it. Nay, who took in everything despite her seemingly guileless round face and innocent brown eyes, knew for certain what Nick only suspected — that he was being left out of meetings and deliberately not told about civic events that might help his campaign. She started to think of him as "the Lone Ranger sitting there all alone in the back." Maybe, she decided, politics interested her after all.

One evening, when all watchful eyes had left, Nay walked into Nick's office and said, "My parents have a house on Pier Street. Do you want to put a campaign sign on my house?" He sent Michael over with the sign a few days later. On her next trip into his office, she was bolder, and asked, "Do you need help on your campaign?" They spent part of the evening in front of the Shoprite on Riverdale Avenue, where Nay watched Nick shake strangers' hands. She was charmed by his enthusisam as he bounded up to shoppers, sometimes carrying their groceries to their cars if it meant they would take a few minutes to listen to his ideas. Soon it was not just Michael, Nick, and Jim, but Michael, Nick, Jim, and Nay.

The quartet worked hard, covering every part of the city. Nick even insisted on going into the projects, despite the fact that they traditionally had a much lower voter turnout than other parts of the city. Nay came along sometimes, to translate to residents who spoke Spanish. More often, Nick went there alone. His only company was his own determination — and the .38-caliber revolver he always wore strapped to his ankle, a habit left over from his days as a cop.

But it was not hard work that turned the campaign around in the middle of the summer. It was Judge Leonard B. Sand, who was running out of patience.

Federal court case 80 CIV 6761: *The United States of America and the Yonkers Branch of the National Association for the Advancement*

Show Me a Hero

of Colored People, et al., AGAINST *The Yonkers Board of Education, the City of Yonkers, and the Yonkers Community Development Agency* was filed back in 1980, when Nick Wasicsko was still driving ice-cream trucks and going to college. Though it would soon shatter his life and redefine his city, he paid little attention to the case at the time. Neither did most of the people in power in Yonkers. They were certain that this problem, like so many other nettlesome problems, did not ever have to be faced, but could be quietly made to go away.

Over time, *U.S. v. Yonkers* would come to stand for everything: Race. Class. Neighborhood. The American Dream. But back then, it was seen merely as "yet another" school desegregation case, albeit with a twist. Brought by the Justice Department in 1980, then joined by the NAACP, it charged that race determined location and quality of education in Yonkers, a charge brought increasingly often, and with mixed results, during the late 1970s. This case, however, did not stop there. The plaintiffs went on to make the unprecedented argument that the reason the schools of Yonkers were segregated was because the housing of Yonkers was segregated. Black and Hispanic children went to the same few schools because black and Hispanic families were forced to live in the same few neighborhoods, and any judicial order to change the schools would also have to change the neighborhoods.

The lottery that distributes cases at the Federal District Court in Manhattan handed this one off to Judge Leonard B. Sand, whose expertise had been in tax law before President Jimmy Carter appointed him to the bench in 1978. A reserved, elfin man, with silver hair and bushy, wizardly brows, Sand could not have been more of a contrast with the raucous and emotional city whose future was now his to shape. Sand was a member by marriage of the powerful Sulzberger family, which owned the *New York Times*. He was a wealthy man in his own right, too, an early partner in the prosperous law firm of Robinson, Silverman, Pearce, Aronsohn, Sand and Berman. Money, however, defined his world far less than ideas. Sand was an intellectual judge, one who reveled in reason and lived in his head. When he was not presiding over court business, he could be found padding around his office in worn leather slippers, and talking jurisprudence with his clerks the way others talk the stock market, or soap operas, or sports. "Now riddle me this," he would regularly say, asking questions rather than making statements, turning thoughts around in his brain, playing with words, delighting in this mental exercise—the law as a meticulously constructed puzzle.

To decipher this puzzle, this riddle, Sand heard the Yonkers case himself, without a jury, at the request of both sides. The trial took up most of 1983 and 1984: 93 days of testimony from 84 witnesses; 140 depositions; thousands of exhibits. By the end it was clear that the city's schools were segregated: twenty-three of the city's thirty-four public schools were over 80 percent minority or 80 percent white. And there was also little question that its housing was segregated: the southwest quadrant, which contained 97.7 percent of the city's public housing, also contained 80.7 percent of the city's minority population.

Sand's job, however, was not to decide if Yonkers was segregated, but *why* it was segregated, why this city of twenty-one square miles and 188,000 people, a city marginally larger than Little Rock or Dayton, came to have nearly all its minority citizens living within one square mile. Why the Saw Mill River Parkway, the sinuous, shaded road that divided east from west, became a barrier of sorts—white and working class to the east of it, black, brown, and poor to the west. If it was happenstance, then there was no wrong to be righted, no damage to be undone. But if it was intentional, the result of purposeful behavior on the part of the city, then Yonkers could be forced to make dramatic, difficult, history-making amends.

Sand decided that is was not happenstance. Yonkers looked the way it did, he ruled, because its politicians, acting on behalf of its very vocal east side voters, wanted it that way. He said so in a 657-page decision, the longest one he had ever written; it weighed three pounds, and contained 166 footnotes, five maps, and five appendices, and when the requisite duplicate copies were filed with the court in November 1985, they were too heavy to be lifted, and had to be wheeled from room to room in a shopping cart.

Most of that heft was a chronicle of what Sand saw as a forty-year pattern: housing sites were proposed for the white east side; outraged residents responded by packing the City Council meetings — 500, 700, sometimes 1,000 people at a time; council members ordered a search for other possible sites; the housing was eventually placed on the mostly minority, southwest side.

He didn't even see it as a close call. There was, he wrote, in the understated but unflinching tone of the judiciary, no "basis for doubt that City officials were aware that the course they were pursuing was one of segregation. . . . It is, to say the least, highly unlikely that a pattern of subsidized housing which so perfectly preserved the overwhelmingly white character of East Yonkers came about for reasons unrelated to race." That said, he ordered Yonkers to redraw the map, to refigure the jigsaw, to rework its view of itself, and to move some of its poor, minority residents from the poor, minority side of town, into public housing, to be built just for them, on the white, middle-class side of town.

Nick was a brand-new member of the City Council back when Sand first issued that order, and he was mostly a bystander to the headlines and hand-wringing at the time. The council voted to appeal the decision to a higher court. Nick voted for the appeal. Martinelli voted against. For a long time afterward, the problem was considered solved — it would somehow disappear into the court system, as so many of their problems had. There were civic spurts of outrage ("We never discriminated against anyone") and defensiveness ("Why is the judge picking on us for decisions made forty years ago?") but almost no self-reflection ("Did our policies cause harm?") and little concern that the new housing would ever actually be built. From where the council members and the voters sat, Sand's decision had nothing to do with *their* Yonkers.

That is because the monumental opinion, despite all its weight and evidence and insight, was missing one thing. The central fact of Yonkers, the one that is the key to all the others, is that it only *looks* like one city. It *acts* like thirty-eight separate cities, or, at best, a loose confederation of neighborhoods, each singular, organized, and proud. Dunwoodie, Seminary Heights, Wakefield Park, Kimball — home to secretaries, bus drivers, teachers, policemen. Lawrence Park West, Sunnyside Park, Beech Hill — where some of the houses are mansions and deer sightings are not uncommon. Runyon Heights—the only middle-class black neighborhood in town. Fleetwood—filled with co-ops and young professionals. Locust Hill—a longtime Hungarian neighborhood. Bryn Mawr, Woodstock Park—mostly Scottish and Irish. Park Hill—Italian. The Hollows—Slovak, Russian, Polish, and Hungarian.

Sand recognized this, but he did not understand it—not in the visceral, organic, unrepentant way that the people of Yonkers did. He saw such cliquishness as the way people lived until they learned how to live better. Born in 1928, Sand spent the first sixteen years of his life in the Bronx, in an apartment so close to Yankee Stadium that, from his bed, he could hear the crack of the bat against the ball. His neighborhood was working class and Jewish. Over by Fordham Road, nearly everyone was Catholic. To the east was a section called Brooke Avenue, and the Irish kids who lived there were called "the Brookies," he remembers, and "once in a while they would come over and we would have a brawl."

When he graduated, he went on to the New York University School of Commerce, which, at the time, was essentially a trade school, and he came out with a degree in accounting. Had it been an ideal world, however, and had he felt he had a choice, he would have taken a different road. "I really wanted to go to Columbia," he says, a place that represented to him the lyrical world of literature and words, rather than the practical world of balance sheets and numbers. But it was also a time of quotas and anti-Semitism, so the Jewish boy from the Bronx did not even bother to apply. That his life turned out just fine—Harvard Law School followed NYU, and partnership in a prestigious law firm followed that—does not dull the what-ifs.

So he ordered Yonkers to do better. To open its neighborhoods, its enclaves, its safe ethnic pockets. To let outsiders enter, and to give them a turn at transforming their lives. To aim toward that ideal world where no one felt rejected before he even had a chance to try. He did not see his decision as "judicial activism," although others would differ. He did not consider himself an activist at all, although others would disagree with that, too. No, he says, he did not start with a conclusion and work backward through a justifica-

Show Me a Hero

tion of that conclusion. He started with the facts, and was led by those facts to the only destination he could reasonably reach. But once there, he found it a comfortable place. It was the logical, rational, right thing to do.

The citizens of Yonkers, however, clearly didn't see it that way. The separateness that Sand saw as a limitation, they saw as a strength. They viewed their barriers and boundaries less as a way of excluding others, than as a way of defining themselves, providing a badge of belonging, a sense of place, a certainty of who they were and where they stood. Those taking comfort in this separateness did not think they were racist. They might have been, and some of the things they did made it look as if they were, but they insisted that this was not an issue of black and white. They did not need lectures on discrimination, they said, since being Italian or Irish or Polish meant a childhood filled with stories of grandparents who could not find jobs or homes or respect because of their accents and their names. Neither did they need lessons from the Bronx. Many of them had also lived a ball's throw from Yankee Stadium, more recently than Sand, and then fled to Yonkers as their neighborhoods became emblems of urban decay. This wasn't about race, they said. It was about their pride in overcoming the barriers this country places before all newcomers, and about the lives they had built — modest, perhaps, but theirs. Mostly it was about their fear that someone was trying to take it all away.

By 1987, when Nick Wasicsko decided to run for mayor, Yonkers was no closer to building the new housing than they had been when the order was first issued two years earlier. Trying to be patient, the judge allowed the city to decide the specifics of the plan: how many new units, where and by what date they would be built. But after numerous court-imposed deadlines came and went, Sand permitted the Justice Department and the NAACP to work out the details instead. On their say-so he ordered Yonkers to build two hundred units of low-income public housing and eight hundred units of moderate-income subsidized housing on the east side. Still trying to be patient, he asked the city to submit a list of specific construction sites. More deadlines were ignored. Yonkers had come to assume that stalling would work forever.

But just before Nick launched his campaign, Sand decided to shake up that assumption. He ruled that since city leaders were having such trouble finding appropriate housing sites, they should hire a consultant to do the choosing. The council conducted a nationwide search, which took a while, then interviewed numerous candidates, which took a while longer. Hours before Sand's Valentine's Day deadline, and much to the judge's surprise, the requisite consultant was actually chosen.

"They hired me," Oscar Newman would say, years later, of his $160-an-hour contract, "with the expectation that I would fail."

Newman still jokes that he got the job because, with his distinctive beard but no mustache, he looks remarkably like Judge Robert Bork, whose conservative views were not thought to be sympathetic to court-ordered public housing. More likely, the council members did not see past the other photo on the jacket of his book, *Defensible Space,* a photo that showed a public-housing project in St. Louis being blown to proverbial smithereens. The politicians who interviewed him came away believing that he would similarly implode the judge's plans to blight their neighborhoods.

If that is what they expected, they were surprised. *Defensible Space* is about using architecture to influence human patterns of behavior, and Yonkers was a chance for Newman to further test his theories on a very large, very public scale. A man of immense vision, immense presence, and immense ego, Newman brought to mind this question: If you think you're brilliant, and you are, is that conceit or merely clear-eyed recognition of the truth? The opposite of the judge in so many ways, Newman soon became one of Sand's closest advisers. They were not friends, because neither was the chummy sort, but Sand admired the brute force of Newman's ideas, and Newman, while he thought the judge far too restrained, recognized the power of the bench and saw in Sand's original decision material that could be worked with.

By spring, the judge had accepted Newman's central philosophy as his own. The large housing projects being planned for the east side were doomed by their very design, Newman argued, and would be a disaster both for the public-housing residents and the surrounding community. The future of public housing, he believed, was a "scattered site" model—small clusters of units that would blend into the community. There would be no shared public spaces, such as hallways or entryways. Every square foot, inside and out, would be private and assigned to individual tenants, meaning each tenant would feel responsible for, and proud of, what was his. At first, this change of plan pleased the members of the council, though not necessarily because they all agreed with the underlying theory. It takes more time to find numerous sites (Newman's plan called for eight) than it does to find one or two, giving the city more time to drag its heels.

Newman, however, found the sites after just a few days. Spending the city's money, he hired a helicopter and pilot and flew low over Yonkers, making maps of vacant areas of land. He identified twenty-six possible parcels, about forty acres altogether. It was pure coincidence, he said, that one of those parcels was next door to one recalcitrant councilman's house and a second was directly across the street from another councilman. The City Council, spending far more of the city's money, hired a team of lawyers, who discovered legal loopholes that would prevent most sites from being used. Newman went back to his maps and compiled a list of additional sites. The lawyers went back to the books and tried to reject those sites, too.

By July, Newman was no longer reporting to the City Council, but was working directly for the judge. What had begun as a three-month contract, for $55,000, had become an open-ended assignment, and the escalating bill was to be paid by Yonkers. Newman installed a separate line in his Great Neck, Long Island, office; Sand was the only person who had that number. Sand announced in open court that he would "keep a phone line open," for Newman; Newman used that line, calling once from the middle of a meeting at City Hall to tell the judge that officials were not answering his questions as he thought they should be answered.

With Newman at his side, Sand's language turned tougher. It

was at Newman's suggestion, for instance, that Sand placed a moratorium on four private commercial development projects that were to have brought an estimated $12 million in tax revenues to the city each year. If there was such a shortage of buildable land in the city, Sand scolded, what's all this talk about building a retail mall? An executive park? The city would first meet its federal obligations, thank you very much.

And, for good measure, Sand, who had threatened Yonkers with contempt fines before, repeated that threat but with greater specificity. The fines would begin at $100 and double every day, he warned. At that rate, the city's entire $337 million annual budget would be wiped out in twenty-two days.

In the escalating debate over the housing, Nick Wasicsko had found his issue—although it took him a while to figure that out. His slogan in this campaign was a variation of the one that had worked in his prior campaign: "Don't Get Mad, Get a New Mayor." Jim Surdoval had the slogan printed on several hundred lawn signs, and, to his astonishment, they were snapped up by east siders who wanted to hammer them into the grass in front of their homes. When the printed signs were gone, people started making their own. Nick was more than just a candidate. He was becoming a cause.

As a result, he began to spend more time campaigning on the east side, reminding voters of the single vote that separated him from Martinelli: the vote to appeal Sand's order. Martinelli believed the housing was "inevitable"; Nick believed the city, the voters, deserved a "second opinion."

As summer became fall, and the noise about the housing became louder, Nick Wasicsko found it easier to be heard. The speeches came more easily for him in the final days of the campaign. Practice had made him more relaxed. It also helped to feel that his audience was actually listening. He traveled from event to event, stressing his belief in the right to appeal, and never really saying what he would do if the appeal was denied. He knew he was leaving anti-housing voters with the impression that he was on their side, that he would continue their fight to the death, but the fact was, he didn't know what he would do. He thought he would be a good mayor. He wanted to be the mayor and the housing issue might allow him to become mayor. He would worry about the rest later.

On November 3, 1987, Nicholas Wasicsko defeated Angelo Martinelli by a vote of 22,083 to 20,617.

"I never thought I'd lose for one minute," he lied to reporters after the votes were counted.

Late on election night, Martinelli drove across town to see Wasicsko and concede the race in person. Shaking Nick's hand, he said, "The voters have lifted a tremendous burden off my shoulders and placed it on yours."

Public opinion polls showed that Nick was elected because of his stand on the housing. He was not the only one so elected. Of the incumbents considered moderate on the issue, four out of five were defeated. Every member-elect of the council was white, despite the fact that the districts had just been redrawn to encourage minority representation.

Nick won, voters told the pollsters, not because of who he was, but because of who he was not. He was not Angelo Martinelli. He knew that was why he won and he didn't care, just as he didn't care that he had $20,000 in law school debt and a new job that would pay him less than that, after taxes. All that mattered to him was that, at age twenty-eight, he was the youngest mayor in the country. He was "The Mayor" now, on and off the basketball court. In a few years, maybe he could change that title to congressman, or senator. In the distance he could see the governor's mansion and the White House.

The first thing Nick did as mayor-elect was ask Nay out to lunch. They were like two giddy kids, all youth and giggles, as they stepped into Louie's restaurant in South Yonkers, where they ran a gauntlet of well-wishers. Everyone in the place wanted to shake Nick's hand or slap his shoulder as he and Nay walked to their relatively private corner table.

When their waitress had come and gone, Nick looked across at

Nay and thanked her. "I appreciate your support, everything you've done," he said. His fingers fiddled with his mustache, as they so often did when he was nervous. This was not sounding nearly as smooth as it had when he'd rehearsed it in his head. "Come work for me," he blurted suddenly. "You're the only one I can trust."

A week later, she accepted the job. It was not the first time, and it would not be the last, that her political instincts were better than his. She understood enough about the ways of City Hall to know that she owed an explanation to Harry Oxman, the man who had hired her in the first place. When she offered one, the conversation turned ugly, and Oxman accused her of chasing after Nick to advance her own career. "That's not it," she answered. "I helped him because I felt bad for him. I thought he was going to lose."

Nay's letter of resignation to Oxman was effective December 31, 1987, but she actually started working for Nick long before then. He put her in charge of what he called "the fun stuff," including planning the inauguration and the party afterward. Nick wanted to do something different, something that symbolized youth and energy, so instead of a traditional gala in a catering hall, he rented a large boat equipped for dinner and dancing. Every day he gleefully read the updated list of people who had paid $150 apiece to attend his bash—people who didn't know him or pretended not to know him at the start of his campaign. His City Hall office was neither quiet nor lonely now that he had won, and he practically strutted from one task to the next: hiring a new city manager, sending out press releases declaring a "fresh start" full of "fresh ideas," schmoozing with the other members of the council, allying himself not with his fellow Democrats, but with a coalition of Democrats, Republicans, and Conservatives who were opposed to the housing.

A phone call came on December 28, a phone call that would change everything, and it was Nay who tracked Nick down and put the lawyers through. It was four days before Nick was to be sworn in as mayor, and the United States Court of Appeals for the Second Circuit had ruled on Yonkers' fate. This was the appeal Nick had staked his campaign on, the appeal he had voted for and that Martinelli had voted against. The appeal that was supposed to persuade the higher court that Judge Sand had overstepped his bounds, and that the housing should not be built.

Instead, the 163-page opinion from the three-judge panel unanimously rejected the city's arguments. Sand's order, it said, was "well within the bounds of discretion," and the city's request to reverse that order was "without merit."

Other members of the council reacted to the news quickly and defiantly. "We will take it to the Supreme Court," said Nick's fellow Democrat Henry Spallone, the beefy former New York City cop who was always ready for a good verbal brawl, whose political views were described by the local paper as "medieval," and who was elected with nearly 80 percent of the vote.

"The whole thing is a farce," said Charles Cola, also a Democrat, who, in keeping with the surreal nature of Yonkers politics, won his seat by defeating a woman who had been his secretary until a month before the election.

The councilmen waited for Nick to join them in their outrage, and the city waited with them, but the young mayor-elect was unexpectedly quiet.

"It is too early to tell whether the city will appeal" was all he was willing to say.

It was probably good that he kept his early reactions to himself, because they were those of a petulant child. "I can't believe the timing," he complained to Nay. "It will put a damper on everything. I don't even get a chance to have some fun."

Quickly, however, he went from feeling cheated to feeling overwhelmed. He was twenty-eight years old. He had never been responsible for his own rent or his own telephone bill, and now he was responsible for this.

Briefly, he thought he should join the shouting. That would be the political thing to do. Take it to the Supreme Court, he reasoned.

Isn't that why the court was there? He was elected because he believed the city had the right to appeal. So why stop with one appeal? Why not go all the way?

But since the day after his election, the expensive team of lawyers working for the city had been warning him that the Second Circuit Court would reject this initial appeal, and those lawyers had been right. Now they were telling him that there were no constitutional grounds for an appeal to the Supreme Court. He suspected they were right about that, too. An appeal would be expensive, and the city had already spent millions of dollars fighting the case. An appeal would also risk Sand's further wrath. The judge would see it as a desperate stalling tactic, which it probably was, and would impose the threatened fines. Vowing to appeal would make him popular for the moment, but would it risk the ruination of the city he had just been elected to lead?

Few men have ever had to grow up so quickly. In his inaugural address five days later, Nick made his answers clear. Yonkers, he said, would comply with the integration order, because "the law is the law" and compliance was the only way to avoid crippling fines. He did not say that he agreed with the decision because he did not. He thought that it was unfair to punish the homeowners of today for discriminatory decisions made by political leaders decades ago. But unfair or not, it was within the judge's power to inflict such punishment.

The phone calls started as soon as he finished his speech. They were venomous and violent, a small taste of what was to come. Nay took one message after another, but drew the line at transcribing the obscenities.

"Tell the mayor to go to hell." "Tell the mayor to go to Harlem." "We should have known better than to trust that child."

"Tell the mayor he's a traitor." "A liar." "A fool." "Tell the mayor to resign." "Tell the mayor we'll impeach him."

He read all the messages, responded to none of them, and wondered if he had done the right thing. As the pink stack of "While You Were Out" slips grew higher, he cheered up. He had beaten the odds against Martinelli, he would beat these odds, too. All his life, he had been able to talk people into seeing things his way. He had to believe he could bring them around now, when it mattered the most.

A City Like No Other

Cities have ways about them, eccentricities and quirks as distinctive and basic as those of the people who live in them. To lament the sameness brought by fast-food restaurants and mini-malls is to lose track of the larger point—that *in spite* of fast-food restaurants and mini-malls, there is an essence, a *something* that cannot be erased. The preening trendiness of Los Angeles. The brash chauvinism of Dallas. The scrubbed friendliness of Minneapolis. Even from the airport, Las Vegas feels different from Chicago. Blindfolded on a street corner, you would probably know whether you were in San Antonio or Salt Lake City.

No place else feels quite like Yonkers, rough-hewn and jagged, a working-class bridge between the towers of Manhattan to the south, and the pampered hills of the rest of Westchester County to the north. Its riverfront, cluttered with warehouses and factories, stares across the Hudson at the majestic Palisades, which rise teasingly out of reach. The Yonkers Raceway, a huge but scruffy harness track that seems always on the brink of closing, is the first landmark visitors see as they approach from the Thruway. It is an apt welcome.

Though the size of a city, Yonkers gossips like a tiny town. After harness racing, politics is the favorite sport here, and, played by Yonkers rules, it is a blood sport. City Council debates have been known to veer off into attacks on a council member's spouse. Past campaigns have included charges of illegal wire-tapping and petition fraud. More than one officeholder has changed parties three times in one career. In sum, there is a defiant nostalgia here, the hallmark of a place that used to be something else, and that, too, is apt. During an era that no one still living actually remembers, but everyone seems to yearn for, Yonkers was a great city.

Its history began with a tribe of Native Americans, who "sold" the land to a Dutch nobleman, Adrien Van der Donck, in 1646. His title was Jonge Heer, or Lord. Eventually Jonge Heer's holdings became known as Yonkeers and then Yonkers.

The city grew with the railroads. The first trains followed the paths of the waterways, and because Yonkers was trisected by the Hudson, Saw Mill, and Bronx Rivers (two of which are now reduced to mere trickles), it had twenty train stations during the late 1800s. By turn of the century, it was the industrial center of Westchester County, with 129 factories counted in 1912. The Waring Hat Company, the largest in the United States, turned out eighteen thousand hats every day. The Otis Elevator Company employed seven thousand people, or one out of every three workers in the city. Another third worked at the Alexander Smith Carpet Mills, the largest in the world, with fifty-six acres of floorspace. Even Nicholas II, Russia's last tsar, had a carpet made in Yonkers.

Waves of immigrants manned those factories and left their imprints. English, Scottish, Polish, Slavic, Ukrainian, Italian—whatever group was escaping the old country in the greatest numbers. Each started at the bottom, in the mills, the smelting rooms, and the refineries, then each group made the climb up, onto the assembly lines and into the managers' offices. As they moved up, they also moved out, heading east of town where, spurred by the age of the automobile, farmland was being transformed into neighborhoods.

When they reached the open spaces east of the Saw Mill River, the groups kept to themselves, forming enclaves that felt less like America and more like whichever country used to be home. The electoral ward system was born of that deliberate separateness, and it helped to keep things that way. For much of the time (until the year Nick Wasicsko was elected), the Yonkers City Council was made up of twelve members who worked more like a confederation than a union. There was a rule back then, not an official one, but ironclad nonetheless, that each councilman had final say over proposals for his electoral ward. It was de facto veto power. If the

Show Me a Hero

councilman from the ward said no, he would not be challenged, and no other member of the council would vote to place a housing project in his territory. And if the voters said no, the councilman said no, unless he had no interest in being reelected.

Some blacks made it across the Saw Mill, into the one black middle-class neighborhood in Yonkers. Called Runyon Heights, its existence is not an example of how blacks were welcomed on the east side, but an example of how they were not. Today, decades later, most blacks and Hispanics in town know the story of Runyon Heights, but few white people do, and those few are often real estate brokers. Judge Sand knows the story. He cited it in the early pages of his decision that found Yonkers guilty of years of deliberate discrimination.

During the building boom of the 1920s, history shows, a developer made a bad purchase—land too rocky and hilly for ranch-style houses with big, flat yards. To salvage his investment, he announced that he would turn the land into a Jewish cemetery, a plan that enraged and panicked the owners of surrounding parcels. Original residents of the area told two versions of what happened next. Some recalled that the developer, angered by attempts to stop him, took his revenge by selling the land to blacks. Others said the developer gave the objectors a choice and it was the neighbors who decided "it was better to live next to live Negroes than dead Jews."

Either way, Runyon Heights was built, a quarter-mile-square area of two-story houses, each on a quarter-acre of land, and each costing $5,000. The quiet winding streets of Runyon Heights looked identical to those of Homefield, the all-white neighborhood directly to the north, but the people of Homefield apparently didn't see the similarities. Or, perhaps, they did and were frightened by them. Whatever the reason, hedges were planted at the end of Moultrie Avenue in Homefield during the 1930s, to prevent movement between the two neighborhoods. Sometime later, the hedges became a fieldstone wall.

Eventually, a four-foot-wide strip of land was set aside by the Homefield residents along the northern border of Runyon Heights. Building was prohibited on that strip. No streets could pass through it. The result is that, even today, every north-south street in Runyon Heights is a dead end. In the spring, the leaves in the strip of land are lush, deceptive, giving the illusion that the woods stretch on forever. But in winter, with the branches bare, the houses of Homefield can be clearly seen on the other side.

Those who made it to the dead-end streets of Runyon Heights were the exception. Few minorities crossed the Saw Mill because they were not wanted and because they could not afford to. The Alexander Smith Carpet Mills did not employ black workers until World War II. Otis Elevator did, but only in the sweltering, grimy factory, with no hope of promotion to the offices upstairs. During the 1930s there was a joke whenever people of color gathered in Yonkers. A friend would ask, in greeting, "How's it going?" The reply was always the same: "White folks still in the lead."

So the minorities stayed on the west side, making their homes in the places that earlier generations of newcomers had eagerly left. In Irving, Cottage, and Wood Place. On Morgan, Garden, and School Street. They lived near where they worked, in tenements behind the factories and the mills, in cold-water flats alongside the railroad tracks and the riverbanks. The east side became ever more middle class and white. The west side became ever more minority and poor.

Yonkers, of course, was not the only place in the country with slums and with a growing gap between blacks and whites. Periodically, the federal government would talk about improving the nation's slums, but nothing was done until the stock market crashed in 1929. In the wake of the subsequent Great Depression, public housing was born. Helping the poor was just a side effect of the program, whose real goal was providing construction jobs and literally rebuilding the economy. More than a decade later, in the aftermath of World War II, public housing was expanded, this time as a way to house returning veterans.

The boom in housing provided the city of Yonkers with a dilemma. The city badly wanted — needed — the money made available for the growing public housing infrastructure, but it did not really want the public housing. So it went about things the Yonkers way. Funds were applied for, and granted, but then came the challenge of finding a place to build. Whatever neighborhood the planning board chose for the housing would convulse with protests and petitions. This happened in other cities, too, but in most of those places the checks and balances of politics meant some neighborhoods occasionally got housing despite the most vocal efforts to keep it out. Not in Yonkers. Not where there was a fiefdom system and the understanding that a councilman's no vote was final.

For more than forty years, therefore, one huge public housing complex after another was built on the west side, the only part of town that offered no resistance. Mulford Gardens, seventeen buildings with 550 apartments, opened in October 1940. Cottage Place Gardens, thirteen buildings with 256 apartments, opened in 1948. The William A. Schlobohm Houses, 415 apartments in eight buildings, opened in 1953. Calgano Homes, better known as School Street, had 278 units completed in 1964. By 1988, not one of the city's twenty-seven subsidized-housing projects for families was located in any of the overwhelmingly white neighborhoods of the east or northeast. In all, the southwest contained 6,644, or 97.7 percent, of the city's 6,800 units of subsidized housing.

The lopsided map came about not because no one noticed, but because those who did notice, and spoke up, were overruled. Members of the city's planning board, for instance, regularly warned that the burden of so many poor people in one place would be the death of business in southwest Yonkers. Rather than heeding that warning, the council voted to sacrifice downtown. When the planning board objected to the School Street site because it was directly in the path of a proposed access road between the highway and the struggling shopping district, the council voted to sacrifice the access road.

And, eventually, when Congress ruled that public funds could not be spent in a way that would create a housing ghetto, the City Council in effect voted to sacrifice the funds. No public housing for families was built in Yonkers after 1964, because that was when the Department of Housing and Urban Development started paying attention to where all such housing was located.

Yonkers, to be sure, is not the only city to cluster its public housing. Others did the same thing, and the year that the Justice Department began its investigation of Yonkers, it also looked at Chicago; Lima, Ohio; Marshall, Texas; Charleston, South Carolina; and Rochester, New York. All were potential targets for the first of what was expected to be a series of groundbreaking lawsuits linking school segregation with housing. Any one of those cities could have been chosen as the test case, but only Yonkers was, less because of what it did than how it did it.

"What got them in deep problems was they couldn't keep their mouths shut," Oscar Newman says. Other cities apologized for their past. Some built a handful of low-income units in middle-class neighborhoods as proof of their regret. Once that was done, the Justice Department went away. Yonkers, however, came out swinging. In one deposition after another, city officials said that low-income housing was purposefully placed in one small corner of Yonkers because that was the poorest corner of Yonkers, hence that's where it *belonged*.

So it was Yonkers, not Rochester or Chicago, that was successfully sued for discrimination in federal court. And it was Nicholas Wasicsko, who always wanted to be mayor of Yonkers, who inherited the legacy of that lawsuit, and who came to learn more than he really wanted to know about his city, and about himself.

For a few weeks at the beginning of 1988 it looked as if Nick might actually be able to do the impossible: to unravel years of tradition, to tame Yonkers, and to unite the council on a vote to implement a housing plan. With the help of the city's law firm, Skadden, Arps, Meagher and Flom, and the city's new city manager, Neil DeLuca, Nick persuaded nearly everyone on the council that voting to comply with the order was the only way to maintain some control over the end result. He accomplished this by doing what he had always done best—talking, schmoozing, debating.

Two councilmen—Harry Oxman and Charles Cola—needed little persuading; Nick had their votes in his corner almost from the start. Oxman, a courtly, quiet man, was the only member of the council who fully favored compliance, and Cola, although he personally disagreed with the plan, represented the district that included all the city's housing projects, so it was his political responsibility to vote yes.

Two other councilmen were never really subjects of Nick's full-court press. Hank Spallone had lived in the South Bronx, and had seen firsthand how a neighborhood could change. He had been a police detective, so he had also seen what happened to the neighborhood after it changed. Had Hank been an actor, his ability to scowl and bellow would have cast him as the thug—the bullying cop, the tyrant father, the rogue politician, the kind of roles always played by Robert Mitchum or Lee J. Cobb. He had been elected because he had vowed to go to jail, if need be, to stop the housing. Nick did not even try to change his mind.

And Edward Fagan was such a puzzle that Nick didn't bother to make an effort. All the relationships on the council were based on business, not friendship, but Fagan, wiry and wary, gangly as a scarecrow, seemed to go out of his way to keep his private life out of the office.

By process of elimination, therefore, Nick directed most of his talking at his two remaining colleagues, Nicholas Longo and Peter Chema. Longo, with black hair and a silver tongue, was probably the shrewdest politician in Yonkers. His "real world" job was as a county employee—a program director at the Department of Environmental Facilities—and that, along with his sixteen years on the council, meant he was plugged in all over the government. Pushing Nicholas Longo was like playing with mercury—he was shimmering but dangerous, and his beads of influence could be found in every crevice and corner. Longo's last campaign had been nasty, and he had won it because he ran full force against the housing. One of his most effective weapons was a cable television commercial which interspersed colorful scenes of a cheery suburban neighborhood with black-and-white shots of a dismal urban ghetto.

Peter Chema, too, was a veteran of Yonkers politics, a world to which he had literally been born. Chema's father had won a council seat when Peter was a child, by defeating the family's next-door neighbor. A decade later, when the elder Chema died of cancer while still in office, his vacant seat was filled by the same neighbor. When the neighbor faced reelection, his opponent was Mrs. Chema. She won, but then decided that the job was too stressful, and resigned after one month, at which time her neighbor was appointed once again. Peter grew up, earned a degree in civil engineering and a black belt in kung fu, then opened a tire business before running for council for the first time in 1979. His opponent—the same neighbor, who finally gave up and moved to Florida. At thirty-seven, Chema was eight years younger than Longo and less certain of himself. His clothes were always perfectly pressed and his hair perfectly coifed, but his expression always looked somewhat startled.

During his first three weeks in office, Nick tried to outpolitic these two long-time politicians. The two hundred low-income units would be built "no matter what," he told them, over lunch, on the phone, in their living rooms, late at night, and first thing in the morning. Many years earlier, he reminded them, Yonkers had accepted federal money to build exactly that number of public housing units on the east side, but although the money was kept, the housing was never built. So Judge Sand saw the two hundred units as payback, and he would not be persuaded to compromise on that part of the plan. Wouldn't it be better, he asked, to have some say over where those inevitable units eventually went?

On January 20, 1988, all this talking turned frantic. The city's annual application for federal community development funds came due that day, and what began as a vote on a routine procedural matter became a showdown on the housing. To qualify for the $10 million renewal, Yonkers had to submit a Housing Assistance Plan, or HAP, which outlined the city's housing plans for the coming year. The city's HAP, drawn up by department employees months earlier, included the statement that two hundred units of low-income housing would be built on the east side. If the council voted to approve the HAP, Sand said, his eyes angry beneath his imposing white eyebrows, he would see that as a pledge of cooperation. If not, he said, he would levy the fines he had threatened during the summer of 1987, fines that would start at $100 a day and double every day until there was no money left in Yonkers.

So, at the last possible moment, the council voted as the judge had ordered them to and as Nick had begged them to. The resolution, cosponsored by Nicholas Longo and Nicholas Wasicsko, passed 5–1. Harry Oxman was absent. The single no was from Spallone, who stormed out of the meeting, face red with rage. "I am not about to be intimidated by any judge," he shouted. "We will not roll over and play dead. If it takes going to jail to prove to America that everyone should have constitutional rights, I'm saying to you 'I am willing to go to jail.' "

Spallone's theatrics aside, Nick was pleased with the results. He must be "one helluva politician," he figured, to have been able to pull this one off, although he had learned enough about his new job to keep those thoughts to himself.

Judge Sand was less pleased. He knew Yonkers well enough to be wary, and although he praised the council's vote, he then asked for more. Stated intentions are fine, he said, but now he wanted specifics. He gave the council a week to develop and vote on a binding "consent decree"—a list of locations where the housing would be built.

The five who reluctantly voted yes held meetings toward that goal and pointedly did not invite Spallone. The list they compiled included seven sites, and 108 of the 200 units would be in Spallone's district. Six of the seven sites had been on Oscar Newman's original lists, but the seventh was a surprise. It was a serene slice of land that was part of the St. Joseph's Seminary, and it seemed like a good idea at the time.

The night before the list was to be presented to Judge Sand, Nick found himself at the Broadway Diner, awkwardly sharing a late-night dinner with Nicholas Longo and Peter Chema. What passed for conversation was, at first, between Wasicsko and Longo, whose political savvy Nick had come to envy. Chema sat there saying nothing, looking uneasy and pale. Nick worried that Chema was going to change his vote, rejecting the list of sites, and therefore reneging on the council's week-old promise to the judge. Longo worried that Chema, the black belt, was going to throw up.

They spent the rest of the evening reminding their uncertain colleague that "we have to stick together. We have to make Spallone look like he's out there by himself."

They asked for, but never received, a promise that Chema would back the consent decree. Their food sat almost uneaten on their plates.

The councilmen and their lawyers appeared in court the morning of January 26, 1988, and presented the list to Judge Sand. He praised the council again, and stressed the importance of having the city make these decisions rather than the court. "A court can order bricks and mortar," he said. "Only the citizens of Yonkers can create an environment that is conducive to good relations."

He gave his blessing to the list, and asked for one more thing. He wanted the city to give up their plans to appeal the case to the Supreme Court. The vote scheduled that night to approve the list of sites would have no meaning, he said, if it were done with the hope that the high court would eventually rule that the consent decree was null and void. That would be like reciting wedding vows knowing you have a date with someone else for next Saturday night. This vote, he warned, must be the last vote. Those who agree to approve the sites must have every intention of building on those sites. Lawyers for the city agreed to waive their right to appeal.

Because the expected crowd would overwhelm City Hall, the meeting to approve or reject Sand's list of sites was to be held in an east side high school gym. As Nick and the others arrived at Saunders High School, they could hear the roar of the crowd before they entered the building. Inside, it was pandemonium. Nine hundred people had passed through the metal detectors at the entrance, and four registered handguns had been confiscated. Five dozen policemen lined the gymnasium walls. Henry Spallone was already at the microphone, whipping the crowd into a frenzy. One man in the audience was wearing a Ku Klux Klan T-shirt.

"We're just one nut away from a riot," Longo thought.

More than sixty people had signed up in advance for the public comment portion of the evening. For more than five hours, they paraded to the microphone to scream, plead, and threaten. For more than five hours, the council members sat there, stone faced, and took it. For more than five hours, Nick glanced with worry at Peter Chema, fearful there would be a surprise when the actual vote was taken.

"Put your jobs on the line tonight," yelled Rabbi Bernhard Rosenberg of the Midchester Jewish Center, his face red and his fists clenched. "Get some guts and stand up to it. Or put it in *your* neighborhood."

Eleven-year-old Judy Guldner, whose neighborhood would get sixty of the two hundred units, stood pale but composed behind a lectern, leaning in toward the mikes from fifteen radio and television stations. "Where are our rights? My parents worked hard for my house. I don't want people who have no morals, and take drugs, in my neighborhood. I used to want to be a politician, but after seeing you it would be a disgrace."

Only one person spoke in favor of the plan—Laurie Recht, a thirty-four-year-old white secretary from south Yonkers. She stood 4'10" and could barely be seen over the crowd. She was even harder to hear as she read her brief, written statement. "Low-income housing in small groups does not necessarily increase crime," she said. "There are good and bad in all races. It is important to realize that no one group should be blamed for all social or societal problems." When she was finished, the jeers were so loud and the faces around her were so frightening that she had to be escorted from the room by the police. As she left, one man shouted, "Send her to Harlem."

At 1:00 A.M., after the list of speakers was exhausted, it was the council's turn to speak. Nick kept it short. "Majority rules in America," he said, "but it cannot rule contrary to law."

Peter Chema did not speak at all.

Last on the list was Hank Spallone. "Nuts to the judge," he boomed. "I swore an allegiance to you and I will keep that allegiance to you. Nuts to the judge! This is a sellout of the worst kind."

With that, the crowd tried to rush the stage, hundreds of people pushing toward the podium at once. Nick could feel the floor shake, and he could see the tension in the officers' faces as they linked arms to hold the protesters back.

The clerk took the voice vote at 1:30 in the morning. Technically it was a vote on a list of sites, but the weariness and tension in the single-word answers of the councilmen made it clear that it was so much more.

"Mr. Wasicsko?" Yes.

"Mr. Spallone?" No.

"Mr. Longo?" Yes.

"Mr. Oxman?" Yes.

"Mr. Chema?" Silence.

"Mr. Chema?"

Nick watched as Peter Chema made a fist, then turned his thumb down toward the ground.

"Mr. Cola?" Yes.

"Mr. Fagan?" Yes.

The consent decree had passed 5–2. The battle was over.

The war had barely begun.

Mary Dorman Joins the Fight

Mary Dorman sat in the front row of the City Council chambers, tapping her sneakers on the blue-and-gold carpet, shifting with edgy excitement on the blue velvet seat cushion, waiting for the latest scheduled frenzy to begin. A sinewy, gray-haired woman, with the denim and khaki wardrobe of one with no patience for excess and the sturdy, roughened hands of one who values hard work, Mary gazed slowly around the room, absorbing every detail.

Above her was an elaborate stained-glass dome, depicting the colorful Yonkers seal. On one wall there was a mural showing Jonge Heer himself buying the land for his eponymous city, and the other wall held a relief sculpture of a large, gold-leafed eagle. Together these flourishes should have created an impressive room, but instead they merely managed to hint of a place that had once been impressive. The stained glass, while beautiful, was cracked in places; the murals, though skillfully drawn, were dulled by years of dirt; and although the eagle was dramatic, even stirring, the surrounding plaster was crumbling from water damage.

Pushing the beige frames of her owlish glasses back up the bridge of her nose, Mary noticed all these things. But as she looked around, she did not see traces of the changing fates of a city as much as she saw the broad strokes of changes in herself. That she was even sitting in this room was because of her own transformation, from a quiet, bespectacled lady into a loud, determined warrior for a cause. Only four weeks earlier, she had never been to a political meeting, and now she was warmly greeting dozens of people by name. Until last month she had certainly never been to City Hall, and here she was, already unfazed by her surroundings, with a specific seat—front row, right side—that she thought of as her own.

Mary had paid no attention to the housing fight until the near riot at the Saunders gym. A few days after that meeting she read a notice in the local paper about a meeting of the 12th Ward Republican Club at the local VFW post. Nicholas Longo was scheduled to speak. On a whim, she went. It was not the sort of thing she would usually do because, until that moment, Mary was not the joining type. Aside from her bowling league and her Sundays at St. John the Baptist, her world was her husband, Buddy, who was an engineer with AT&T, her grown daughter, Maureen, and her job as an assistant to her brother-in-law, who was a veterinarian.

Twenty years earlier, when she and Buddy first moved from the not-yet-dangerous Bronx to the comparatively open spaces of Yonkers, they had lived in an apartment over the same animal clinic where she now worked. It was the Dorman family "bouncing-off place," a rent-free apartment for family members wanting to save for a house of their own. Maureen, an adolescent back then, took the only bedroom, and Mary and Buddy slept in the living room, on a pull-out couch. They tried not to waste much time complaining about the lack of space. To their mind, sofa beds were simply where you slept while you worked for something else.

Whenever they talked of moving, Mary would say, "If I can't have a brick house on St. John's Avenue, I don't care if I never have a house." To her mind, St. John's was one of the city's prettiest streets, a winding boulevard lined with neat, modest Georgians and Cape Cods, ending with a flourish at the spires of the St. John the Baptist Church. But although she talked about her fantasy house often, she never actually searched for it.

Then, on a snowy day in 1978, she saw a sign at the local drugstore offering a one-story, two-bedroom brick house on her perfect street. The pharmacist said, "Why not take a look?" She and Buddy fell in love with it at first sight, but the $58,000 asking price was more than Buddy was willing to pay. When Mary heard that another buyer had already bid the asking price, Mary went back to her suddenly cramped apartment, shattered.

Within days, the owner of the little house called. The other buyer had talked about tearing out the arch over the kitchen door. Would Mary and Buddy be willing to pay $53,000? The house became hers because she loved it as it was. She swore she would never let it change.

Now two of the seven sites on the consent decree list were within walking distance of that house, and she was drawn to the meeting at the VFW post because she wanted to keep her word— to protect the house, its neighborhood, her dream. To Judge Sand, the battle of Yonkers was about what was right. To Nick Wasicsko, it was about what was realistic. To Mary Dorman, it was about her home.

At that meeting, and at all the others that followed, she fell in with a group called the Save Yonkers Federation, a coalition of thirty neighborhood associations from throughout the city. Its leaders said they had one hundred thousand members, and Mary believed them, having seen how easily they could mobilize a pressure-cooker crowd on almost no notice. Save Yonkers was an odd testament to the fact that Judge Sand, in a most unintended way, had united at least part of the city.

Her attraction to the group was its loyalty to Hank Spallone. There were a lot of politicians doing a lot of talking, she decided, and Spallone was the only one who seemed to make any sense.

Mary's days were soon shaped by Save Yonkers. She found herself attending meetings, sometimes nightly—at the VFW post, at the Grinton I. Will Library, at the Lincoln Park Jewish Center, at St. John the Baptist Church—where she listened to speeches to the converted by people who had been strangers before the fight but now described each other as good friends.

Her first meeting in hostile territory—at City Hall—came two weeks after the one at Saunders, on the second Tuesday in February. This was a regularly scheduled council session, although there was nothing regular about it, and she arrived at 5:00 P.M., three hours before the actual meeting was scheduled to begin, one hour before the public comment portion of the evening. She was there early because she was determined to be one of the eighty people who actually sat inside the chamber, not one of the hundreds who stood and chanted outside. As she waited with her new compatriots in what would quickly become her usual seat, someone handed her a small American flag, a symbol of the right to appeal to the Supreme Court. That had become the rallying cry in the weeks since the council forfeited that right by approving the consent decree: "Appeal. Appeal. Appeal." No matter that there were few identifiable constitutional issues in the case, or that the Supreme Court agrees to hear only 3 to 5 percent of the cases brought to it each year. "Appeal. Appeal. Appeal," they shouted, demanding their constitutional right to try to beat those impossible odds.

Mary Dorman shouted along with them. She waved her flag, she booed, she screamed, she closed her eyes and joined the others in a tuneless hum to drown out any councilman other than Peter Chema or Hank Spallone, the two who had voted against the consent decree. When Nick Wasicsko tried to speak, someone from the back of the room hurled pink disposable diapers at him. Mary snickered. "Go back home to your mother," she yelled. Her fists clenched, her veins popped, her anger was raw, white hot, and oddly cleansing. For fifty-four years she had been a polite woman, the type who said "Excuse me" when she bumped into furniture, so she was amazed at how easily she took to the rhythms of disobedience. It was exhilarating to believe so completely. This was not the first time Mary had felt this angry, but it was the first time she had ever shown such anger to strangers. "I didn't know I could act that way outside," she said, meaning outside the intimate circle of family. "You might get mad at your kid, or your husband, but you wouldn't lose your cool outside."

She was intimidated only for a moment that first night, when a group of protesters near the back of the room stood up on their chairs, linked arms, and looked defiantly at the thirty policemen and their leashed police dogs. The protesters knew that most of the officers were Yonkers homeowners, too, and the officers knew that they knew it. Mary kept her feet on the floor, transfixed by the drama, watching the cops approach lawbreakers who were also their relatives and their neighbors. It was over in a moment, as several dozen protesters were taken firmly by the wrists or elbows and escorted out of the building. As they left, they chanted. "Appeal. Appeal. Appeal."

The mayor adjourned the meeting soon after that, leaving much of the agenda as unfinished business. When Mary got outside there was a party of sorts going on, lit by the roaming television cameras that were attracted by the prospect of imminent flame. In the glare of the spotlights, those who were ejected were being high-fived and hugged. They were heroes. Mary was already looking forward to the next meeting. There were still limits on what she would do for this cause, but she knew as she stood on the steps of City Hall, slapping her new friends on the shoulder, that there were fewer of those limits than there used to be.

The next two weeks went quickly, filled with meetings and phone calls and plans. Now, on the fourth Tuesday of the month she was back in the council chambers again. She was sitting in her seat, holding her flag, waiting for the meeting to start. Waiting, most of all, to feel that liberating anger once again.

While Mary was out front, getting ready to chant, Nick was in his office in the back, getting ready to take it. He knew he shouldn't allow the protesters to feel they were disrupting city business, but there was no way to hide the fact that they were. All but one entrance to the building had been closed during the past month, and

Show Me a Hero

the metal detector, which had at first been rented by the day, was now the paid-in-full property of the city.

Despite the precautions, there were bomb scares, the most recent one that very afternoon. The call to police headquarters came at 3:15, an unidentified man warning of a bomb in City Hall, set to detonate in twenty minutes. It was all declared a hoax at 4:05, but by then most of those who worked in the building had gone home, just to be safe.

There were death threats, too, letters that were stamped but not postmarked, all arriving through the mailroom and addressed to the five who had voted yes. Laurie Recht, the secretary whose short speech at Saunders had so enraged the crowd, received threats of a different kind.

"You're dead, bitch," said one snarling caller.

"I don't feel dead," she answered, then crashed the receiver into its cradle.

And there were bullets. The three white envelopes that were left in the men's washroom at City Hall were identical but that each bore the hand-lettered name of a different council member — Nicholas Longo, Charles Cola, Ed Fagan. Each had a single Winchester .22-caliber bullet inside.

Just as the temporary metal detector became permanent, the periodic police escorts assigned to the five council members, and to Laurie Recht, also became full-time. When Nay visited Nick at home—they were a couple by then, but a deliberately low-profile one—she was frisked by armed guards before she was allowed to walk in the door. When she left early the next morning, she would have to pass the guards again.

If it was impossible to mask the effect of the protests on the government, Nick was determined to mask the effects of those protests on his life. At home he stood in front of a mirror and practiced keeping his face impassive, so he could better pretend that the protesters weren't there. He rehearsed a calm, steady tone of voice, one that would not waver as the volume in the room became unbearable and as Pampers and insults were thrown his way.

He spent the minutes before eight o'clock collecting that poker face. Then he took a long, deep, unsteady breath and walked through the door from his office into the packed council chamber. This was just a routine council meeting, he reminded himself. Get through it, then get out.

As soon as the mayor appeared, Mary leaped to her feet with the rest of the crowd, joining in the catcalls and the boos. When Nick put his hand in place to salute the flag, Mary waved her own miniature flag over her head and chanted, "Appeal. Appeal. Appeal." He didn't flinch, Mary noticed. Though she could not hear him recite the Pledge of Allegiance, she saw his lips form every word.

The moment of silence was anything but. "You can't keep us quiet," the crowd yelled. "We will be heard." When it came time for the business at hand—a list of twenty resolutions, none of which had anything to do with public housing—the noise from the spectator seats was so loud that the city clerk had to leave his seat and walk up to each councilman in order to hear and record his vote.

The meeting was supposed to conclude with a ceremony honoring city firefighters and police officers for acts of bravery in the line of duty, but that too was drowned out by the crowd.

For a moment, Nick lost his cool. "These men risked their lives for the city of Yonkers," he screamed into the microphone. The boos became even louder.

Seeing the young mayor become flustered felt like a victory to Mary, and she leaned over the railing that separated the public from the council. "Wasicsko, you're crazy. You're a sleaze," she yelled.

"Would the officers please eject this woman," Nick thundered back. Moments later, there was an officer on either side of Mary Dorman as they walked her out of the building.

Mary had seen something in Nick's face that she thought was regret, and, on a whim, she called him the next morning. She expected to leave a message, but, instead, he answered the phone himself. He had been answering it whenever he could since he had become mayor, just as he had when he was a councilman. Nay had tried to get him to stop, but he insisted. No one was going to accuse him of being inaccessible or out of touch.

Show Me a Hero

"I just called to tell you that you're wrong to support the housing," Mary said.

"The law is the law," he responded.

"Do you think Yonkers is guilty of racism?" Mary asked.

"I think Yonkers is getting a raw deal," he said. "But the judge ordered it, and the appeals court upheld it, and the law is the law."

"Why can't you say you think it's wrong. Let people know that, at least?"

"That's not what a leader is supposed to do. I'm supposed to be a leader."

It was not the answer Mary was expecting, and, for a moment, she was quiet.

"You threw me out of the last meeting," she said, finally.

Nick heard something in her voice that he thought was sympathy.

"Which one were you?" he asked.

"I'm older, gray hair, glasses. I always sit on the righthand side, first row."

"That's you?" he said. "I promise I'll never have you thrown out again."

Alma Febles Struggles through the Night

The eight red-brick buildings of the Schlobohm housing project stand within sight of Yonker's City Hall. Mary Dorman passed the hulking eight-story structures on every trip to the council chambers, but had never been inside. Fighting to keep "those people" out of her neighborhood became her all-consuming goal, yet she had never thought to detour the one block north off Yonkers Avenue to see "those people" for herself.

Alma Febles, in turn, could see City Hall from her bedroom window in Building One at Schlobohm. The lights were on late whenever there was a council meeting, which means they were on often during February of 1988, but Alma never noticed. She paid as little attention to the protesters at City Hall as the protesters paid to her. The few blocks were a lifetime, another world, a strange land. She saw no connection between the goings-on at City Hall and the events of her own life, a life that was crashing down around her.

While lights were burning, while Mary was chanting, while Nick was worrying, Alma Febles was crying. She had cried every night in the weeks since she came back from Santo Domingo—the weeks since she left her children behind in Santo Domingo—the tears streaming so constantly that she sometimes ceased to notice them and did not even bother to wipe them away.

If fate had placed her in a different life, Alma Febles would have been a beautiful woman, with dark black hair that fell in perfect rings around her caramel-colored face, accenting her dramatic, magnetic brown eyes. But the life she'd been handed had dimmed all hope from those eyes, and left them puffy and red. She'd barely eaten since she'd returned home, replacing food with two or three packs of cigarettes a day. She avoided sleep, too, because when she managed to fall asleep, she would dream: Frankie getting lost, Virgilio getting hit by a car, Leyda getting sick. She would wake up with a sour taste in her mouth and a pain in her stomach.

One night, in a sobbing rage, she stripped all the pictures of the three children off the walls, because she couldn't stand the blame she imagined in their camera-ready smiles. Another night found her frantically stuffing their clothes into boxes then cramming the boxes into closets, as if she could pack her guilt and loneliness away, too. The bursts of activity calmed her for a few moments, but then the tears would come again, and she would wander the empty, smothering apartment until dawn.

During the seven years she had lived there, Alma rarely called Apartment 151 at Schlobohm "home." She called it "the apartment," as in "I'm going back to the apartment." Never "I'm going home."

That was because the two-bedroom flat, with its muddy green walls and temperamental bathroom door, was not home, not to Alma Cordero Reyes Febles, thirty-one years old and still a dreamer, still sure there was a place for her to live that would bring her a feeling of peace. Alma was chasing a memory, trying to catch the days when she was a child in Santo Domingo, the capital of the Dominican Republic. Her mother owned their modest house back there, bought with money from the family factory, which made uniforms for stores. Alma, close to the youngest in a family of two brothers and six sisters, would wander the streets without worry, feeling safe, or so she remembers it, in the invisible cocoon of neighborhood.

Although Alma loved life on the Caribbean island, her mother decided the children should have more, and slowly the family began to emigrate to the United States. Alma's aunt Mela already lived in New York City, and she brought Alma's oldest sister, Rosario, over first. Then came Dulce, the second oldest. Because Dulce and Rosario were here, Alma's mother and youngest sister were permitted to come. Alma stayed in Santo Domingo while her mother worked to bring the rest of the children stateside, one by one. Alma was eight when her mother left. She was fourteen when her mother sent for her.

Life in Yonkers was different from life in Santo Domingo. Alma knew no English and, although she was a serious student back home, she was miserable at the city's huge high school. She hated the winters. She hated sharing a two-bedroom apartment with her mother, three sisters, two brothers, and one cousin. Her goal in life, one that would elude her for at least the next twenty-six years, was to find a place with a room all her own.

The pull of home brought her back to the island for frequent visits, and when she was sixteen, she met Virgilio Reyes there. They were from the same neighborhood and had friends in common. They were married in Santo Domingo when she was nineteen. Virgilio was born two years later. Like Alma's mother, Alma's new husband was drawn to the United States, so, against Alma's better judgment, the young family moved back to Yonkers in 1979. At first, they lived on the top floor of a five-story walk-up. The $212 rent was the most they could afford with Virgilio's job at a local factory. The apartment was freezing all the time, and before she could bathe her baby, Alma had to turn on the kitchen stove and prop open the oven door.

Eventually, the young family moved to 188 Ashburton, into a $260 ground-floor apartment with a small backyard. Leyda was born there twenty days later. Although Alma's surroundings were somewhat better, their marriage was significantly worse. "That's when we started to hate each other," Alma says. She and the children shared one bedroom, while Virgilio senior slept in "the babies' room." Suspecting she would soon need to take care of herself, Alma started working toward a degree in special education at a local college. In 1981, when Leyda was a year old, Alma and her husband were divorced.

Alma took her children to Santo Domingo for Christmas that year. When she came back to Yonkers at New Year's she found that a fire in the boiler at 188 Ashburton had destroyed everything she owned. As a result of the fire, she moved into Schlobohm, as far from her dream as she was likely to get.

To enter her building she had to walk through courtyards that seemed to radiate dread and despair. Then she had to pull open the unlocked main door, a door whose milky Plexiglas had turned opaque from harsh detergents that never quite won the fight against the graffiti. To get to the elevator, she practically tiptoed through dank entryways, which were piled with garbage—old mattresses, beer cans, the detritus of so many disordered lives. Everywhere, the smell of trash mixed with the smell of urine, which mixed with the smell of the disinfectant that failed to wash the other smells away.

Apartment 151, two bedrooms, no view, was supposed to be a short-term stopping place, but Alma was still living there three years later when she took another trip to Santo Domingo and met Jose M. Febles. They married within months; their son, Frankie, was born within a year; they were divorced by the time he was five months old. Now there were three children to feed, and Alma quit school and took a job selling office furniture at a Yonkers showroom.

For a few years she managed to keep Virgilio, Leyda, and Frankie sheltered from the world outside. They were not allowed to leave the apartment without their mother, and they rarely left it with her, because Alma feared that the small, ill-equipped playground in Schlobohm was really gang territory. Joining her on errands was usually out of the question, too. If she took them to the supermarket, they simply begged her for things she couldn't afford, and everyone went home miserable. Instead they would sit in the cramped apartment, watching television or visiting with their cousins, who also lived in Schlobohm, and who were the only neighborhood children Alma trusted in her home.

When Virgilio and then Leyda reached school age, Alma walked them each to the bus stop in the morning before she left for work. Frankie spent the day at cousin Miriam's apartment, and when the school day ended Miriam would meet the older children at the bus stop and walk them to her house, too, carefully locking the doors when she returned.

But no number of locks could shield them completely, and by the time Virgilio was nine, Leyda was eight, and Frankie was four, their heads were filled with scenes that children are not supposed to see.

Leyda: "Once the elevator doors open and there was a drug deal happening inside and they tried to pull me in but they didn't."

Virgilio: "There's gunfire every weekend. I've never seen anyone shot but I hear about it sometimes. One time the kids started jumping off the fence and flattened a car."

Frankie: "Me and my aunt saw two guys knocking on a door. Nobody answered. They went in and we heard a scream. I don't know what happened then."

There was no one moment that made Alma move back to Santo Domingo in 1987. Instead, it was the gradual grinding down of the soul, the growing realization that her short-term solution was quickly swallowing her children's childhoods. Once back on the island, she rented a peach-colored house on Calle J-1, the street she grew up on and to which her mother had temporarily returned. If Alma stood on the big front lawn she could look down the block at her mother's window and wave. Although the house had three bedrooms, Alma still did not have a room all her own. She and Leyda shared one of the bedrooms, Virgilio and Frankie shared another, and the third was for the sleep-in baby-sitter, a common arrangement on the island. The woman would watch the children while Alma worked as a teacher's aide from seven in the morning until seven at night.

Virgilio and Leyda loved the freedom of the island, and spent their days as Alma remembered spending hers. They went to school from 8:00 A.M. to noon, then played happily in the poor but safe neighborhood. Frankie also loved his freedom — a little too much. His wild streak was broader than his brother's or his sister's, and his favorite game was to hide from his worried family. They would search the area for hours, yelling "Frankie, Frankie," only to return home and find him crouching under the bed. Soon Alma found one school that would take Frankie in the mornings and another that would take him in the afternoons.

Because the children were safer, it took Alma a year to face the fact that she was not earning enough to afford the life she wanted to build. Her salary was less than 2,000 pesos a month, which was about $300 at the time. Her rent on the house was 350 pesos, her electricity was 40 pesos, the baby-sitter was paid 100 pesos. The highest monthly cost was food, and each weekly trip to the grocer cost more than 500 pesos, meaning that each month she spent slightly more money than she brought home.

One of the reasons for the high grocery bills was the cost of imported foodstuffs, because a large foreign debt had depressed the Dominican peso against the dollar. That fact, while her undoing, could also be her solution. American dollars went far in Santo Domingo in 1988, and if she went back to Schlobohm alone and began to work again in the furniture store, the $1,200 she would earn each month would be enough to house, clothe, and feed her children back on the island.

Alma resisted the obvious for several months. She was still angry at her own mother for leaving her when she was eight. And she sharply remembered the scenes six years later, when they were reunited in Yonkers and Alma pretended not to love her mother, punishing her for the scars of separation. But her own plan was to leave for a few months, not a few years, she told herself. She could save enough money to provide a needed cushion, she reasoned, and the money could do more for her children than her presence could. She was not the first woman to come to understand her mother better once she became a mother herself.

On a February day in 1988, when tropical breezes were blowing in Santo Domingo and the temperature was below freezing in Yonkers, Alma boarded a $550 American Airlines flight. She cried through the entire three-hour trip. She returned to the apartment she had fled a year earlier, and which, never fully believing her escape would be final, she had sublet to some cousins. She spent her days at work, and her nights weeping. When her first monthly phone bill came she disconnected the telephone in the apartment, because she was wasting hundreds of dollars in nightly calls to the tiny peach house on Calle J-1.

Removing the phone did not stop her from calling, however, it just made the calls more dangerous. She would sleep, then dream, then awaken in fear. More often than not she would race off to the pay phone on the rough streets near Schlobohm. It was the only reason she would ever dare to venture outside in the projects in the middle of the night.

Norma O'Neal's Veil of Black Lace

Dawn was near in the darkened apartment across the street from Schlobohm, and Norma O'Neal was in the halfway place between awake and asleep. She was lying on the couch in her patient's living room, her eyes still closed, and she sensed the time without looking. It had been a quiet night, a typical night in this job as a home health aide. She had arrived, as usual, at eight in the evening, after the day nurse had bathed and fed the elderly patient and gotten her into bed. Norma's only real duty was to give the woman her nighttime medications, two pills that were already counted out and placed into a container, then to help the woman to the bathroom and to be nearby if she woke during the night.

Most nights she didn't, and although Norma never slept soundly when she was on duty, she rarely slept soundly in her own bed back in Schlobohm, either, so this was a perfect job for this stage in her life. She had her own list of ailments—diabetes, hypertension—the ones that plague poor blacks everywhere, and which she saw as an expected part of life. While no one of her health problems was crippling, in combination they were debilitating enough that most other jobs were impossible. At forty-seven, Norma looked far older. She was short, stout, and unmitigatingly stoic, with deep pockets of worry under gray-brown eyes and far more silver than black in her hair. Her voice was so crackly and shaky that she always seemed to sound as if she was laughing, which, despite her trials, she very often was. She knew she couldn't be a day nurse, but this arrangement helped pay the bills and made her feel, after a lifetime of work, that she was still useful.

The radio alarm clock came on, confirming for Norma that it was 6:00 A.M. As always, the set was tuned to a local station, the source of the most useful weather reports. Norma didn't care about the wind chill in Times Square. She wanted to know what was doing closer to home in Getty Square. Before the weather came the news, and the man at the microphone said something about a noisy meeting the night before at City Hall. Norma had been following the controversy a little, and knew that "the white folks" wanted to stop the building of new housing on the other side of town. To Norma that didn't really qualify as news. As far as she knew, white folks were always trying to stop black folks from doing something.

She opened her eyes as she turned off the radio, and that was when she noticed that something was very wrong. The room, which should have been light, was still dark. The gray, blue rays of early dawn were not coming through the window as they usually did, and she couldn't see a thing. Slowly she stood, groped her way to the wall switch, and flipped it on. Her panic rose as she realized that the problem was not with the light, but with her eyes. She turned her head right to left, she squinted, then opened her lids wide, but whatever she did, the room still looked like it had been draped in thick black lace. She put her fists to her temples, her way of calming herself. She was afraid to admit all this to her patient, or maybe she was afraid to admit it to herself, so she pretended she was fine, trusting her sense of touch and her memory to give the woman her morning medicine.

When the day nurse arrived two hours later, Norma took the elevator to the first floor of the building, then waited at the corner until she did not hear any cars. Holding her breath, she crossed the street, grabbed the fence on the other side, and clung to it, hand over hand, until she reached her building near the end of the driveway. She went upstairs and spent four days in bed.

The marred vision didn't go away, although it did clear a little. She still saw a veil of black lace, but it was of a looser weave. Norma finally confessed all to her patient, who asked her to stay on in the job anyway. It is hard to find someone to come at night near Schlobohm, a fact that Norma knew well. Most pizza places don't deliver to the neighborhood. Taxis say they'll come, then they never show. This elderly woman had been assigned many a night health aide in recent months, but Norma was the only one who actually arrived as promised.

So every evening after that, Norma's nephew, who lived in another building in Schlobohm, would walk Norma to her patient's apartment. He would be her eyes while she dispensed the medication, then he would leave the two ailing women alone for the night.

If she had slept poorly before, Norma barely slept at all now. She lay on the couch, eyes closed, with her ears alert to the sleeping woman in the next room, and her mind wandering across her own earlier years. The more she lost sight of the present, the more clearly she seemed to see the past. She could spend hours staring inwardly at her memories, which were vivid and in focus. She saw the burgundy velvet curtain in the front room of her parents' five-room house down in North Carolina, and the remembered colors were so rich she reached out her hands in front of her for a moment, as if to feel the softness of the fabric. There was white in her memories, too—white Chantilly bedspreads with flowers, white sheets, and white diapers, scrubbed by hand and hung on the clothesline.

She was Norma Frances Smeets back then, the oldest of the

seven children of a handyman and a housekeeper. Everyone called her Frances. Her family was poor, but there always seemed to be enough food. The garden out back supplied string beans and tomatoes, and the nearby fields held blueberries and blackberries, all of which filled Norma's memory as a kaleidoscope of green and orange and mouthwatering purple. At Easter there were baskets and no less than four dozen pastel-colored eggs. Norma's new dress was always pink. Janice, the second oldest, always chose yellow. At Christmas there was somehow money for a doll for each girl, and a toy dump truck for each boy.

Her later memories were darker, but no less clear. Her mother died of a heart attack when Norma was thirteen and her baby sister not yet two. Then, after high school, her father sent her away. There was no future in North Carolina, he told her, nothing for a young black woman to do but work in the fields or do "days work," cleaning white people's houses and tending to their children. He sent her to a tiny town in Pennsylvania, which Norma remembered in grays and browns—the soot gray of the dirtied snow days after a storm, and the muddy brown of the mushrooms she packed into cans at the local factory. There was family there—an aunt, two uncles, and three cousins—and her father hoped they would watch over her more closely than he could.

They couldn't. She had been living in Pennsylvania for just over a year when she became pregnant. Her baby's father was twelve years her senior, a friend of the family, a man she hardly knew before and rarely spoke to after. She was a teenager who had never had a talk with an adult about sex. When Dwayne was born, in the winter of 1962, his father gave Norma thirteen dollars.

Declaring that motherhood made her independent, she left Pennsylvania and moved north to Yonkers, where another aunt was living. The aunt watched Dwayne at night and took him to a baby-sitter during the day, while Norma, who found a job as a live-in maid, saw him only on weekends. Lying on the couch near Schlobohm, she could still feel the five crisp ten-dollar bills that the rich lady placed in her hand every Friday all those years ago. She remembered grasping them tightly in her pocket as she rode the bus home, where she would hand two of the five bills to Dwayne's baby-sitter.

Somehow Norma managed to save some money, and she found her own apartment at 159-163 Duropa Street, number 4D. It was clean but small, with one bedroom, a living room, a bathroom, and a kitchen. Most important, it was safe, "one of the safest places this side of town," she says. Visitors had to ring the bell and wait to be admitted by buzzer. She had loved the sound of that bell—the sharp, jarring buzz of security. There was security, too, in the friendship of the woman in the apartment next door, who watched Dwayne all day, for free.

In time, her new friend set Norma up with Jimmy O'Neal, whom Norma disliked immediately. A boisterous man, the type who always seems to be laughing louder than everyone else in the movie theater, Jimmy had a good job at a factory in southwest Yonkers, making dresses. He won Norma over with his affection for Dwayne, and the two were married in May of 1966.

They lived all over southwest Yonkers. Like Alma, Norma was looking for the contented feeling of home that she'd had in her youth and, years later, she would remember each apartment down to the knobs on the cabinets and the tiles on the floors. First, the cold-water flat on Croton Terrace, $50 a month, where two families shared the hallway bathroom, and, also like Alma, the only heat came from the kitchen stove. They only stayed six months, because Bruce was a newborn and needed to be kept warm. Then the pretty apartment on Pollrock Street, in a four-family house, with two bedrooms and a beautiful blue bathroom. But after two pleasant years, Norma's two youngest sisters, precocious at fourteen and fifteen, were sent north from Chimney Rock by their father. So the extended family moved to the gritty apartment on Ashburton, where heat was included in the rent, but the landlord rarely turned it on. They moved after seven months, to the housing project of Mulford Gardens.

She had happy memories of Mulford Gardens—ocher and rose, like the sunsets over the redbrick buildings on summer nights. Back in the 1970s, public housing was a goal, a step up from the crumbling apartments people like Norma could afford, and when it was warm the children could play outside until ten or eleven o'clock, hundreds of children racing and laughing, while their parents sat on nearby benches and watched. Tasha was born during Norma's years in Mulford, and Norma would often leave her sons downstairs to play while she took the baby inside, bathed her, and put her down for the night. Then she would collect the boys, tuck them in as well, and spend several more hours outside, talking with her neighbors, unworried about her sleeping children upstairs.

Jimmy was a good provider, and life took on a comfortable, predictable routine. When Norma was working, either housekeeping or at a factory, she refused to cook on Friday and Saturday nights, so the whole family dined someplace special, like White Castle on Fordham Road. The children would each have four of the tiny, square, onion-topped burgers, and Norma and Jimmy would each eat eight. There were french fries and milkshakes for everyone. Norma, who had developed her diabetes when she was pregnant with Tasha, would usually try to skip the milkshake.

Because Jimmy was so generous toward the children, Norma simply ignored the other women in his life. She knew from the time they met that all of his married friends were unfaithful, and Norma told herself that this was just her husband's way of saving face in front of those friends. The hurt it caused her was not worth the cost of confronting him.

Then, in 1974, when Tasha was less than a year old, Jimmy lost his job and announced he was going back home to North Carolina to find work. When he was settled, he would send for his family. At first he called frequently, then less often, then not at all. When he had been gone for three months, Norma had the locks changed. For years he sent each child a hundred dollars at Christmas and another hundred at the start of school, but he stopped doing so, Norma believed, because his girlfriends disapproved. He and Norma continued to speak on the phone occasionally and to see each other when Jimmy came to visit the children, once or twice a year. They never did get around to getting divorced.

In the years after Jimmy left, Norma went on and off welfare,

Show Me a Hero

taking countless jobs that barely paid enough to pay the baby-sitter. One of Jimmy's brothers worked as a butcher, and he would periodically arrive at Norma's apartment with a sack of meat and a few needed dollars. Jimmy's other brother had daughters older than Tasha, and he would give Norma their hand-me-down clothes. When she wasn't working full-time, Norma would baby-sit, off the books, first in Mulford, and then in Schlobohm, where she moved when Tasha was two and a half. Eventually she found steady, well-paying work as a home health aide. She would leave her oldest child to care for her younger ones, then go spend the night at the bedside of an elderly patient.

That was where she was the day her world went black, and where she continued to be in the weeks and months that followed, because she couldn't think of anything else to do. The doctors that she paid with Medicaid said that her optic nerve had been damaged by all those years of diabetes. They gave her laser treatments, which helped a little, and then they told her that there was no cure.

Her initial panic gave way to resignation. She didn't complain, because, she had learned, complainers were "tiresome" and self-pity never fixed a thing. So she saved up happy moments to tell her children about when they called, her way of proving to them, and to herself, that she was fine. And, most of the time, she really *was* fine. This was one more obstacle life had thrown at her. She would just have to find a way through.

The War

Pent-up anger explodes. Unleashed anger expands and multiplies. Every day there was more anger in Yonkers—more protesters at every official and unofficial meeting, more bullets in the mail, more Pampers and condoms and tiny American flags. As the weeks passed in 1988, as winter became spring, the web of anger widened. It moved beyond the council, beyond Yonkers, beyond control.

In February, it went to Washington. At 7:30 one morning, five hundred protesters boarded ten rented buses and caravaned to the Capitol building, where they held signs that pleaded "President Reagan, Help Yonkers, N.Y." Mary Dorman was part of that crowd, standing windblown but determined in her jeans and sneakers, her chapped hands crammed into the pockets of her white ski jacket. A small group of coalition leaders arranged a meeting with the state's senator Daniel Patrick Moynihan, and Mary, emboldened by her new passion for a cause, tagged along inside the Senate building. She and a few other stowaways got as far as the senator's door, but were asked to wait outside while the actual talks took place. Mary came away as unimpressed with the Senate as she was with the council. Moynihan made it clear there was nothing he would do to help Yonkers fight the judge.

By April, the anger had ensnared the Catholic Church. Mary and her compatriots had come to blame the Church for the consent decree, because the agreement was made possible by the donation of land by the St. Joseph's seminary. What the Archdiocese of New York saw as a gesture of goodwill, the protesters of Yonkers saw as an act of betrayal, and when Cardinal John J. O'Connor happened to visit the seminary for a reason that had nothing to do with the housing, he was met by fifty protesters holding signs with such messages as "Catholic Americans, Stop All Donations to the Church." As his car drove through the gates and up the long drive, the protesters chanted, "Support the people who support the Church." In the weeks that followed, parishioners throughout Yonkers defiantly kept their wallets closed when the collection plate was passed.

In June, the anger reached Judge Sand's front door. This time there were two hundred protesters, and their purpose was to show Sand that they knew where he lived. They also wanted to show the world how well he lived. Following a hand-drawn, photocopied map, they drove north, to Pound Ridge, an affluent pocket of Westchester where most homes cannot be seen from the road, and where the driveways are a quarter mile apart. They stood in front of his fence for two hours, waving their fraying American flags and carrying placards that compared Sand, who is Jewish, to Adolf

Hitler. They blew whistles, shouted "Integrate Pound Ridge" into bullhorns, and heckled neighbors with chants of "No Justice, No Peace." The vehicles that brought them from Yonkers lined the narrow, curving road for half a mile. On the trees and mailboxes along that road, they taped signs saying "Low-income housing to be built on this property, courtesy of Judge Sand."

As the circle of anger widened, the entire country began paying attention. Mail arrived on Nick's desk addressed "City Council, Yonkers," or "Yonkers, New York."

A letter writer from Arcadia, California, described Sand's order as: "Nothing but garbage. These Federal judges are doing everything they can to take over our lives. Instead of dealing with all the crime in the streets, they're more interested in molding society to their views."

A farmer from Mountain View, Missouri, wrote that federal courts were leading the country "right down the drain." Judges like Sand were "just a bunch of dictators who won't be happy until they ruin our lives," he continued. "The Yonkers City Council took a fair and square vote and Judge Sand should mind his own business."

From Long Beach, California: "We need a few nice places to live in this country, and our judges need to be replaced when they take such ridiculous stands as Judge Sand."

From Memphis, Tennessee: "Public housing is wrong and I would not permit it in my neighborhood without a fight."

Nick's days had become a spiral of less sleep and more vodka, and he became the first to bend. It was the only practical way, he decided, and he still believed he could subdue this tiger if he could find the practical political way. After all, he had ridden the anger into office in the first place. He had seen it only as a means to election then, and had not understood its depth and fury. Whatever his miscalculation, however, he had controlled it once and needed to find a way to control it now. If a symbolic appeal to the Supreme Court would calm the frenzy, then he would go to the Supreme Court. One night, at the end of a particularly draining council meeting, when one hundred forty people were on the speakers' list and another two hundred were outside chanting, he quietly announced that the city would ask Sand to restore the right to a Supreme Court appeal.

In a written statement to the judge, Nick blamed himself for "sorely underestimating" residents' fears. "They are very frightened people who can see in the court's decrees . . . a callous government destroying . . . the only real asset which [many of] these people have managed to acquire. Any efforts at fence mending are doomed to failure in such an environment." Hoping to reach the judge's practical side, he added, "If the furor is not dispelled, the hostility will scare away prospective public housing tenants and destroy chances of racial harmony—the goal of the case."

Sand turned down the request. He was worried about the young mayor, whom he saw as trying to do the right thing—despite being worn down by the force of the crowd.

"To allow [the appeal]," Sand wrote back, "would reward intransigence, reward threats of violence and reward conditions which lead, rather pitifully, the leaders of Yonkers to say 'Help us, court, we can't govern.'" An appeal, he said, would not stop the protests or solve the housing problem. "I can't believe they would simply fold their tents and stroll away if the appeal were announced and the Supreme Court said 'denied.'"

The City Council heard Sand's response, then decided to appeal to the Supreme Court anyway. They knew they risked contempt charges, and they knew the high court probably wouldn't help them, but that did not stop them from filing the papers. Nick, simultaneously relieved and worried, had an extra vodka the night the appeal was filed. Nicholas Longo, when asked by a reporter why the hopeless appeal was necessary, summed up Nick Wasicsko's feelings, too: "Why don't you look at all the people ready to riot in the streets?"

The next to blink was the Catholic Church. In a full-page advertisement in the *Herald Statesman,* Cardinal O'Connor said he had been misled. He was not given all the facts, he said, before he allowed the seminary site to be included in the housing plan. At the time he gave his consent, he said, he didn't know that 108 units, more than half the total, were planned for a single Catholic parish—the one square mile around St. John the Baptist Church. O'Connor said in the article that he was "deeply puzzled by the concentration" and feared such a plan would not work. "I certainly would have been concerned by its designation had I been aware of the concentration. I don't like having been misled."

The Church threatened to withdraw the seminary site. Sand ordered Yonkers to condemn the property and seize it. The archdiocese appealed to the New York State Supreme Court, charging that condemnation proceedings would be contrary to Church law, which requires the permission of the Vatican for any transfer of Church land. What had been a tug-of-war between a city and a judge was becoming a shoving match between Church and State.

Nick, a lapsed Catholic, but still a Catholic, was personally troubled by that fight. But he was much more troubled by the effect the standoff was having on Nicholas Longo, who had so reluctantly voted in favor of the consent decree and who was now regretting that vote. Longo, who was as tired as he was of the yelling, the threats, the bullets in the mail. Longo, who had voted for the consent decree because it would theoretically give the council control, only to find that they were being ordered to seize land from the Church.

"As a Catholic," Longo said, "I in good conscience cannot proceed against the Catholic Church. A hostile takeover was never our intention, never, never, never."

Nick suspected that Longo and the others were actually more interested in saving their council seats than in saving their souls, and that the entrance of the cardinal into the conflict was not their reason to back out, but their excuse. He believed that all the more completely when Sand offered to drop the seminary site from the plan if the city found a replacement. Instead of being relieved, Longo was outraged.

"No more sites," he said. "That's it. Period. Sand is anti-Catholic, anti-Christian, and ought to be removed from the bench."

From there, the showdown between judge and city was inevitable. The next weeks were a cascade of events, one after another, each taking the city further and further from compromise.

On June 13, the Supreme Court announced it would not even hear the Yonkers case. The next night, the City Council voted a moratorium on the housing, officially refusing to cooperate with the judge. Sand immediately answered back, instructing the council to take a vote reaffirming support for the consent decree. As ordered, a vote was taken, and the tally was 5 to 2 *against* the housing. For good measure, the councilmen also voted to halt the proceedings designed to take land from the archdiocese. That resolution, introduced at high volume by Hank Spallone, referred to Sand as a "philosopher king," who was "illegally engineering the destruction" of the Catholic Church.

"If Judge Sand wants to hold me in contempt of court, he can," said Spallone. "This is nothing more or nothing less than what happened in Nazi Germany." Then he compared Sand to Hitler again, saying that both aimed to confiscate Church property. "Perhaps," he said, "Judge Sand forgot what a swastika means."

The grenade was now in Sand's court.

Michael Sussman, the lawyer for the NAACP, hoped this would be enough to push the judge to do what he had refused to do so many times before—to use the full force of his office and finally take control of the housing away from the City Council. That is what other judges had done in other standoffs. In Alabama, for example, during the early 1980s, a U.S. district judge took control of the state's mental hospitals after patients sued for better treatment. At first he gave hospital officials three months to come up with a proposal to improve conditions. Nine months later, when there was still no plan, he devised his own, specifying such details as hospital staff qualifications, clothing allowances for patients, and the amount of money to be spent on food.

Similarly, a federal judge waited three years but then took full charge of the Arkansas prison system, which had been found guilty of such abuses as filthy bedding, insufficient clothing, and rampant brutality by so-called honors prisoners against other inmates. And in Boston, U.S. District Judge W. Arthur Garrity Jr. took control of the city's schools from the elected Boston School

Committee in 1974, after finding that the city had segregated blacks in inferior schools within its system. He retained that control for eleven years, during which time he issued more than four hundred orders relating to such things as busing, budgets, and school curriculum. He finally relinquished control in 1985, when the city's first black school superintendent was hired.

Sand seriously considered the same route. He even asked one of his law clerks to draft an order that would establish a commission to oversee the housing. But, in the end, he did not sign that order. In part it was because he agreed with the other plaintiff in the case, the Justice Department, which argued that setting up the commission would be "effectively letting the city off the hook" allowing them to "flout" the court's order "with impunity." What persuaded Sand to forgo the commission, however, were not the arguments in open court, but the discussions with his clerks back in his chambers. To be effective, he concluded, a commission would have to be given authority over everything from local zoning laws, to building and fire code inspections, to the system by which asphalt is bid out and purchased for the new roads to the new developments. It would all but devour the government of Yonkers.

From the begining of the case, Sand had believed that the only way the housing plan would work was if it came *from* the city, rather than being forced *on* the city. The point of this exercise, he reasoned, was not to punish Yonkers, but to change it, or, more accurately, to coax Yonkers into changing itself. His intention was not to erect some buildings and declare victory, but to make those buildings into homes, and make those homes part of a diverse but unified community.

"Diverse, yes," architect Oscar Newman would comment later. "Unified was something else again."

Newman saw the latter goal as unattainable. More than that, he believed that the idealism behind that goal was the judge's deepest flaw. "He's a mixture of naiveté and hope," he said with a frustrated sigh. "He very much wanted the city to see the light. To see that they had erred, that they had sinned, and that this remedy would really cure them if they could only see the light."

In the end, Sand's decision to fine Yonkers, not dismantle it, was more than just a philosophical one. Like Nick, he thought he was taking the practical route. He was wagering that fines, hefty fines, would work. A student of judicial history, he knew that in every other case when sanctions were imposed for obstruction of a federal desegregation order, the showdown fizzled within hours after the fines took effect. Sometimes, even the mere threat was enough to change some minds.

In 1964, for instance, Alabama's governor, George Wallace, backed down when charged with contempt of court, and he reopened the Macon County school system, which he had closed in order to prevent its integration. In 1970, Florida's governor, Claude Kirk, backed down in the face of $10,000-a-day fines, and he reinstated the Manatee County School Board, which he had dissolved to prevent court-ordered desegregation.

In Boston in 1974, Judge Garrity held three Boston School Committee members in contempt for refusing to approve a citywide school desegregation plan, and said he would fine the members if they did not approve the plan within weeks. They did, and the threat of fines was dropped. And in 1981, the Cleveland School Board's treasurer and its twenty-six-year-old president were held in contempt and actually put in jail for twenty minutes for refusing to pay outside desegregation experts as ordered by the judge. They were released on bail, and the experts were soon hired.

So it was with an external scowl but internal optimism that Judge Leonard B. Sand announced what he would do to Yonkers. If the council did not vote to reaffirm the consent decree by August 1 he would impose personal fines of $500 a day against each recalcitrant councilman—the first time an individual legislator had been fined in a federal desegregation case. To underline his point, he added the threat of jail time for the councilmen if they remained in contempt for ten days. In addition, the long-threatened fines would be imposed against the city, starting at $100 a day, then doubling every day. The money would be nonrefundable. It would take an act of Congress to recover even one dime.

On Day 1, Yonkers would owe $100. Day 2, $200, for a total of $300 paid. After a week, on Day 7, a daily fine of $6,400, for a total debt of $12,700. By Day 14, the daily fine would top $1 million for the first time, $1,638,400 to be exact, for a total of $3,276,700 paid. On Day 22, the daily fine of $209,715,200 would bring the total fine paid to $419,430,300, more than the $355 million in the city's budget. By Day 29, the total fine would be $53,687,091,100, which would be greater than the U.S. trade deficit with Japan. By the end of the month, the total fine of $107 billion would be more than the gross national product of Finland.

Hours before the midnight deadline on August 1, 1988, the council met again. Nick's months in office had taught him to expect the worst, and driving to City Hall that night he wondered why he was bothering to go at all. Hank Spallone, Peter Chema, and Nicholas Longo had each been clear and public about their plans to vote no. Nick and Harry Oxman were planning to vote yes. Charles Cola had said once or twice that he was worried about the effect of the threatened fines on the city's bond rating, but otherwise he had been firm in his opposition to the housing, and Nick did not expect Cola to provide him with a miracle. Only the ever-mysterious Ed Fagan had refused to say which way he would vote.

That left the most optimistic projections at three votes in favor of compliance and four votes against. Another death threat had come in the mail for Nick recently, scribbled on an invitation he had sent out for a political fund-raiser that would double as his twenty-ninth birthday party. "This is your last birthday" had been scrawled across the card in the place of an RSVP. A small-caliber bullet was in the envelope. It was hot outside now as he drove to City Hall, thinking about that bullet. He was sweating in spite of the air conditioner. He wanted to go back home.

Before he saw the protesters, he heard them singing. There were hundreds of them, more than the steps or sidewalks could hold, and they were standing in the center of Nepperhan Avenue, kept there by thirty police officers as cars streamed by on either side. Linking arms, they sang "We Shall Overcome," then "God Bless America." When Spallone's car passed, they sang "Happy Birthday," because he, too, had recently had a birthday.

Inside City Hall, four floors up, Nick could still hear the singing.

Only eighty people could fit in the council chamber, a relief to all after the riotous meeting of nine hundred at Saunders High School, but the small crowd felt threatening in its own claustrophobic way. Here the protesters sat almost nose to nose with the councilmen, separated only by a six-foot barrier of klieg lights and television cameras. The air inside was stifling, and became even more so when Nick was forced to close the windows to drown out the shouting from the street. Michael Sussman, the lawyer for the NAACP, was barred from the chambers by the police, who feared that his presence would be an excuse for violence. Laurie Recht was asked to leave, too, after she sparked a shoving match when she tried to take a seat.

First came the speeches, familiar faces saying the same things they had said before. But this time there was a cockiness where there used to be only desperation. This time they believed they would win.

When it came time to vote on the reaffirmation of the consent decree, Nick voted yes, as did Henry Oxman. Charles Cola, to Nick's amazement, voted with them. Nicholas Longo voted no, relieved that with that one simple word the catcalls and the bullets in the mail would finally stop. Peter Chema did the same, and smiled when his vote was greeted with cheers from the crowd.

The vote was tied, three for and three against. Even the jaded newspaper reporters held their breath.

The last to vote was Ed Fagan, who had remained a puzzle during the week before this meeting. He had said he wanted to weigh his options, but Nick assumed he was silent because he was hoping for a crescendo moment just like this. The clerk called Fagan's name and he paused dramatically. One second. Two seconds. More. Then he leaned his long body toward the microphone, stared into the spotlight, and delivered an emphatic "No."

The single word shot through the silence with the force of a starter's pistol. The crowd went wild, giving Fagan a standing ovation, and dancing in the narrow aisles. Like a jolt of electricity, the news traveled out of the council chambers, down the stairs, and onto the street: the council had taken on the judge. The whoops of

Show Me a Hero

celebration could be heard even through the closed windows of City Hall. People screaming inside. People screaming outside. Soon it sounded to Nick as if all of Yonkers was screaming.

Alma Goes Home Again

Alma Febles was far from the screaming on that deafening August night. She was back with her children in Santo Domingo, spending precious vacation time she had earned by working Monday through Saturday every week during the endless months in Yonkers. She would have gladly worked Sunday, too—anything to keep her away from the apartment—but the furniture showroom was closed.

She brought few clothes with her when she arrived for this visit to the island. Her suitcases were crammed instead with the tastes of home that her children craved, and she spent her first night filling the cupboards with boxes of cereal, cans of tuna fish, assorted soups, spaghetti sauces, and salad dressings. The cartons of cigarettes—she was up to three or four packs a day now—she hid where she hoped they would not find them. She was hiding other secrets, too. What Virgilio, Leyda, and Frankie missed most, she knew, was not in her suitcase. Eventually she would have to tell them that she could not stay.

When she first left her family, back in February, Alma had intended to return permanently to Santo Domingo by August. Six or seven months, she calculated, would give her enough time to save the modest nest egg needed to live together on the island. But she had miscalculated, mostly because she hadn't counted on the phone calls. Disconnecting the phone in her Schlobohm apartment hadn't stemmed her need to talk to the children, and neither had her fear of the pay phone on the corner. It became her routine to call collect to the peach house every day, sometimes two or three times a day. If they were not there when she called, she would call back later. If just Virgilio was home, she would call again until she spoke to Leyda and Frankie, too.

Alma knew her children missed her. Virgilio, quiet and brooding like his father, stopped writing to her for weeks at a time. When she asked him where his letters were, he said, "I was mad when it was time to write and I didn't know what to say." Frankie, wild and impulsive like *his* father, tried to run away from home once or twice so that he could go and find her. Leyda, who was most like her mother, with the same lustrous hair and huge eyes, was the one who missed her the most. When the little girl was sad she would close those eyes and picture Alma, back in Schlobohm, feeling sad too. "I knew you were feeling the way I was feeling," Leyda would tell her. "Sometimes I'd cry, and wish you could see me, too, and that you would come. But you didn't come."

Leyda wrestled with her despair by trying to become her mother, acting particularly protective of her little brother. When the maid cooked something that Frankie didn't like, Leyda would stomp around the kitchen shouting "Leave him alone. If he doesn't want to eat it, don't make him eat it."

Often the fights became physical, and if the maid slapped Leyda, Leyda usually slapped back. The incident would inevitably be reported to Alma, who would try to calm her daughter long-distance. The girl would not be soothed.

"Why don't you come here and hit me yourself if you're my mom?" she cried into the telephone.

The children were so happy to see her at the start of this visit that Alma could not bear to tell them of her change of plans right away. She settled in as if she were staying. They never asked why she hadn't brought more with her from Schlobohm.

The days took on a lazy routine, because her Santo Domingo was not the activity-filled Santo Domingo that the rich tourists saw. On her slice of the island there was no snorkeling or parasailing, no discos or roulette wheels. The only way that world intersected with her own was when the electricity in her neighborhood was turned off periodically during times of peak energy demand at the resorts.

Show Me a Hero

Each morning, Alma served the children buttered rolls and hot chocolate. She had grown up drinking hot chocolate for breakfast and it comforted her to give it to her own children, even in the heat. At night, she made spaghetti and meatballs, a favorite of theirs from Yonkers. During the sunny hours between the cocoa and the pasta, Alma would tidy the house, do the laundry, walk down the block to her mother's, gossip with childhood friends.

After all her years up north, Alma reveled in the friendship of people who had known her all her life. In Schlobohm she had allowed herself no friends, and the only women she spoke to were her sister Dulce, her cousin Miriam, and her own mother (who, now that Alma and her sisters were long grown, preferred to spend her time back in Santo Domingo). Alma had forgotten the connectedness of real friendship. On the island she allowed people into her home, something she would never do back north in the projects. More important, she let them into her life, sitting for hours over coffee and conversation, sharing gossip and finding guidance.

It was from these friends that Alma learned more about the lives of her children during the months when she was gone. About how the maid had started to lock Frankie in the house to keep him from climbing the fence and running away again. About how Leyda stayed out after dark, and about how all three kids climbed onto the roof to pick mangoes from a towering tree and snuck into a neighbor's yard to steal wild strawberries.

Knowing that they were flirting with danger made Alma even more heartbroken about her inevitable news. One night, over dinner, she told them. Frankie ran from the table and hid under his bed. Virgilio silently played with his food. Leyda looked stricken and said, "I understand that you *think* this is the best way to take care of us."

The children cried during the long bus ride to the airport, and during the longer wait for the plane. When the voice over the intercom announced Alma's flight, she stood up and turned to give each child a kiss good-bye. Frankie sank to the floor, grabbed her leg, and shrieked. Leyda threw her arms around Alma's neck and sobbed. Alma's last glimpse of her children as she entered the jetway was of her mother holding them back, keeping them from rushing onto the plane.

The Homeless Motel

Doreen James sat on the bed at the motel for the homeless, bouncing, slowly, against the surprisingly firm mattress. Doreen was a large, imposing, fleshy woman, made rounder still by her very recent pregnancy, and she held Jaron, her newborn, in her ample arms, snuggling him against her chest, trying to keep him from crying. She bounced sluggishly, but rhythmically, and she did not change her pace as his screaming grew louder.

Some young women, alone with an infant for the first time, would be frantic, but Doreen was not the frantic type, and she reacted to this as she did to most of the unpleasantness in her life— she sighed more deeply and moved even more slowly. Up and down, up and down on the big motel bed. "You be quiet now," she said, without anger, or even intonation. "Quiet, quiet," she repeated, patting the wailing baby with her dark brown hands.

As she bounced, she glared at the pot of water bubbling lazily on the hot plate across the room. Stubbornly, it was proving the rule, and refusing to boil. Until the water boiled, then cooled, she could not mix the powered baby formula. And without the formula, she could not quiet Jaron. Leaving her parents' home, with its fully equipped kitchen and two extra pairs of helping hands, had seemed like a good idea at the time, an overdue declaration of independence. But here, in this state-funded motel room, with only a contraband hot plate to care for this baby, she was having second thoughts.

She knew when she decided to move that the only home she could afford would be in public housing, and that idea did not bother her at all. Doreen was born in Yonkers in 1965, and had spent her childhood in the projects on School Street. It was different there then, she remembered: "No drugs, no dogs, and they

Show Me a Hero

didn't have all that traffic." Her father and several other men took turns patrolling the hallways at night. The most dangerous past-time when she lived in the projects was riding on the tops of the elevators.

Doreen was the fifth child in a family of four girls and two boys, and her memories of public housing were ones of safety and to-getherness. Alma Febles wanted out of Schlobohm; Doreen James wanted in, or thought that she did.

A life spent in and around public housing meant she knew how to navigate the rules, and she understood that there were two ways to get the apartment she wanted: the regular waiting list and the emergency one. The first route could take years, and Doreen needed to transform her life quicker than that. So she went to the Yonkers Department of Social Services and presented herself as an emergency case—a twenty-one-year-old new mother who was homeless. Her grandmother helped with the plan, writing a letter to Doreen's caseworker explaining that there was not enough room in the grandmother's apartment for two more. The caseworker im-mediately found a room for Doreen and Jaron in a motel for the homeless in the upper reaches of Westchester County, a temporary stopping place until an apartment became available.

What Doreen never mentioned to the caseworker was that there was an entire bedroom available for her at her parents' house, a room her parents said would be hers to call home whenever she wished. And she also failed to mention that her parents were leery of her entire plan. Pearl and Walter James had struggled to get their children out of the projects and they could not understand why their youngest daughter was hell-bent on moving back in. Doreen had been ten years old when her father took a job main-taining a golf driving range in New Jersey, proudly moving his wife and children to Essex County, where they lived in a two-family house. Doreen, not yet slowed and saddened by the disappoint-ments of life, had thrived away from School Street. After school each day she would race to the backyard where she jumped rope and rode her bike until dark. She didn't spend much time then worrying on the future, but when she did think about it she saw herself as a social worker, "helping people" all day, then coming home to "a husband, a son and daughter, nice house, two-car garage, me working, him working, kids doing well in school."

Despite their move, however, the James family did not cut off all contact with Yonkers. Sheila, the oldest of the children, was nearly twenty when her parents decided to move, and she stayed behind. Doreen went back to see her often, visits that grew more frequent after Doreen's high school graduation. She tried the helping professions for a while, attending school to learn to be a medical office assistant, but she discovered she had an unconquerable fear of needles, so she dropped out after three months. Next, she became a home health aide, and enjoyed that work until one of her patients died. For months after that she worked as a salesclerk in a fabric store, where the only needles were used for sewing.

During one of her visits to Sheila, she met Joe Bailey. He was the brother of a mutual friend, and he was a symbol of how the projects had changed. Joe sold drugs, cocaine mostly, on the corner near School Street. Doreen didn't really mind his profession, because he rarely sampled his wares himself. "He's nice to me, he's a good listener," she would explain in her languid, laconic way. Then she would shrug her shoulders.

A year after the couple met, they decided to marry. They never set a date, but they did choose a solitaire diamond ring, which they put on layaway. Soon after that, when Doreen learned she was pregnant, Joe was thrilled. Doreen was less so. "This wasn't part of the dream," she tried to explain to Joe.

In her seventh month of pregnancy she went to the hospital clinic for her prenatal checkup. It was a crowded, uncomfortable room, and she hated her appointments there. She kept them only because Joe insisted. He had suffered from asthma for years, and, his source of income aside, he was always preaching healthy living. So Doreen went to the clinic as scheduled that morning, fitting her expanding girth into a small molded plastic chair and waiting for her turn with the nurse practitioner. When her name was finally called, however, it was not by a nurse, but by Joe's father, who made his way across the room to her, his face sagging with the weight of his news. Joe was dead. Asthma. All of a sudden. Doreen gripped the flimsy chair so tightly that the edges bent. She tried

Show Me a Hero

not to faint. As she sobbed in the arms of her fiancé's father, he patted her kindly but awkwardly and warned, "Don't you have this baby on me right now."

That same night, she escaped back to New Jersey. "Mommy and Daddy to the rescue as always," she said. The jewelry store would not refund the money for her ring, so she exchanged it for a gold cross for her baby, a last gift from his father.

Jaron was born early in the summer of 1988. At first, Doreen burrowed into the cocoon of home, the chance to be a child while she cared for her child. Then one night she dreamed that Jaron called his grandparents "Mommy" and "Daddy." Despite her parents' objections, she applied for her own apartment.

The motel in Yorktown Heights, the stopping place on the way to her new life, was nicer than she had expected. It had two double beds, a matching desk, nightstand, and dresser, and a shiny bathroom, tiled completely in white. Attractive as it was, however, Doreen felt trapped in the quaint rural town, which was nearly an hour north of Yonkers.

She spent her days trying to feed her child with only a hot plate, and she spent her nights worrying about noises from outside. Someone had told her "there was Klansmen in the woods," and, after a few sleepless nights, she left. She had to *say* she was homeless, she reasoned, but she didn't have to *live* like she was homeless. She could room with her parents in New Jersey until her name reached the top of the emergency waiting list.

The Glare of the Spotlight

The gaze of the world is a fickle, intoxicating thing. As the television cameras turned their attention to Yonkers, they magnified and electrified events, changing the body language of the combatants and sharpening the tone of their words.

Nick first watched that transforming power on the night of August 1, 1988, the night that the council voted to defy the judge and face the fines. There had been some attention from the press before then, mostly local newspapers and television. But the night that the city hurled itself into contempt there were fifty reporters in the chamber to watch the vote, including one from the *Jerusalem Post*. Yonkers was now international news.

The next morning, August 2, the council members were summoned to Judge Sand's chambers to have the fines officially imposed. The press was there, too, and their presence intensified the drama. In the middle of the hearing, Hank Spallone walked out, lured by the call of the media. A U.S. marshal soon found the AWOL councilman in a nearby telephone booth, where he was chatting on the air, live, to radio talk show host Barry Gray.

From then on, there seemed to be reporters everywhere. They were clustered on the steps of the federal building after the August 2 hearing, and each councilman had to run through the barricade of microphones and blinding lights. Spallone barreled past with his hands raised above his head like a newly titled boxer. Fagan and Longo, the two who changed their votes, received cheers and handshakes while the cameras rolled. Nick tried to answer questions while a hundred people chanted against him.

"They've had their moment of glory, if that's what they're looking for," he said of the defiant councilmen.

A reporter asked if he thought people would still consider moving to Yonkers.

"If they do, they have rocks in their head," said a voice from behind the mayor. One of the protesters had made it through the knot of journalists and was standing inches from Nick, towering over him.

"Get out of my face," Nick said softly, aware of the cameras.

"Fuck you," the protester said, live on some cable stations. The press stepped back, anticipating a fight, and Nick and the much taller protester glared at each other, until a nearby police officer came and escorted the protester out of camera range.

Nicholas Longo talked on his car phone during the entire hour-long drive home from the courthouse, giving an interview to a radio station in Denver. His smooth, concise message: "If it can happen to us, it can happen to you."

By the time Hank Spallone arrived at his office, there were thirty telephone messages waiting. He started at the top of the stack, and worked toward the bottom: Channel 2, Channel 4, Channel 11, the MacNeil/Lehrer Newshour, the *New York Times,* the *Los Angeles Times, Newsday, Time* magazine, the *San Francisco Chronicle, Good Morning America, Good Day, New York.*

"I have to say this about Judge Sands," he said, adding, as was his habit, a mocking, dismissive extra letter to the judge's name, "he couldn't have given us more free publicity than he did with this."

There were no meetings scheduled that first afternoon to find a compromise that could stop the fines. Instead there were appointments with CBS, NBC, and ABC. Nick had two meetings set up in Washington, D.C.—with New York senators Alphonse D'Amato and Patrick Moynihan—but he canceled them both. Nay didn't eat lunch until three o'clock that afternoon, and Nick didn't get to eat at all. Nick knew that every reporter who called him also called Hank. Hank knew that anyone who quoted him would also quote Nick. By the following morning, their remarks would appear under a single headline, their faces would be shown in the same video segment, one right after the other, point-counterpoint, a debate in front of the entire nation between two men who had more or less stopped speaking months ago.

The lawmakers were not the only ones caught in the seductive pull of the spotlight. Over the days and weeks that followed, the entire city became a backdrop for the cameras, a massive soundstage for the serial drama that was playing to a worldwide audience. Wherever the defiant councilmen went, people did double takes, they wanted to pat them on the back, introduce them to their grandchildren—"Junior, this is the man you saw on *television.*" Nicholas Longo dined out on spaghetti one night soon after the contempt vote, and a woman at a nearby table came over to thank him for his stand, then handed him a check for a thousand dollars to help him pay the court-ordered fines.

For months, from the January meeting at Saunders until the August 1 showdown at City Hall, the protesters had been posing only for the council. Now they were posing for the cameras. During the second week of August, Hank Spallone brought his small Kodak Instamatic over to Schlobohm, where he took photos of peeling paint, overflowing trash bins, and broken windows, then glued the snapshots onto a huge piece of oaktag. Mary Dorman was on the national news that night, holding the collage in front of City Hall. Shortly after that, producers from the CBS program *48 Hours* came to town, and Mary Dorman was on in prime time, talking in her kitchen. She yelled at Phil Donahue one morning and Morton Downey Jr. one afternoon.

Mary welcomed the cameras, sought them out, courted them, but each encounter left her a little stunned and bruised. Her purpose was to show the world what she thought, but the video lens can be a two-way mirror, and what Mary often saw reflected was what the world thought of *her*. Until the cameras came, she had assumed that everyone believed as she believed. It was an easy assumption, because nearly 70 percent of Yonkers residents believed the city should disobey the judge.

But then the reporters descended, and they were not from Yonkers. They stood before their microphones during these early days of August and used the word *racism* a lot. They compared this city to cities like Selma and Montgomery, and they compared this fight to the one to integrate Little Rock's Central High School.

Mary did not think of herself as racist. To her, this fight was not about race at all, it was about *principles*, and the same naiveté that allowed her to believe that also allowed her to believe she could make all the reporters see it her way.

One sweltering afternoon, in the middle of the media madness, a writer for the *Boston Globe* sat with Mary and Buddy in their kitchen for several hours, talking above the roar of an aging air conditioner. The woman ("a nice black girl," Mary said) asked a lot of questions about the east-west division between the races in Yonkers. Mary, her worn hands folded on the Formica in front of her, tried to explain that there were black families on the east side, and that they lived in lovely middle-class homes, not projects, not tenements. Those homes were on this side of the Saw Mill, her side of the Saw Mill, she said. Then she took the reporter to Runyon Heights, the black middle-class enclave that had been effectively walled off from its surrounding neighbors all those years ago.

Mary had been there before, to drop off members of her bowling league, and so she thought she knew her way around. But she quickly got lost, unable to find the homes of anyone she knew. Despite that, she thought the visit had been a success.

"I think I helped her understand," Mary told Buddy, that it isn't only white people who choose to live with others like themselves. When black people move across town, she said, "they also stick together."

The reporter wrote her article, but did not mention Runyon Heights. "Mary Dorman is white and lives on a pleasant, tree-lined street on this city's east side," the front-page story began. "Her view on housing desegregation, voiced one day last week in the air-conditioned parlor of her modest brick home, is this: 'I don't think you should take people with one lifestyle and put them smack in the middle of a place with a different lifestyle. You have to expect them to resent us.'"

Another woman, the article continued, "is black and lives on a busy, treeless street on this city's west side. Her view on housing desegregation, voiced in a steamy hallway outside her apartment, is this: 'I think all people should be together and equal as one.'"

The Emergency Financial Control Board and the Supreme Court

Nick Wasicsko stood on the spectator side of the waist-high partition that, on more usual days, separates the council from the public. The room looked different to him from back there, more somber and imposing, despite its peeling, tired edges. It looked more like a center of justice and government, and less like the place where he happened to go to work every day. He stood there, one hand playing nervously with his mustache, one hip pressed against the railing, trying to seem at ease with the role of outsider.

It was Tuesday, August 9, Day 8 of contempt. The city had paid $12,700 in fines (another $12,700 would be due by 4:30 that afternoon), and the councilmen had paid $3,500 each. Later in the day, in the opening scene of what would become a multiact legal drama, the Second U.S. Circuit Court of Appeals would put those fines on hold, pending an appeal. The halt was simply a delay of the inevitable, however, and did not stop the goings-on in the front of the council chamber.

There, at the seat graced by a sign that read "Nicholas Wasicsko, Mayor," sat a woman who was clearly not Nicholas Wasicsko. She was shuffling her pens and arranging her pads with the manner of someone comfortable being in charge. The other council seats were filled with other people whose names did not appear on the nameplates in front of them. They were there to take control of the city's finances.

More generally, they were there because the council's game of chicken with Judge Sand was not the first time Yonkers had flirted with bankruptcy and dissolution. The city had careened within inches of disaster more than once, and always managed to find a last-minute rescuer to save them from their own foolishness. During the winter of 1976, Yonkers was technically in financial default for one weekend, because it had spent years simply rolling its deficit into the next year, until the debt reached $83 million. That time, Governor Hugh Carey stepped in and bailed the city out. Then, in the spring of 1984, the Yonkers Board of Education announced it would close the schools in April instead of June, because the City Council would not provide the funding needed to complete the school year. The schools remained open when Governor Mario M. Cuomo signed a financial bailout and the council agreed to enact a local tax surcharge.

The bailouts of 1976 and 1984 came with strings attached. At the request of the city itself, the state legislature established an Emergency Financial Control Board for Yonkers, which was authorized to keep an eye on the city's finances and to step in, when necessary, to prevent another crisis. The board had the authority to approve or reject every dime of proposed spending in the city, and for years it had been reviewing, advising, and overseeing all financial decisions. Now, on Day 8, its members had come to Yonkers to wield the *full* force of their authority for the first time.

It was not the solution Nick had wanted. He and Neil DeLuca had asked Cuomo—begged Cuomo—to save Yonkers from itself, as other governors had done before. Neil was particularly persistent in his pleas. A former director of the Yonkers Youth Bureau, Neil had left that job because there was no money to be made in government service. Nick had to do a lot of arm-twisting to persuade Neil to come back and take this job as interim city manager, the person who runs all the day-to-day operations of Yonkers.

Neil was a sometime drinking buddy of Nick's, and the two looked so much alike they could pass for brothers. But while their looks were the same, their temperaments were dramatically different. Restless and intense, Neil had the air of a boxer itching for the match to begin. Nick was still more like that boxer's manager, strategizing in the corner, coolly sizing up the opposition. Neil accepted the job on two conditions: first, that it would only last a few months, and, more important, that it would not involve him in the fight over the housing. That was eight long months ago, during which time Neil had worked round the clock on the housing.

On the first day of the contempt crisis, Neil publicly asked Mario Cuomo to remove defiant councilmen from office, "to save Yonkers from bankruptcy and further national embarrassment." The same day, Nick called the governor and asked him to come down to Yonkers himself to "talk some sense" into the rebellious four. That he was neither awed nor thrilled to have the governor on the phone was a measure of how jaded and exhausted the young mayor had become since he took office in January. Cuomo turned both men down.

On Day 3, Neil warned that the city would have to lay off half the city's workers in two weeks. Once again he asked Cuomo to intervene, and once again the governor said no. It was the same answer Cuomo would give in the coming days and weeks, although the reasons for the answer changed often. First Cuomo said he would not fire the councilmen while the appeal to the Second Circuit was still pending. ("Let them have their day in court.") Then he said he would gladly help, but only if Sand would change the consent decree so that the housing was more thinly spread throughout Yonkers. ("We'll be glad to participate if he ever chooses to modify the order.") Later, he suggested that it was Neil DeLuca's job to fire the councilmen. ("DeLuca could do it without charges, without a hearing, instantly.") The last idea made no sense to Neil, who had been hired by the councilmen in the first place. "If I tried to fire them, they would fire me first," he said. "And I'll be damned before I let that happen."

Each of Cuomo's comments made it clearer to Nick that this governor wanted to stay as far away from the mess in Yonkers as possible. He sent that message not by what he did, but by what he did not do. A phone call here, a press conference there, but not a single visit to Yonkers in these first weeks of the standoff. It was all far less than the nation's most compelling orator, known as a defender of the poor and disenfranchised, could have done if he had chosen to.

Cuomo's problem was that this battle had lined his two natural constituencies up against each other. If he had said what some would have expected him to say—that racism, however it might be cloaked or sanitized, is still racism and is still evil—then he would also have been saying that working men and women, most of them immigrants like his parents, could sweat and save only to have their labor be for nothing. And if he had said just the opposite, that good, honest, hardworking people had a right to protect their dreams, he would also be saying that other good, honest, hardworking people, who happened to be black, or happened to be less educated, or happened to be stuck in a cycle of discrimination and poverty, were not entitled to dreams of their own.

Given that choice, he said both. He stayed distant enough from Yonkers that he had that luxury, one that Nick Wasicsko and Neil DeLuca didn't share. They didn't understand why one day Cuomo warned the councilmen that "the rule of law" must prevail in Yonkers, and why the next day he called Judge Sand and warned that the plan, in its current form, would hurt property values. What they *did* come to understand, was that the governor was not going to bail them out. They had asked to be rescued, and in answer Cuomo had sent Gail S. Shaffer, New York's secretary of state and the chairman of the Emergency Financial Control Board. A tough-as-nails woman who was used to playing hardball up in Albany, everything about Gail Shaffer—from her bloodred manicure to her perfectly coiffed brunette hair—showed she was in control. It was she who sat in Nick's chair, looking stern and ready for business, while Nick stood outside, looking in.

He had expected that the board members would take over the city, but he had not expected them to take over his seat. There were, in fact, other places they could sit. The morning of this meeting, a long table had been set up in the middle of the room for these intruders, on the inside of the horseshoe formed by the desks of the councilmen. But Gail Shaffer knew Yonkers, had come to know it during the years she had spent on the control board, and knew she had to send some strong messages from the start.

What the city saw as quirky independence, and Sand saw as discriminatory obstinacy, Gail Shaffer saw as simple immaturity. Politics in Yonkers resembled a preschool classroom, she thought, and when she prepared for her visits there she would tell her staff, "I'm going to teach Potty Training 101." Like children, the politicians in Yonkers were incapable of taking responsibility for their own actions. "What they always do in Yonkers is do a great punt on any major policy decision that has the slightest political impact," she said, and the very fact that her "baby-sitting job" on the control board existed was a sign of their childishness. Her goal was to dissolve the control board, to push Yonkers to the point where it was mature enough to act like "a normal locale," one that could "take charge of its own destiny and make these decisions themselves," she said.

Clearly, however, that was not going to happen in August of 1988, so Shaffer set about this initial meeting like a kindergarten teacher on the first day of school. She wanted to make it very clear who was in charge. Seating has symbolic importance in government chambers, it sets a visual pecking order, which led Shaffer and the rest of the board members to ignore the chairs at the temporary table and make themselves comfortable in the front of the room.

By the time the meeting was over, the board had taken away almost all financial authority from the city manager and the City Council. The city was still allowed to pay employee salaries, court judgments, and previously approved bills and bond payments, but nothing else. All other spending, every single item over $100, would have to be personally approved by Gail Shaffer. Hiring a new employee, increasing the salary of a current employee, authorizing overtime, negotiating contracts (the firefighters at the time were working without a contract), even buying bulk rate postage stamps — everything would need written approval. Yonkers was like an adolescent without an allowance. A teenager who had been grounded. A city no longer trusted to run itself.

The vote was 5 to 1 in favor of the restrictions. One member was absent, and Neil DeLuca, who was a member of the board by dint of his office, was the only vote against. Rather than snatch away the city's purse strings, he said, the board should ask Mario Cuomo to step in. The idea was not even brought up for a vote.

If the governor wouldn't come to the rescue, there were always the courts. "Appeal, appeal, appeal," the protesters had shouted at countless rallies, and on August 17, 1988, more than two weeks into the crisis, dozens of lawyers had their chance to do exactly that. Attorneys for the city and attorneys for the councilmen filled the courtroom of the U.S. Court of Appeals for the Second Circuit and explained why nothing about this situation was their clients' fault.

Like schoolmates caught in the act of pummeling each other, like the children Gail Shaffer thought they were, they stood before the three-judge panel and pointed indignantly at the other guy. "He" started it, the city said of the councilmen. No "he" started it, the councilmen said of the city. So, both sides argued, only "he" should be punished.

Michael Skulnick, who represented the City of Yonkers, told the court that his client *wanted* to obey Judge Sand but was "powerless to comply with the order." Compliance required a majority vote of the council, he argued, and there was nothing the city

Show Me a Hero

could do to change the four council members' minds. To fine the city under those circumstances, he continued, was like blaming a hostage for failing to flee. As much as the city would love to end this mess, he said, it couldn't, and fining it into bankruptcy would not change that.

"You talk about [the councilmen] as if they're emissaries from a foreign country," said Judge John O. Newman.

Skulnick agreed that they were. "I have serious questions about their concern" for Yonkers, he said, "if they are willing to let the city go bankrupt."

Then Hank Spallone's lawyer, Anthony J. Mercorella, stood up and argued that the city, not the councilmen, should be fined. "If the city has failed to act, then punish the city," he said.

The judges shook their heads. "*You're* telling us the city should do something, and the city is telling us *you* should do something," Judge Roger Miner said, making no attempt to hide his annoyance.

Amid the testy exchanges it was easy to lose sight of the fact that the hearing was more than a chance for grown men to act like adolescents. Beneath the layers of finger-pointing and name-calling, the Yonkers contempt case raised significant questions of philosophy and of law, of the essence of government and the power of the courts.

To rule on the appeal, for instance, the judges would have to decide exactly who *is* the city of Yonkers. "The city" was powerless to comply, Skulnick had argued. "The city" was at the mercy of the council. But who *is* "the city"? Is it a collection of bureaucrats and elected officials, people like Nick Wasicsko and Neil DeLuca? Skulnick's arguments suggested that it was.

But Judge Sand's order, in fact nearly all of his actions, were based on a view of the city as something more. When Sand leveled fines against "the city," he was leveling them against its people, the ones who packed the council meetings and marched in the streets and made it clear how they wanted their representatives to vote. Actions have consequences, he was telling them. You protest at your own peril.

An equally complex question raised by the case was that of the right of a legislator to vote his conscience. It was clear that Judge Sand had the right to order the housing into Yonkers. This same appeals court had upheld that right just before Nick took office. Also clear was that he had the power to ignore the council and "build" the housing himself. But he had not chosen to use that power; he had chosen, instead, to allow the council to participate in the process. The question before this court was how much muscle he could use to ensure that participation. It was a straight-forward question, but an unprecedented one: Does a judge have the right to tell an elected representative how to vote?

"Never before has a federal court commanded a city council-man, or other state or local legislator, how to vote on legislation," Mercorella argued on behalf of Hank Spallone. "A legislator has only to answer to his own constituents and no one else. What we have here is an attempt to erode the integrity of the legislative process."

Michael Sussman, speaking for the NAACP, responded that Sand was not really telling anyone how to vote. He was simply requiring affirmation that the city would implement something—namely the consent decree—that the councilmen had already voted for. The city had made an agreement and was now trying to renege on that agreement. Sand, Sussman argued, must now force the council to keep its word.

"Does he"—meaning Hank Spallone—"have a right to ignore the consent decree?" Judge Miner asked Mercorella, after both sides had presented their arguments.

"In his role as legislator, yes," the lawyer answered.

Said Miner, throwing out his hands in frustration: "I don't un-derstand how anyone keeps their word in this group of people."

In the end, the circuit court upheld the fines against the council-men, an affirmation of Sand's right to have implemented the fines in the first place. At the same time, the judges tinkered with the fines against the city. Saying that the formula Sand had used could reach "unreasonable proportions," the panel limited the fines to a maximum of $1 million a day, meaning the city would go bankrupt on Day 79 rather than Day 20.

Show Me a Hero

Knowing that both sides would appeal their decision to the only remaining rung on the American judicial ladder, the judges extended the stay on the fines until the Supreme Court had its chance to rule. The appeal to the Supreme Court was filed within hours, and the decision was issued at 11:55 P.M. on the night of September 1. In that decision, the justices unanimously rejected the city's request to continue a delay on the fines. Although technically that was not a rejection of the city's broader point—that the fines were unconstitutional in the first place—the practical effect was the same as a rejection, because by the time the court would finally hear the full arguments against the fines (sometime in the fall, when such hearings were traditionally scheduled), the city would already be bankrupt.

The decision surprised Nick. He never believed that the fines would be found unconstitutional, but he had hoped—he had assumed—that the Supreme Court would continue the stay until October, giving him a month of maneuvering room. Instead, tomorrow would be Day 9 of the fines, and a messenger would deliver a check for $25,600 to Judge Sand's courtroom, made out to the Department of the Treasury. The next day, the check would be for $51,200. The day after that, $102,400. The day after that, $204,800.

If the first part of the Supreme Court's decision surprised Nick, what the justices said next left him nearly speechless. After ruling that the fines should be reimposed on Yonkers, the justices turned around and lifted them from the councilmen—granting them the stay that they had denied the city as whole. The councilmen were freed while the city kept paying. The calculator continued to *kaching* in Nick's head. On Day 13, the city would owe the court $409,600. Day 14, $819,200. Day 15, $1 million. Day 16, $1 million. Day 17, $1 million.

Reporters started calling for his reaction, and all he could muster was "I had hoped that it would be the other way around."

The decision also distressed Judge Sand. Judges commonly say (in public, at least) that they do not regard it as a personal slap when they are reversed on appeal, and that it would not cross their mind to keep a mental win/loss ledger. Just as commonly, no one believes them. Before judges were judges, they were lawyers, and the competitive edge that drew them into their profession does not evaporate with the donning of a black robe. Add to that the fact that federal judges have lifetime tenure, meaning they will receive few promotions and no merit raises, none of the things that tell driven people where they stand. Their rate of reversal on appeal is often the only measure there is of how they are thought to be doing.

Sand's irritation at the ruling of the Supreme Court stemmed only partly from ego, however. He was far more distressed that the justices had removed the part of the sanctions that Sand felt was most likely to work.

"Had the Supreme Court not issued a stay, the matter would have been resolved within the next two days," he would say when the events of 1988 were long over. Faced with the reality of paying $500 a day every day, he said, he was certain that a councilman would have changed his vote.

Nicholas Longo had a different reaction altogether. Awakened by a reporter at two o'clock in the morning and asked for his opinion on the Supreme Court's ruling, his answer — something about the rights of legislators to vote as they see fit — was not what he was really thinking. The court, which was theoretically above petty politics, had issued a decision that Longo recognized as a stroke of political brilliance.

In lifting the fines against the councilmen, but not the city, the justices simultaneously did two things. They freed the councilmen from the fear that changing their votes would make them appear to have buckled to save their own wallets. At the same time, the decision stripped them of the mantle of martyrdom.

The way Judge Sand had set things up, while the city suffered, the councilmen suffered, too, making them look like selfless warriors for a cause. The way the Supreme Court set things up, the city continued to suffer, and the councilmen were the reasons why. Now they were more likely to look like stubborn roadblocks, watching the city swerve toward bankruptcy, while their own checking accounts were safe.

Show Me a Hero

"Well I'll be damned," Longo thought, with a mix of fear and admiration.

In his gut he suspected this was the beginning of the end.

Norma Waits

It was nearing noon at Schlobohm, and although the September sun was high and bright outside, Norma O'Neal's apartment was gray and dark. Even before she lost her eyesight, it had always felt to Norma that the sun's rays stopped at the outer windowsills of Schlobohm, as if they did not dare to enter. Now that shadows had become a permanent part of her day, the lack of sunlight was all the more striking.

Across the living room, against the glaring backdrop of the window, she could make out the silhouette of her oldest son, Dwayne. Because he was so big and muscular, and because his skin was so dark, Dwayne was the only one of Norma's three children she could still recognize on sight. She was always mistaking Bruce, the middle one, who had a smaller build and lighter tone, for a stranger. "Bruce looks like a little Spanish boy to me," she would say, and black/Hispanic tensions being high in Schlobohm, that led to frightening moments. One night she got into the elevator with Bruce, but did not know him. When he followed her to her door, she hit him with her purse. It was the same with Tasha, the youngest, who had to identify herself to her mother every time they passed in a public place.

The saddest part about losing your vision, Norma was learning, is losing the faces of your children. She missed that more than she missed her hard-won independence, which she was loath to admit was also slipping away. She had worked for several months after her eyes went cloudy, but eventually stopped, in the middle of the summer, when her patient's medications became more complicated. She still did her own shopping, but now a visit to the supermarket took all afternoon. "Excuse me, miss," she would say to a passing stranger. "I don't have my glasses with me, could you tell me the price?" Then she would stop someone else and ask: "Could you tell me which brand this is?" Pride and practicality kept her from asking anyone more than one question.

Once, when she needed a pair of jeans, she borrowed the six-year-old son of a close friend and took him to the store. "Eugene, look for a size two-oh. A two and then a zero. Two oh," she said in her peppiest, shakiest voice.

Eugene found one.

"Okay, I want you to tell me the price. Do they say one nine nine nine?"

No, Eugene said, they say two oh nine nine.

Norma instructed Eugene until he found a pair of size 20 jeans on sale for $19.99, the most she was willing to pay. Next, they searched for a blouse, size Four Two.

When she returned from these shopping trips, she always told her children about them, burnishing the tales from one telling to the next until they became comic adventures. Her message: "I can fend for myself." But back home in her apartment, the small things were becoming big things, and she could not will them away with a rollicking good story. She burned herself while cooking. She missed buttons while dressing. Her morning shower made her feel awkward and nervous.

In time, she realized she needed someone to do for her what she had spent years doing for others. Her children were relieved, and helped her fill out the required Medicaid paperwork, but Norma knew finding an aide would be more complicated than any form. She understood firsthand how hard it was to find a home care worker in Schlobohm.

Now that Norma was on the other side of this reality, Dwayne had come during his lunch break to wait for the home health aide who Norma knew would never show. He sat in the window for nearly three hours, hoping to prove her wrong, but he did not see a single woman enter Building Two who looked like she might be from the agency. Unable to take more time from work, he called the agency himself, and was told that the worker scheduled to see Norma had in fact been at Schlobohm that day. When she got into

Show Me a Hero

the elevator, someone tried to rob her, so she fled. Or so she told her boss.

Dwayne repeated the story to Norma, who shook her head slowly and said, "Liar." She wasn't angry. She certainly wasn't surprised. She didn't really feel anything at all.

Shutting Down the City

Every time anyone in the Yonkers government wanted to spend more than one hundred dollars, they needed the permission of the Emergency Financial Control Board. As a result, Gail Shaffer's desk was covered with piles of paper, and she spent a large part of every day saying no.

No to new trash bags for the meals-on-wheels program, to postage stamps for the Board of Elections, to photocopying supplies for the license bureau. No to repairing potholes, upgrading fire hydrants, repainting the walls of traffic court, buying materials to cordon off vacant lots.

No to the Department of Parks, Recreation and Conservation, who wanted $325 to charter a bus to take forty senior citizens to the Platzl Brau House restaurant for lunch. No to the same department for the $3,000 to fund the thirteenth annual Afro-American Heritage Festival in Trevor Park. No, again, to a performance in Coyne Park by the Buster Long Big Band, which would have cost the department $1,325.

Each no was met with howls of outrage.

"To the people of Yonkers who look forward to concerts in their neighborhood, the concert is an essential service," moaned a city spokesman.

"The festival does an awful lot for the community, it's a beautiful thing," wailed one of its organizers.

"This isn't saving any money, they're just nickel-and-diming us," grumbled the parks commissioner.

"I don't think a $325 bus ride for senior citizens is going to run

Yonkers into bankruptcy," griped the head of one anti-housing group.

Shaffer was in awe at the depth of the denial. "What the hell's the matter?" she asked aloud, drumming her lacquered nails impatiently on the desktop. "Isn't there anyone in that city who understands the gravity of the situation? Isn't anyone in that place listening?"

Though each individual no would not make a dent in the city's looming problem, she knew, together they were far more than just nickels and dimes. As Sand had envisioned and intended, they were a glimpse of the city's possible future. Each rejection should have given the people of Yonkers a taste of what would be if fines swallowed the entire budget and the government they had pilloried for years suddenly was not there.

But the indignant whining made her wonder whether that message was getting through. Yonkers, she feared, was like a millionaire after the market had crashed, still hiring limousines because "they don't really cost *that* much more than cabs," when the reality was that Yonkers couldn't even afford the cabs.

"It's time to take the bus," Shaffer said. "When the money runs out, the money runs out."

On September 2, when Judge Sand received the Supreme Court's permission to reinstate the fines, bankruptcy grew more likely. What had seemed like a most far-fetched scenario began to look more like destiny. Now that the fines were once again devouring the budget, the control board's cuts grew deeper. The visions of what was yet to come grew more ominous. The concomitant shouting grew louder and louder.

Hoping to make the point that Yonkers had entered another realm, Gail Shaffer effectively forced some city workers to take the bus. A memo from the control board ordered nearly all sixty-eight city executives and administrators to turn in their city-owned Plymouths, Fords, Dodges, Chevrolets, and Pontiacs, the ones stamped "NY Official" on the license plates. Nick Wasicsko and Neil DeLuca, along with the police and fire commissioners, were among the few who were allowed to keep their cars. The six members of the council were not, and they did not take it well.

"What next?" Peter Chema asked. "Cut off our legs?"

A pool of cars was created for workers who required them during the day in order to perform their jobs. Not surprisingly, the workers' idea of "need" was worlds apart from the control board's. Thirty requests for pool cars were received on the first day. Only one was approved, allowing the city clerk to go to a meeting at the Board of Elections office in White Plains.

Everyone else had to find another mode of travel or stay put. Reality was becoming impossible to ignore. The Plumbing Bureau lost its three cars, and shortly after 6:00 P.M. that day a water line burst at the Bowling Green Storage and Van Company, spewing one million gallons thirty feet into the air. It took inspectors two hours to get there.

The Bureau of Housing and Buildings, which lost eight of its twelve cars, canceled all routine building inspections because its inspectors couldn't get to their appointments. Only emergency calls, like post-fire inspections or ceiling collapses, were being answered.

"Taking away our cars like this is like taking the guns away from police officers," warned the head of the department. "If an elevator is broken down and we can't get there, senior citizens will have to use the stairs, and, believe me, that's the number one cause of heart attack."

The safety of the city was not the only concern raised by the control board's order. There was also a question of the safety of the cars. Once surrendered, they were placed in city-owned lots surrounded by fifteen-foot fences which were topped with barbed wire. No guards were posted at the lots between midnight and dawn, however, because there was no money for their overtime. Vandalism and theft seemed inevitable.

A solution soon made itself clear when the Police Department began running out of gas. The control board had refused to authorize a hefty fuel contract for the next several months, saying that until the crisis had passed, gasoline should be purchased in weekly allotments, instead. Precinct 3, which covers the city's west side, had an empty gas pump and was borrowing from two other precincts that were also low on gas. The control board approved the precinct's emergency request for $2,189 to buy 3,127 gallons of gas, but the fuel supplier, spooked by all that was happening in Yonkers, refused to make the delivery.

Desperate, the precinct bartered an agreement allowing it to use the pumps at the Department of Public Works (those pumps were full, because the department's cars weren't going anywhere). In return, officers of the precinct agreed to guard the cars that city workers had surrendered.

As the cuts mounted, so did the fines. "What's $200,000?" asked the local paper on Labor Day morning, September 5, Day 11 of the contempt crisis. On Day 12, $192,000 would be hand-delivered to Judge Sand's office, Room 626 of the Federal Courthouse in Manhattan's Foley Square. Once it was delivered, the city would have paid the aggregate sum of $204,700, which led the *Herald Statesman* to do some math.

How much is $200,000? Slightly more than $1 a person, enough for each resident of Yonkers to buy a $1.35 pack of cigarettes, a $1.21 gallon of gas, a 73-cent quart of milk, or an 89-cent pound of fresh tomatoes. How much is $200,000? In 1988, it took sixty-five average Yonkers homeowners to pay that much in property taxes. A family with that much saved could pay cash for a two-family home in the neighborhood around Kimball Avenue.

It would pay the salaries of ten employees at the Department of Public Works Animal Shelter. It was the budget for the city's Plumbing Bureau, which inspects plumbing jobs and grants plumbing permits, and it was the annual payroll of the six-person Public Works Bureau, which grants engineering permits. It would cover the yearly operating costs of Nick Wasicsko's office, including his salary, Nay's salary, and the paychecks of his four other employees.

Two hundred thousand dollars was the clothing allowance for the city's 401 uniformed firefighters. The fuel bill for diesel-powered vehicles in the Department of Public Works. The 1988 capital construction program for the city's sewer system. The yearly budget for the Division of Youth Services.

How much is $200,000? A lot of money. But within a day, when the daily fine reached $409,600 it would seem like nothing. Then, two days after that, when they reached $1 million a day, the old level of $200,000 would be looked on with nostalgia. One million dollars a day was roughly $30 to $40 for every citizen of Yonkers. It was as if every one in the city received a parking ticket every day.

In two months, when the total fines reached $66 million, the city's entire cash supply would be gone.

All that money, which could buy so many other things, being sent off in an unmarked envelope transported by an anonymous courier.

And not one cent was refundable.

When the Supreme Court upheld the fines, when the totals reached $200,000 and more, the councilmen began to talk. Not to the cameras, not to the shouting crowds, but to each other, for the first time in a very long time.

It was not just the pressure of the escalating fines that brought all these usually voluble men awkwardly, tentatively into conversation. It was also the fact that Judge Sand had given them something to talk *about*. The day after the high court ruled, Sand held a short, public session in his courtroom where he officially restarted the clock that was ticking away the treasury. He quickly adjourned that meeting and gathered the major players in his back office for a second, private one.

The councilmen "still have a responsibility to the citizens they represent," he said, looking even smaller than usual now that he was not behind his raised courtroom bench. "It should be clear that the first step that must be taken is compliance with the law."

If it would make compliance easier, he said, he would allow what he had considered and rejected so many times before—the court-appointed commission that would take most housing-related matters out of the council's hands. He did not go so far as to order the overseer into existence, however. The councilmen would still have to exercise some of the responsibility he was trying to teach them, by voting to approve the commission and to submit to its authority.

So they would have to talk. But they were out of practice. Never a fraternal group, the men responsible for Yonkers' future moved in separate social orbits. Only Neil DeLuca and Nicholas Longo were true friends (they played racquetball once a week). Nick Wasicsko and Neil were friendly (they had met because, long before Nay, they had both been dating the same woman). What tied everyone else together were the posturings and protocols of politics. In Yonkers, those rules of civility had been a little frayed to begin with; by the time they were most needed, they had all but unraveled. "Traitor." "Liar." "Demagogue." "Embarrassment." Those were just a few of the things that the defiant councilmen had called each other in recent weeks. Even those on the same side were barely speaking.

Most of the animosity dated back nine months, to the January vote on the consent decree. Hank Spallone was still angry with Longo and Fagan for acceding to the plan in the first place. Longo and Fagan, in turn, had not forgiven Chema for bolting at the last wrenching minute.

"His word means nothing," Fagan said of Chema.

More recently, Fagan had begun accusing Longo of "conspiring" to force Fagan to change his vote, through methods that Fagan never exactly made clear. "He knows the things I mean" was all he would say.

Longo was far more specific about his view of Fagan.

"He's in outer space," he said. "He's not the tower of maturity."

When asked if he was talking to his fellow councilman nonetheless, Longo said, "If I was getting two hundred dollars an hour, I might be."

There was a similar chill on the other side of the issue. Nick's relationship with Harry Oxman and Charles Cola had been frosty since the start of his administration, when he spurned them in favor of his short-lived coalition. By far the most complex feud, however, was between Nick Wasicsko and Neil DeLuca. In theory, the two men who looked so much alike also wanted the same thing —a vote of affirmation that would end the fines. But Nick could not see past the fact that Neil remained cordial to Nicholas Longo, which Nick saw as betrayal in the interest of politics.

"He wants my job," Nick told Nay, certain that the city manager was planning to run for mayor.

Neil, in turn, was furious that Nick could not understand that politics was about maintaining relationships, not severing them. The young, overwhelmed mayor had been standing alone so long, Neil believed, that he refused to recognize when someone, namely Neil, was standing with him.

It was hard to talk, yet Sand left them no choice but to talk, so most of them did. Neil and Nick managed to be civil long enough to agree upon a strategy—they would ignore Hank Spallone and Ed Fagan and concentrate on swaying Peter Chema and Nicholas Longo. They targeted Chema because he represented southwest Yonkers, where none of the proposed housing would be built. He was the councilman who could change his mind with the least political fallout. And they targeted Longo because they expected that Chema would not have the stomach to switch his vote alone.

On the afternoon of Labor Day, the councilmen all but locked themselves in City Hall. They started their conversations in Neil DeLuca's second-floor conference room at about one o'clock, then broke into small groups. For the next few hours, these clusters of twos and threes met, broke apart, came back together—a kind of cocktail party in hell.

At one point, Longo and Chema retreated to the men's room with Wasicsko and Cola for some particularly intense conversation. Ed Fagan loped in. He was asked to leave.

"It felt like a bunch of high-school kids," he said, pouting, as he retreated back out to the hallway. "Everybody was standing around, smoking and talking, and the only thing missing was the graffiti and the guys singing a capella doo-wop in the stalls to get the echo."

As the councilmen went from room to room and group to group, they talked about more than just the judge's proposed commission. The four who had voted no were focused on what amendments might be made to the plan to induce them to change their minds. They talked of reducing the number of units, scattering them across a larger geographical area, not building any housing at all, but using money to upgrade housing that already exists, instead.

The three who had voted yes focused on returning the talk to reality. The judge seemed in no mood to entertain any amendments to the plan, they warned, until after the council voted to reaffirm the consent decree. There was no possibility of negotiation until someone changed his vote. In the midafternoon, Spallone and Fagan walked out, saying that unless Sand changed the plan they would not change their minds.

Those who remained talked for several hours more, then sent out for pizza and gathered to watch Spallone and Fagan on the six o'clock news.

"I'm staying with my position," they saw Fagan say as he marched out of the building.

"The only thing Judge Sand gave away was ice in the wintertime," they saw Spallone say, following close behind. "No deal."

At 8:30, the meetings finally ended, and the exhausted councilmen had their turn to face the media.

"There's no resolution to the problem," said Longo.

"It's impossible to predict what the outcome will be," said Chema.

The sticking point, said Wasicsko, glancing over at his worn-out adversaries, "is that they want to show their constituents that they accomplished something with their defiance. I think the court is reluctant to give them that appearance of victory."

Sensing some momentum, the Emergency Financial Control Board added its own extra push. On Wednesday, September 7, when the fines reached $409,600, Gail Shaffer announced sweeping layoffs for Saturday, when the fines would be $1 million. It was no less than the first step in the slow deconstruction of the government of Yonkers. On Saturday, 447 people would lose their jobs—almost a quarter of the municipal workforce.

Shaffer made this announcement despite her suspicion that she might not really have the right to do so. The board was established to oversee the city's affairs, not to arrange them, but Shaffer had run out of patience with those who would split such semantic hairs. The legislation establishing the board could not possibly have envisioned a situation where Yonkers was poised to commit municipal hara-kiri, she reasoned, so the rules could be bent. "We're in uncharted terrain here," she told her staff, explaining that they should "legally, but creatively, push the envelope."

When the fines against the city had resumed a few days earlier, Shaffer had asked Neil DeLuca for a "Doomsday Plan"—a day-by-day list of exactly who would be laid off and what services would be cut as the debt mounted. A few days after that, on Tuesday September 6, he had given her one, and when she read it she resolved that the board must do what the city would not.

DeLuca's goal was to save as many jobs for as long as possible. He would have laid off 40 people the first week, and 200 people the next week, a savings of $8.6 million. Under his scenario, the city's money would run out, and all services would cease, in two months.

Shaffer's goal was to keep the city functioning, albeit at a bare minimum, for as long as possible. Her plan meant laying off 600 people in the same two weeks, and cutting between 109 and 439 more per week until November 5. By then the only remaining city employees would be the police officers and firemen necessary for bare-bones protection. The money to pay them would last a month longer than under Neil's plan—until the end of the year.

But there was more to Shaffer's strategy than just saving money. Dramatic, immediate layoffs, she hoped, would change the political equation for the "spineless" council and force them to change their vote faster than would gradual, threatened layoffs.

The two plans were brought to the control board for a vote, but DeLuca's never really had a chance, and he was the only board member who voted against Shaffer's more dramatic timetable. Watching the vote, Nick was stunned at the schedule of cuts, which would systematically erode every corner of life in Yonkers. If the council did not comply by the control board's deadline—Saturday, September 10—all the libraries would close immediately, saving the city $3.6 million. The Parks Department would close that day, too ($4.15 million), along with the Real Estate Department ($50,000). Everyone at the Planning Department would be laid off, except for the director and one clerk ($200,000 saved). The Personnel Department would be all but eliminated ($500,000) as would the Civil Service Department ($150,000). The offices of Fiscal Services, Management, and Information Systems, city manager, corporation counsel, and finance commissioner would be cut by one-third ($2.2 million). That would leave Neil with just himself and one secretary. The Community Services Bureau would be sharply reduced ($350,000) and the Department of Public Works would have a fraction of its usual staff to handle such tasks as street cleaning, garbage pickup, and staffing the animal shelter ($5.4 million). Some streetlights would go out as that budget was trimmed by one-third ($470,000). City Council clerical employees would be allowed to keep their jobs, but their salaries would be cut by one-quarter. Every employee laid off from his job would also lose his benefits, an additional savings of $3.7 million.

It would only get worse from there. During Week Two of the Doomsday Plan more streetlights would go out, as would many of the employees in Nick's own office. During Week Three, cuts would begin in the police and fire departments.

There was only one way to prevent all this, Shaffer reminded the city. The councilmen knew what they had to do.

"The city of Yonkers must confront reality in a very decisive way," she said. "The time for finger-pointing is over. The time for punting is over. We must save Yonkers from itself."

The results of that extra push could be seen twenty-four hours later, on Thursday evening, September 8, at the next meeting of the City Council. Nick sat in his chair—the one he had temporarily claimed back from Gail Shaffer—and watched the mayhem.

At first, it seemed like business as it passed for usual in Yonkers: the room was packed to overflowing, the police strained to keep order, the heat was oppressive, and tempers were short. But as he called the meeting to order, and the members of the public approached the microphone to speak, Nick heard that something was different.

Instead of yelling at the council, the people were yelling at each other.

"I'm tired of these idiots supposedly representing my interests,"

Show Me a Hero

shouted Martha Darcy, a librarian whose job was scheduled to be cut by the weekend. She pointed not toward the front of the room, but toward the spectator seats in the back. Not toward those who favored compliance, but toward those who had been protesting against it.

One by one, frightened city employees took the floor.

"I have a wife and two kids. How am I going to feed them if I'm laid off?" asked Russell Deutchen, a motor equipment operator in the library.

"Sixteen years with the city is going down the tubes," said Mary Rudasill, a single parent who worked in the city's Office of Human Rights.

"I'm a taxpayer, too," said Gloria Graham, her boss. "Settle the mess."

There were a large number of people speaking against the housing, too, trying to rally the crowd to their view that the layoffs were a noble sacrifice that some would have to make in the name of a greater cause. Unemployment checks and food stamps would help pay the bills, they said, and when the judge gives in and lifts the fines, the workers could all be rehired.

Nick let them shout for a while, then acted to end the meeting. He was getting smarter. The judge had ordered the council to meet once a week until someone changed his vote, and for a while Nick had polled the members anew each time until he realized that he was providing them a forum for troublemaking speeches. More recently he had learned to say, "Does any councilman desire to change his vote today?" With no vote on the agenda, no councilman had the parliamentary right to talk, since there was officially nothing on the table for them to talk about.

He asked his question, received no answer, then ordered the meeting "recessed indefinitely." He did not adjourn it, since the rules required twelve hours advance public notice before a new council meeting could be scheduled, and Yonkers did not have that much time.

Despite everything hanging over his city—despite his exhaustion, despite the fact that no solution was in sight—Nick left the room feeling something close to hopeful. He had always known they were out there, the Deutchens and the Rudasills and the Grahams. He had often sat in these meetings and wondered where they were.

By the time he got home he was bordering on optimistic. This had been the best meeting he'd had in months.

On Friday, September 9, 1988, Day 15, the fines reached $1 million and the layoffs began. Black flags of mourning were hoisted at all three library buildings, which were ordered to close at noon. Announcing the closures, one member of the library's board of trustees warned, "The bleeding of city services has begun."

At the Grinton I. Will Library, on the east side, a group of senior citizens refused to leave. They had been playing bingo in the ground-floor senior center there when the building officially closed, and they spontaneously decided that if their councilmen could be defiant, they could show support for those councilmen and be defiant, too.

"If they want me out of here, they're going to have to carry me out like they did those kids in the 'sixties," one septuagenarian said.

The bingo game continued, and the winners joked that they would chip in and buy a cemetery plot for Judge Sand. As they played, laid-off workers interrupted to say good-bye and offer encouragement. One employee, who had worked for the library system for seven years, sent in sandwiches.

"If the cops are going to take you away, I want you to have full bellies," he said.

The police did come, at 5:30 in the evening, and the residents started chanting "Hell no, we won't go."

The leader of the group, sixty-six-year-old Harry Preis, shuffled up to the three officers, waving his cane.

"What if we said 'we're not going'?" he asked.

"Oh, we have tear gas we can bring in," said Lieutenant George Kovalik, tongue firmly in cheek. "Everybody who goes to jail today is getting cornflakes. Without milk."

"Will you please escort us out of here?" Preis asked.

Kovalik took his arm.

"Atta boy, Harry," people yelled.

The library was dark and empty by six o'clock.

While the bingo players were chanting, the councilmen were talking. The million-dollar-a-day mark had brought on what Peter Chema called the "chill of reality." It was finally time for Yonkers to choose its fate: desegregate its housing or dissolve its government.

They knew they could not talk at City Hall. There were too many eyes there, and too many cameras. It was like talking naked in a glass room. Paul Pickelle, one of the city's many lawyers, offered his Tudor-style home in nearby Scarsdale, where the press and the protesters would not think to go.

Michael Sussman, the lawyer for the NAACP, was the first to arrive, at 8:00 A.M. on Friday. He and Pickelle, adversaries for years, took off their jackets and shot some hoops in Pickelle's backyard.

"I was going to offer to play you for the housing plan," Pickelle joked. "But then I saw how well you play."

Neil DeLuca arrived at 9:00 A.M., as did Michael Skulnick, the city's lawyer on the housing case, and lawyers for Nicholas Longo and Peter Chema. All these men had been talking secretly during the week, at hush-hush dinners arranged by DeLuca at restaurants in neighboring towns. Now, over coffee and donuts in the Pickelles' kitchen, they refined the compromises that had been sketched out during those dinners. They agreed to suggest the following to Judge Sand: that the 200 townhouses be reconfigured as 100 townhouses plus 100 units scattered throughout mixed-income developments; that the controversial seminary site be dropped from the plan; and that a nonprofit corporation be created to oversee it all.

After two hours of talking, the lawyers phoned Longo and Chema, who had spent the morning at home, waiting for word. That done, they broke for sandwiches and coffee in the Pickelles' backyard. One thing they forgot to do was update Nick Wasicsko, who was holding the fort back at City Hall. When he found out about the off-site meeting, he was furious. He had called a council meeting for noon because the council had to vote to release the

$819,200 needed to pay the contempt fines for that day. But DeLuca, Pickelle, Chema, and Longo were nowhere to be found.

Nick had been suffering from stomach pains all week, burning jolts so severe they left him momentarily unable to speak. With no time for a checkup, he had called his doctor, who prescribed ulcer medication over the phone, but that made a small difference at best. He'd had to keep excusing himself from the meeting so he could run to his office and double over in private agony.

"Four of the key players aren't here, and I don't know why, and the national press is twenty-five feet from the tip of my nose," he fumed at Nay. Noon came and went. Nick swallowed more pain pills. Then he went back out and recessed the meeting "until further notice."

At 2:30, Michael Sussman arrived to fill him in. Chema and Longo came soon after. The payment was authorized, and a check was sent to Foley Square. Nick again recessed the meeting, reserving the right to resume it again on a "two-hour call."

At 3:30, the lawyers gathered once again at the Pickelle house, bringing Peter Chema and Nicholas Longo with them. They all sat in the living room, which had been immaculate that morning but which by the afternoon was strewn with soda cans, beer bottles, and snacks. By 4:20, the deal was done. The two councilmen had agreed to the reduction to 100 townhouses that had been worked out by lawyers for all sides earlier in the day. After months of stalemate, it almost seemed easy.

They should have known that nothing in Yonkers is that simple. At 4:30 the lawyers held a telephone conference call with Judge Sand, who was in Pennsylvania at a judicial conference. Oscar Newman joined in from his office on Long Island, and Brian Heffernan, who represented the Department of Justice, was on the line from Washington, D.C.

Michael Sussman began the call by telling the judge that the city and the NAACP had been negotiating in good faith. The proposed changes that came out of those discussions, he said, "might make it a better plan, more acceptable to the community."

Michael Skulnick spoke next, and began to tell the judge the specifics of the compromise. Sand cut him off. He was angry. He had expected a phone call pledging complaince, and instead all he was hearing was a proposed list of changes. Just because the NAACP agreed, and the Justice Department agreed, did not mean that *he* agreed. It was too late for that.

"The court will not entertain" any mention of changes, he said, "until the council votes to comply."

Skulnick knew enough to change the subject. In light of the recent progress, he asked, might the judge consider suspending the fines.

Sand said no, he would not consider that.

Would the judge consider not sending the checks on to the U.S. Treasury? Would he consider putting them in escrow — where they might eventually be refunded—instead?

No, he would not consider that, either.

Might the council be allowed to adopt a resolution of intent, promising to adopt the plan if the amendments were worked out?

No, Sand said.

The conference call was over seven minutes after it had begun. The judge's message was clear. Comply first. Negotiate later.

"The judge was in no mood to hear new plans," Pickelle told Longo and Chema, who had been required to leave the room, and who were pacing in a nearby hallway while the lawyers made the conference call. "He has said from the beginning that before there could be any consideration of a different plan the law had to be obeyed. This is his tough medicine."

About twenty minutes later, Sand's law clerk called back, saying the judge was willing to compromise a smidgen. The court would forgive Thursday's $819,000 fine, as well as Friday's $1 million fine, if the council voted to comply at a meeting that began before midnight on Friday night.

Sand had finally figured out how to play political hardball in Yonkers. What seemed like a concession was really the most intense form of pressure. The council had a $1.8 million vote on its hands.

With seven hours left until midnight, all remaining energy in the Pickelle house was spent pressuring Chema and Longo to change their votes without any promise of a future compromise.

Yes, the weary councilmen agreed, they wanted to end this, they wanted to stop the financial hemorrhage, but they didn't want to break their word. Nick Wasicsko arrived at six o'clock, with news that upped the stakes even further. Gail Shaffer, he said, had promised she would suspend the layoffs if the city complied that night. A vote within six hours could now save $1.8 million, and 630 jobs.

Paul Pickelle's wife, Karen, made beef stew for dinner. At 7:30, fifteen-year-old Matthew Pickelle turned on the Mets game, and Longo, a rabid fan, kept wandering off to watch the TV. At 9:55, Nick realized that he had five remaning minutes in which to give the required two-hour warning that there would be a council meeting, or he would miss the midnight deadline. At ten o'clock everyone left for City Hall, with no commitment from either Peter Chema or Nicholas Longo.

Nick went home for a quick shower and another dose of medication. Then he drove to City Hall. He arrived at the same time as Neil DeLuca and Paul Pickelle. The three men raced up the steps of City Hall together, past a sea of workers who were about to lose their jobs.

Nick called the meeting to order at 11:57 P.M., three minutes shy of Sand's deadline. At 11:58 P.M. he called for a recess, so that the clerical staff could type up the resolution on which the councilmen would vote.

It was an arcane resolution, listing specific building incentives that would promote the construction of the 800 units of low- to moderate-income housing, but it's overarching meaning was clear—by voting these incentives into effect, the council agreed to comply with the judge and move forward with the housing plan. It took more than an hour to type, copy, and circulate the resolution, and Nick spent most of that time in his office, urging the police chief to keep the protesters quiet "so they don't spook Nicky Longo."

Longo and Chema spent most of that same hour in Neil DeLuca's office, being spooked. "Do I have any other choice?" Longo asked DeLuca more than once. "Is there anything else I can do?"

Chema called his wife twice while he waited. During the first

Show Me a Hero

call he said he would change his vote. During the second call he said he "couldn't do it."

Just before the council was to reconvene, one of DeLuca's assistants came in and handed everyone in the room a list of the 630 workers who had received pink slips earlier in the day. Both Chema and Longo turned pale and shook their heads as they scanned the pages of names.

"We're about to go from martyrs to murderers," Longo said. "We're about to economically murder six hundred families."

At 12:45 A.M., the councilmen returned to the chamber. Police lined the walls. Nick's gavel could barely be heard against his desk when he reopened the meeting.

As the council members took their seats, Mary Dorman found herself putting her hands over her eyes and staring out through her fingers. She couldn't bear to watch, but she couldn't bear not to.

"Does any council member wish to change his vote?" Nick asked.

Longo gave a short speech. Until tonight, he said, the fines, the threats of bankruptcy, the layoffs, the cutbacks, all of those had been distant and abstract. Now they were terrifyingly real.

"These are people I've shared backyard barbecues with," he said, and Nick knew the fight was finally over.

"I have attended their weddings, the christenings of their children, not as councilman but as their friend," he continued. Mary, defeated, let her hand slip, motionless, into her lap.

The historic vote came at 1:15 A.M. on Saturday, September 10, 1988.

Nicholas Longo voted yes. Moments later, Peter Chema did so, too. They would comply with the judge's order. The housing would be built.

Mary left the building, and, out of habit, stood with the crowd on the street for a while, but her heart was not in it. She had been troubled all night by something more than just the outcome of the vote. All around her in the chamber people she thought of as her friends were expecting—demanding—that *other* people sacrifice their jobs. "We turned into animals in there," she thought.

She was still a novice as a protester, and she understood that in any cause there must be sacrifices, but this did not feel right. The deeper doubts would come later. For now, all she knew was that the chanting in the street seemed harsher to her tonight than it had the night before.

Nick stayed in his office until 4:00 A.M., trying to wait out the crowd. He had expected to feel exhilaration when the end finally came, but all he felt was exhaustion. When the protesters showed no signs of leaving, he accepted a police escort for his short ride home. The officer took the wheel and inched the car out of the City Hall parking lot. Angry fists banged on the hood, the doors, the trunk, and threatening faces were pressed against the windows. The car shook from side to side, nearly flipping over. Nick, who was sitting in the back seat with Nay, reached over and gripped her cold, shaking hand. He, too, was terrified. They had been trying to keep their private life a secret, but he didn't care who might see.

After several minutes, Nick's car was clear of the insanity, and the dark streets of Yonkers seemed eerily quiet. Nick had won something tonight. But he was beginning to understand that he had also irretrievably lost something. He would not understand exactly what he had lost, how completely he had lost, until later. All he knew now was that he would never see his hometown the same way again.

1 9 8 9

A House on a Hill

The house at 175 Yonkers Avenue is hidden in plain sight. It sits on one of the west side's busiest streets, at the top of hill, making it visible for miles. But the only way to reach that hill is via a steep, private road, which is unmarked and easily missed. Nearly everyone can see the house. Practically no one can find it.

Only because of a Realtor's arrow did Nick and Nay make their way up that pitted yet imposing driveway in the first place. At the time, they were not in the market for a house. They were in the middle of Nick's reelection campaign, and were headed to the Cross County Shopping Center, on the east side, to shake some hands. Nick had come to hate those campaign stops across the Saw Mill. A few weeks earlier, a passerby had actually spat at him in an east side neighborhood, and he would be very happy never to have to cross the highway again. What he was looking for was not a house, but a detour, an excuse. When he saw the "Open House" sign he made a U-turn across four lanes of traffic and drove up the hill.

Once there, it was love at first sight. Nick and Nay were both instantly smitten by the huge, unkempt building, with its withered green shingles and peeling green brick. They knew they couldn't afford it, and they had no idea how to begin repairing it. They also knew they had to buy it.

Nick, who had never lived in a house before, loved the space as much as he loved the idea of homeownership. Most of all, they both loved the privacy. At the time, they were tenants in the upstairs apartment of a two-family split. Coming home each night, they would use one key to open the main front door, then climb a flight of stairs and use another key in their own lock. It felt like a safe arrangement until the day they found a "Spallone for Mayor" sticker on that second, upstairs door. Sleep was a rare luxury for them after that. Nick would lie awake worrying about the campaign. Nay would toss and turn, then get out of bed yet again to check the locks.

There was one thing more that drew them to this house, something beyond privacy, security, or space, something they both thought but did not say out loud. One seventy-five Yonkers Avenue could be a grand house. Beneath the hideous linoleum on the floors and beyond the cracking acoustic tiles, they sensed there was a mayor's house. Maybe a home worthy of a senator, or a governor, or a federal judge. Buying the hilltop estate would be more than the usual investment in the future. It would be a statement of faith that there *was* a future. If the weary, wind-worn home could be returned to its days of glory, then it would follow that Nick Wasicsko could be returned to those heady days just after his first mayoral election, when there was nothing but possibility.

The day Nick and Nay first saw the house on the hill, nearly a year had passed since the night that Longo and Chema changed their minds. Nick had assumed—naively, he now realized—that once it was over, it would be *over*. Instead, the skirmishing and posturing continued. Property owners near the sites filed suit to block the plan. A group of pro-compliance taxpayers sued the recalcitrant councilmen for $166 million, charging dereliction of duty. The Save Yonkers coalition launched a petition drive to recall Nick Wasicsko, even though recall elections are not legal in New York State. A local congressman introduced a bill to refund the fines that Sand had declared nonrefundable. Only one of the many suits and petitions met with any real results. The Supreme Court agreed to hear the appeal by the four councilmen who had incurred personal fines and who wanted their $3,500 back

In the middle of all of it, just in case Nick had somehow missed the absurdity of his city, came word of Laurie Recht. After she made her lone plea in favor of the housing, Recht had become a local celebrity. She was called a hero in the *New York Times* and

Show Me a Hero

she was honored as the commencement speaker at a local college. But the spotlight brought heat as well as light, and Recht filed twenty-four police reports in the nine months after she stood up to the crowd. Most were for threatening phone calls, but one described a bomb threat, another described a swastika painted outside her fourteenth-floor apartment, and a third detailed an attempt to run her car off the road.

Secretly, police put a tap on her telephone and installed a video camera outside her apartment door. Soon after that, Recht reported receiving three threatening calls in one day, but no such calls were recorded on the wiretap. The video camera did catch a guilty party, however. Reviewing the tape, the police clearly saw a person looking around, then scrawling a threatening message and a swastika on the wall. That person was Laurie Recht.

How fitting, Nick thought, that the only other person who stuck out her neck for this cause was now being led away in handcuffs.

He never really decided to run for reelection. That was not how he phrased the mental question: "To run or not to run." Instead he saw the decision as one of "hanging in or quitting." A first-term incumbent was supposed to run again, expected to run again. To do otherwise would be an embarrassment, a declaration of failure. It would give Hank Spallone, who was threatening a primary challenge, too much satisfaction. Nick was too tired for a fight, but he would also be damned if anyone would think he was giving up without one.

Once it became clear that Nick was going to run, some of the old adrenaline came back. It was a different kind of energy than that which had propelled him through his first mayoral campaign, because he was a different kind of man, reforged by the fires of the past two years. He still looked like a teenager, but there was a battle-scarred man inside. His first race had been about *him* — could he do this, was he smart enough and crafty enough, could he say what people wanted to hear? It was a campaign by a boy on the playground who might be too short for basketball, but who had the undefinable something that made the other kids nickname him "The Mayor."

What the housing fight had shown him, however, was that the

rush of victory only lasts through election night. After that you have to stand for something. Nick had come into office with ambitions. While he was there, he developed beliefs. It was a journey that had sobered him, but it had not bleached him into a saint. He still wanted to win. He still wanted to be the mayor, entranced by everything the office meant and all that it might lead to. And he was still determined to prove something, but this time it was a different something. He needed to prove he had been right. Elected the first time because of who he was not, Nick wanted to win this time because of who he was.

The first thing he did was spend $15,000 on a poll with the hope that it would prove there really was a silent majority who supported his stand on the housing. What he learned was not as straightforward as that. Back in August of 1988, his results showed, 42 percent of voters had backed the defiant councilmen and 37 percent had agreed with Nick. Slightly more encouraging was the fact that by the spring of 1989, when Nick's pollsters called, 48 percent said it was time to accept the court's order while 39 percent wanted to continue to fight. The most useful result of the poll was the fact that although the general electorate was split between Nick (29 percent) and Hank (33 percent), among the Democrats who would decide the primary—the voters that counted—40 percent supported Nick and only 28 percent supported Hank.

The Wasicsko campaign deliberately leaked the results of their poll and waited for the fallout. Hank Spallone, rather than simply dropping out, as Nick expected he would, switched parties and became a Republican instead.

Nick officially launched his campaign in front of City Hall. A crowd of one hundred fifty stood on the steps around him, holding brooms and chanting "Clean Sweep." He was proud of his speech, a portrait of a city at a crossroads. "Our road leads to Yonkers once again being a fine city," he said. "Their road leads to Yonkers once again being a city fined. Our road leads to electing a City Council of lawmakers. Their road leads to reelecting a city council of lawbreakers."

Show Me a Hero

He tried to ignore the fact that seven hundred people were in the crowd when Hank Spallone launched *his* campaign.

Nick was challenged for the Democratic nomination by Dominick Iannacone, a former councilman whose last run for mayor was a loss to Angelo Martinelli in 1977. Typically, primaries are, at best, a necessary evil, draining money and momentum from the eventual candidate. This particular primary, however, had an invigorating effect on its winner. Wasicsko defeated Iannacone with 70 percent of the vote, and the victory gave him confidence, energy, hope. He was on a roll. He could do this.

Slowly, the endorsements came. His own party leaders were noticeably silent, but he received high-profile union support—from District Council 37 of AFSCME, Local 1199 of Hospital and Health Care Employees, and the Yonkers Federation of Teachers—as well as praise from big-name Democrats outside Yonkers. Senator Daniel Patrick Moynihan called the race one of "national importance." Governor Mario Cuomo called Nick "clearly the superior candidate." Moynihan's words thrilled him, and Cuomo's support amused him, given how distant the governor had been a year earlier. He found fitting irony in the fact that, for a variety of logistical reasons, the Wasicsko fund-raiser at which Cuomo spoke was held in Tarrytown, ten miles to the north. Nothing, it seemed, could bring Mario Cuomo to Yonkers.

As the campaign unfolded, Nick tried to concentrate on these satisfying parts. Keeping his gaze on the high points meant he would not be distracted by the creeping ugliness. He tried not to react, for instance, when his posters were torn down overnight in one east side neighborhood and replaced with stickers that said "Vote Henry Spallone." He tried to shrug with nonchalance when his name was mistakenly left off the absentee ballot. What required the most concentration was pretending not to see the group of protesters from Save Yonkers who appeared at all his east side campaign events, to catcall and jeer. It was one of that group that spat at him. He found that more unsettling, not to mention downright disgusting, than the Pampers had ever been.

In short, his campaign was going well and he was feeling confident—as long as he stayed away from the east side. Nay would find him lying on the couch, unshaven and ill-tempered, when he was scheduled to appear across town. "I don't want to go," he would say. "What's the point?" If he did agree to go, he would make sure to strap his .38 to his ankle, dazed by the irony that the weapon he had previously used to protect him in the projects he now needed in the safest parts of his city.

More often, he would skip the east side events entirely. Jim Surdoval, who had steered Nick through his first two campaigns, was managing this race, too. Every Friday, Jim would give Nick a stack of proclamations for him to present at the stops on his weekend campaign schedule. On Monday morning, the papers were still lying on the seat of Nick's car.

That avoidance instinct was what led him to his fixer-upper house on the hill, where he placed a $210,000 bet, in the form of a bid-to-purchase, that everything would work out okay. It was money he and Nay certainly did not have, so they borrowed the down payment from Nay's parents—more a gift than a loan.

The house provided them a distraction through the rest of the summer—passing the inspection, filling out mortgage forms, planning renovations. On good days they imagined their home as a political salon, a center of power. On bad days they thought of it as an escape, a retreat.

Increasingly, the days were bad. A poll after Labor Day showed Nick losing to Hank by nearly ten points, 41 percent to 32 percent. Eighteen percent of voters were undecided, 3 percent favored the Right to Life candidate, and 7 percent refused to answer the pollsters' questions. His level of campaign contributions, which had been disappointing, became even more so. Hank had already spent $90,000 while Nick had spent $60,000, and $40,000 of that had been during his Democratic primary.

Since he had little hope of reaching that undecided 18 percent on his own dime, Nick put his hopes in the one televised debate he would have with Hank, a Cablevision News event that would reach 35,000 subscribers. He dressed carefully that night, trying to look young and energetic. He insisted on pancake makeup and powder, concerned that he would sweat. He and Hank were in different rooms for the debate—the Cablevision producer thought the clash

Show Me a Hero

would be more dramatic that way—and when Hank's florid face come up on the monitor, Nick was pleased to see that it looked slightly shiny. Television image made all the difference in the 1960 Kennedy–Nixon debates, he remembered.

The tone turned nasty, early, when Spallone noted that the Supreme Court had agreed to hear his appeal of the personal fines, and hinted that this might help the city stop the housing. Wasicsko blasted his opponent for giving the voters false hope.

"The Supreme Court has ruled on all issues of liability and remedy," he said. "That is forever closed. Mr. Spallone's case involves $3,500 of his money but the housing situation in Yonkers will not change."

Talk then turned to school desegregation.

"The system is not functioning," Spallone said. "It's not helping anyone and the mayor is saying it's a wonderful system and the record shows it doesn't work."

"I'm not saying—" Nick began

"It doesn't work, Mayor," Spallone shouted.

"I'm saying we can make it better," Nick said.

Later, the two candidates were asked why they sought the job. Nick said it was "the most important election in Yonkers history" and said his reelection would "send a signal to the world that what happened in the last two years is not the norm here in Yonkers."

Spallone responded to the same question by again raising his Supreme Court case. Nick accused him of using the housing issue to "advance your own personal political career. You're willing to bankrupt the city in the process."

As the mayor spoke, Spallone shouted, "The mayor has lost his mind."

In his closing remarks, Nick talked about putting history, and the housing, "where it belongs, behind us."

Spallone closed with these words: "It's time you recognized that you failed as a leader, and I think if they vote for you again you'll be a disaster upon this city."

The debate seemed to have an effect, and a new poll found the race to be a virtual dead heat. Spallone was still ahead, but by only two percentage points, which was statistically insignificant in a poll with an error margin of 4.1 percent. Eighteen percent were still undecided.

Nick went to bed the night before election day thinking he might be able to defy the odds one more time.

He was wrong.

Nearly 70 percent of Yonkers voted in the mayoral election of 1989, twelve thousand more people than two years earlier. Fifty-three percent of them voted for Hank Spallone, and 45 percent voted for Nick Wasicsko.

A ward-by-ward map of the mayoral vote showed a city divided in half by the Saw Mill River Parkway. Nick beat Hank on the west side of the city, winning in each of the six west side wards. Hank made an equal sweep of the east side, winning there by the same ratio. There are more voters on the east side of Yonkers, and a higher percentage of them came out to the polls, a fact that decided the election.

Nick made the first concession speech of his political career shortly after 11:00 P.M. "Do not despair," he told the crowd of 250. "I believe I was there when the city needed me. I have no regrets. I endured death threats and all sorts of abuse. I think in the long run history will prove me right."

He didn't really blame people for not hearing his message. "Obey the law and do what has to be done, it's not the kind of issue that gets to people," he said, after he left the microphone. "It's like 'Eat your vegetables.' You do it because you have to, but hey, it sure ain't pleasant, and people are not going to get highly motivated and that's really what worked against me."

Whatever the reason, the loss hurt. That is the risk of running on an idea, not just a strategy. When you lose, you lose a lot more.

On the morning after election day, Nick and Nay moved into the house on the hill. For her sake, he tried to be cheerful, a man starting a new chapter with the woman he loved. But despite his best efforts, even his jokes were tinged with his pain. At lunchtime the couple took a break on the sunporch, where the windows were milky and cracked with age. "It's a lot like the city of Yonkers," he said, his mouth smiling but his eyes dark and sad. "With a little bit of work, it could be gorgeous."

Then he stood up and walked to one of the windows, squinting through the years of grime toward the busy street below.

"People driving to and from City Hall every day are going to see my house," he said. "People are going to know right where to find me."

Billie Rowan Meets John Santos

Throughout the eight buildings of Schlobohm, throughout all the public housing in Yonkers, people are living where they are not supposed to be. The official rules are clear on the subject: allowing someone who is not on your lease to live in your apartment is grounds for eviction. But it is a rule that is difficult to enforce and, therefore, one that is regularly ignored. Home is a fluid and relative concept in Schlobohm. And that is how Billie Rowan first came to meet John Mateo Santos Jr. during the summer of 1989—because so many people were where they were not supposed to be.

Billie was technically living with the rest of her family, over in Building Six, but she spent as much time away from there as she could. Nineteen-year-old Billie was a teenage whirlwind, partial to cornrows, colorful African print scarves, and glittery costume jewelry. She was happiest when she jangled and sparkled, and it was her goal in life to find a way to be forever happy. For nine years, since she first moved to Schlobohm with her parents, brother, and two sisters, their three-bedroom apartment felt cramped and claustrophobic to Billie. Now that she was fighting with her mother, it felt even more so. Janet Rowan had not approved of Billie's decision to drop out of school four months earlier, seeking adventure and time to shop. She insisted that her daughter get a job, and

Billie spent each weekday as a nurse's aide at a home for mentally retarded children, the same work that her mother had been doing for years.

Billie hated it. One of her dreaded responsibilities was to bathe a ten-year-old boy who banged his head against the wall and wailed while being washed. It was all she could do not to let him slip under the water, and by the end of each bathtime Billie was usually crying, too.

"I don't have the patience for this," she would yell at her mother, begging to be allowed to quit and just hang out with her friends.

"This is the real world," her mother yelled back. "Live with it."

The tension at home was why Billie spent most of her time in Building Four, with her best friend, Meeka. John Santos spent a lot of time there, too. Meeka's boyfriend, known as Mambo, was among John's best friends, and although John was officially on the lease in his mother's apartment over in Building One, he spent almost every night in Meeka's spare bedroom.

It was there one hot Saturday night in July that John heard Billie and Meeka talking in the living room. He had been drinking and worse since early evening, and now, at three o'clock in the morning, he could not sleep. So he pulled on a pair of shorts and found Meeka and Billie simultaneously watching *Star Trek* and passing a joint between them. John turned off the volume, but not the power, so that the picture from the TV and the red-hot shimmer of paper turning to ash all glowed silently in the otherwise darkened room.

"Anyone for a beer?" John asked, as he turned to help himself to the contents of Meeka's fridge. Billie said she would like hers in a glass, and he decided right then that she was "quality." Soon Meeka hurried to her bedroom. Mambo was one of those men who didn't like his woman being social when he wasn't around. Billie and John sat alone.

His baby face was smooth, his big brown eyes were sexy, but what attracted her first, and what would hold her for years to come, was his voice. It was a voice that was both innocent and dangerous, that blended Yonkers with Puerto Rico, that was filled with an anger that Billie confused with strength.

John could convince her of anything with that voice, and, that first night, he used it to tell her that he was nineteen, when, in fact, he was only seventeen. He also told her that no one called him John, nearly everyone called him Hot. The nickname, his street name, was given to him by all the girls who could not stay away. It was short for "Hot Stuff."

He went on to explain that his constant fights at school, ones that led to his expulsion, were not *really* his fault, because the "white guys always provoked me." And he also explained how the robberies he and his friends "sometimes did" weren't *really* robberies, because "we're a group, and if there's another group, and we fight, then the ones that we end up beating, we take what they have." Not like "armed robbery or nothing," he said. More like the spoils of war.

He was the smallest, but the toughest, he said, describing the day that he fought off a gang of seventy-five wildmen in the schoolyard, all of whom "had bats, pitchforks, you name it." He became tough, he said, because his father "used to beat on me," when he was young. Not until he was in his teens, he said, did he learn it was because he was not his father's son.

His mother was only fifteen when he was born, he said. Abandoned by the man who'd gotten her pregnant, she was already five months along when she met John Mateo Santos Sr.—the man John long thought was his father. That man, in turn, walked out on the family when John was twelve. "But he gave me his name," he boasted to Billie. "John Mateo Santos. First name, middle name, and last. I was named right after him."

John junior's own son, Noel, was born on Christmas Day of the year John himself turned fifteen. The baby's mother wanted to get married, John explained. He had lied to *her* about his age, too. "She thought I was older," he said, "but then I told her the truth. I said, 'Now that you know how old I am, don't you think I'm too young for all this stuff?' "

Even then, entranced and stoned, Billie realized that a lot of what John was saying didn't quite ring true. A mob armed with pitchforks? Who has a pitchfork in Yonkers? And she also sensed that all his stories had the same central theme—nothing that happened to John, not the fights, not the baby, was ever his fault. But that didn't matter to Billie. Not yet. She was mesmerized by his stories, spellbound by his words. Everything about his life was so much *more* than hers—more tortured, more intense, more exciting. He talked as if he knew about the world.

As the hours passed, John gradually moved from the sofa, to the love seat, and finally to a spot on the floor at the base of Billie's chair. He looked up at her and asked, "May I kiss you?"

Billie was impressed because most guys she knew were never gentleman enough to ask.

He tapped her lips with his. A deep tap.

Then he did it again.

Billie decided she would be with him forever.

A Night without Dreams

Doreen James was also having a sleepless night at Schlobohm. It had been months since she had slept the way she knew other people did—from bedtime until morning, awaking rested and alert. Most nights she did not even bother to get into bed at all. She sat in the living room of her hard-won apartment in Schlobohm and stared sadly at the few furnishings—a table and chairs, a couch, some curtains—that she had bought at garage sales near her parents' home.

All through the summer of 1988—during the months that began with Joe's death and stretched out after Jaron's birth—Doreen had been wrapped in a blue, weepy mood. She had no appetite, yet she seemed only to gain weight, as if her body were swelling to match her heavy spirits. Leaden with depression, she had grabbed tightly to the idea that a new apartment, her own apartment, could magically lift the sadness. When she finally moved to Schlobohm, in November of 1988, she spent weeks sitting listlessly in her living room, as if waiting for the very walls to make her happy. Had she been able to see more clearly, she might have understood that she had never mourned the loss of Joe and the loss of her dream. "This was not the way my life was supposed to be," she thought, but would not say aloud. "I was supposed to have my college degree. His father was supposed to be here."

Now, during the summer of 1989, the sadness lingered, and Doreen had abandoned the illusion that an apartment would make it go away. The rush of feeling came most often at night. Nights like these. As was her ritual, she cried for a while, then fumbled in the drawer by her bed, where she kept things away from her one-year-old's curious fingers.

She was proud that she hid her stash from Jaron. It meant she was not so utterly lost that she couldn't protect her son. For the same reason, she held fast to her other rules, too. She would not make a buy unless there were Pampers and baby food in the house. Only an addict, she told herself, spends the diaper money on drugs. And she would not start to smoke unless she was certain that Jaron was deeply asleep. Only a hopeless soul does crack in front of her children.

Slowly, almost drowsily, Doreen took the single crack vial from her drawer. Tonight there would be just one, because five dollars was all she could scrounge. There wasn't much money left after the baby food and Pampers, and she had been borrowing from her sisters too frequently lately. She would die of shame if they did the math and told her parents. Despite Doreen's current address, Pearl and Walter James still thought of their daughter as a child of the suburbs, not the projects. They would never understand how she had got so lost and had wandered so far from where she belonged.

Lumbering over to the window, Doreen pulled the garage sale curtains shut, so that her parents, miles away in New Jersey, could not see. Then she poured the tiny amount of white powder into the bowl of her smoke shop crack pipe, and lit a match. Her heavy hands shook, as they always did when she held the flame to the powder and inhaled. She coughed, then inhaled again.

When the familiar sound of bells filled her head, she leaned back on her secondhand couch and sighed. Soon everything would look crystal clear, as if someone had washed the windows of her soul, turned up the volume on her world. She would be lifted out of herself, out of her life, to a place that was shiny and brightly lit. Five dollars bought only a few minutes there, and when they were over she would be more depressed than before. But for those few minutes, she could escape, leaving Schlobohm, with all its disappointment and confusion, behind.

Defensible Space

Nick thought little had been accomplished during his last year as mayor. In fact, a lot had been accomplished, although very little of it happened at City Hall. Across town, in the squat mustard brick building that housed the Municipal Housing Authority, steady, quiet progress was being made toward complying with the court order. Now that the list of sites was complete (Judge Sand had unilaterally replaced the seminary site without asking the council), the bureaucrats, not the politicians, were in charge. The detail work—drawing up blueprints, soliciting developers, awarding the contract—would all be done not by City Hall but by Municipal Housing. And behind every detail of that work, with his finger in every pot and his ego on the line, was Oscar Newman, the towering architect with the Amish-style beard who had infuriated the city with his helicopter search for housing sites.

To Newman, the Yonkers desegregation fight had never been about desegregation at all. It had been about his chance to test his worldview. Thirty years earlier, another set of townhouses had caught his eye, those of Carr Square Village in St. Louis. His observations about those townhouses would become his life's work. Newman, an assistant professor of architecture at Washington University at the time, was struck by the fact that those older, smaller buildings remained safe and livable while during the same decade the brand-new, towering Pruitt-Igoe project across the street was ruined by vandalism and crime, and was soon torn down.

The demographics of both projects were the same—poor families in need of public-housing assistance. There was no difference in their surrounding neighborhoods, either, because they were directly across the street from one another. The only real difference was the type of structure that comprised the housing project— two-story row houses on one side, eleven-story apartment buildings on the other. What was the dynamic of those designs, Newman wondered, that meant the difference between success and failure?

After years spent walking through Pruitt-Igoe, and Carr Square Village, and countless other housing complexes, Newman thought he'd found the answer. Crime, mischief, menacing behavior—they all require anonymity, the feeling that no one is watching and no one will interfere. In public-housing high-rises, he concluded, there is too much space that belongs to everyone, and, therefore, to no one. Hallways, elevator lobbies, stairwells. Large, unassigned public areas without such luxuries as doormen, elevator operators, or superintendents, hence all visual clues say that no one is in charge.

He'd had his first chance to test his theory of "Defensible Space" at the Clason Point public housing project in the South Bronx in 1969. The project consisted of forty-six buildings, mostly row houses, with a total of 400 apartments. All the buildings were constructed of exposed cement, reminiscent of army barracks. In fact, Clason Point was built to house munitions workers during World War II, and was never torn down. Because few of those workers had cars, few of the apartments faced the street, but looked out on a grid of internal walkways, instead.

Oscar did not demolish a single building at Clason Point, but by the time he was finished everything looked new. First, he resurfaced each building with a stucco-like substance that could be made to look like stonework or brick. The material came in a variety of styles and colors, and Newman let the tenants of each row house select the color of their home.

Out front, he used ankle-height slabs of stone curbing to turn the neglected communal lawn into semiprivate front yards. In back, he did much the same thing, using inexpensive hollow tubular steel, which looked like stylish iron, to create a series of smaller backyards. The desolate grid of walkways was transformed into a kind of promenade. Down the center he placed benches and decorative streetlamps, each only eight feet high and made of real, breakable glass.

The New York City Housing Authority had never installed such an accessible, vulnerable lighting fixture before, and officials there tried to talk Newman out of it. Lights in housing projects are placed high enough that they are not easily reached and are fitted with plastic covers that can withstand potshots. Fragile, decorative *glass* fixtures were unheard of.

But Newman argued that the reliance on the shatterproof devices was part of the reason that vandalism occurred in the first place. "The materials are vandal resistant—and ugly," he said, "and people go out of their way to test the resistance capacities."

The Housing Authority at Clason Point had similar objections to nearly all the other changes that Newman proposed. The stated reason was that his plans were too expensive, but Newman believed the real reason was far more complicated, and reflected a way of thinking that was much more difficult to confront.

It has always been understood that public housing must not be too nice, that it must not have frills like balconies or bay windows, the kind of things that inspire envy or hostility in the taxpayers who paid for it. Although those in charge of the country's public housing would never phrase it this way, the unspoken philosophy is that we as a society look down on people who need help paying their rent, and we want their housing to be different.

It is this "stigma of ugliness," Newman argued, that was largely responsible for the crime rate in many housing projects. Making a project look as different as possible from its surroundings, he said, "marks it off as clearly as if by quarantine." Unfortunately, he explained, "this practice not only 'puts the poor in their place' but brings their vulnerability to the attention of others."

Oscar Newman is a forceful personality, and over time he persuaded the Housing Authority to try it his way. In the first year after Newman made his changes, crime in Clason Point dropped 54 percent. Polls of the residents, before and after, found that the percentage of people who felt they had the right to question strangers increased from 27 percent to 50 percent. The tenants planted grass on the lawns that they now thought of as their own. When that grew, they went on to plant flowers and bushes, and to add small white picket fences. There had been a 30 percent vacancy rate in the project before the redesign. Soon there was a waiting list of several hundred families. The streetlamps were not vandalized.

Over the years since he revitalized Clason Point, Newman had redesigned countless neighborhoods. But Yonkers was different. It was the first time he would have the luxury of starting from scratch. Instead of doing the best he could to correct existing mistakes, he was being handed the chance to create something entirely new.

When others of his redesigned projects failed, he could hand off some of the blame, pointing out that the original project had flaws that even he could not fix. If Yonkers failed, he would have no such excuse, and he would face the failure of a lifetime of theory. But if it worked, if the townhouses were all he expected they could be, then the credit would be his alone.

While others in Yonkers fought for their homes or their political philosophies, Newman fought for his theories. He was not fighting to desegregate Yonkers. He was not even a champion of public housing. He never dwelled long on the question of whether there *should* be public housing. Instead he started from the reality that there *would* be public housing and worked from there, battling ferociously for his ideas.

In Yonkers, Newman's most public fights were with the council, but he spent far more time arguing with HUD, the Justice Department, and the NAACP. The first thing he did, of course, was to persuade Judge Sand to make the buildings townhouses in the first place. When he entered the case in 1987, the plan on the table was for two high-rise apartment buildings to be built on one site, and a three-story walk-up to be built on another. Those designs had the support of the NAACP, the Justice Department, and HUD. Newman explained to all of them, as he had explained to the housing officials in charge of Clason Point, that such large, anonymous structures would serve only to destabilize the surrounding neighborhood. But the more he explained, the more officials he managed to alienate.

HUD was wary because what he was proposing would set a bad—read "expensive"—precedent. Although the housing itself would cost less, the land would cost more, because the townhouse design would use more land.

The NAACP, in turn, was hostile, saying Newman himself was racist in his suggestion that a large pocket of poor people in a middle-class area would create a de facto subculture tolerant of crime and drugs.

"He is putting a respectable gloss to basically racist sentiments," blasted Michael Sussman, the lawyer for the NAACP. "It's that kind of fearmongering garbage that reflects Oscar Newman's ideological baggage."

In the end, it was the judge who made the decision to adopt Newman's scattered-site approach, a decision that led to the endless search for buildable sites and that eventually led to the contempt crisis. Over those years, Michael Sussman came around to Newman's point of view, saying that the NAACP had always supported scattered sites, but worried that the approach would result in too many delays. The rapprochement was helped along by the fact that Newman stopped talking of the evils of high-rises, and emphasized the benefits of low-rises, instead.

Although resigned to a scattered-site strategy, HUD continued to lobby for two-story walk-ups rather than townhouses. The expense would be less, they said, because more walk-up units could be built on the same amount of land.

Newman responded with long memos to Judge Sand. He cautioned again and again about too many poor, single-parent families in large anonymous spaces. Walk-ups have communal entries, stairwells, and yards, he said. The townhouses, as he envisioned them, would each have its own front and rear yard. Each front door would be close to and visible from the street. Each backyard would be defined by a small fence, and small groups of yards would collectively be fenced off from the surrounding streets by a taller, six-foot fence. There would be no common sidewalks in the clusters of yards.

That last part, about the shared sidewalks, was a lesson learned the hard way at Clason Point. He had made a mistake, Newman decided with hindsight, when he created communal gathering places behind some of the buildings. Many of the areas fell into disrepair because no family saw the space as theirs.

"I had forgotten my own basic rule," he said. "The smaller the number of families that share an area, the greater is each family's identity with it and the greater its feeling of responsibility for maintaining and securing it."

He would not sidestep his own rules again. In Yonkers, he insisted, there would be only individual front and backyards. He finally won his point when he learned to argue not in terms of philosophy, but economics, the language HUD spoke most fluently. In a fifteen-page memo to one of the many deputy assistant secretaries who revolved through the case over the years, he explained that in the long run, walk-ups were in many ways more expensive to build than townhouses. He pointed out that "when calculating the cost of walk ups vs. row houses, HUD was using only the initial construction costs, whereas the big savings in the use of row housing was in the consequent reduction in maintenance, vandalism and security costs. HUD spends millions of dollars per project every few years repairing the destruction wrought by the residents in public areas of high-rise and walk up buildings. Our housing would have no such public areas."

Eventually, HUD agreed. Newman's next challenge was to communicate the plan to prospective builders, and bureaucracy got in the way, here, too. The Municipal Housing Authority typically bids out such work by issuing a "Request for Proposals," with only the most basic guidelines given for the job. All the detailed decisions would be left to the developer preparing the proposal. The purpose of this method is to allow the developer to build what he knows best, at a lower cost than if he were told to follow the authority's more specific, predetermined plans.

This approach worried Newman. The usual sketchy details given to prospective bidders would never result in the "Defensible Space" experiment that he envisioned. Looking for a way around the process, he turned to Peter Smith, the executive director of the Yonkers Municipal Housing Authority. Smith, too, had his own mixed agenda when it came to the housing. A former priest, whose ministry had included the west side of the city, Smith knew the need for decent housing and wanted this experiment to work for the simplest of reasons—it would mean better lives for those who moved. But Smith was also a native of Yonkers. He still lived on the east side. He sent his children to school there, and he confessed to some nostalgia for the old days when a person's ethnic history could be read in his street address. He had another motive for wanting the housing to work. It would spare him further lectures from his east-side neighbors every Sunday when he went to church.

No one knew the bidding system better than Smith, and he and Newman tried to persuade HUD to allow them to include a schematic drawing in the bid packages, to give builders a better idea of the eventual goal. To an architect, they argued, a picture is unquestionably worth a thousand words. HUD rejected the idea, saying that the entire point of this process was to let each developer do it his own way. A compromise was reached, in which HUD allowed more detailed language than was common in the Request for Proposals, giving Newman a chance to incorporate some of his most central ideas.

He tried his best. He filled dozens of pages with descriptions of the "two-story townhouse units," each its "own entity" and each with "its own front and backyard." There were to be no "lobbies, stairways or corridors." And they were to be attractive ("brick veneer at the first story") and different from one another ("variation in window sizes, color, texture, etc."). The front yards should face the street "so as to facilitate normal patrolling by police cars." Rear

Show Me a Hero

yards should be individual but grouped together "to create a collective private zone."

The developers' response to this words-only description was what Smith and Newman had predicted. The designs submitted were nothing like what was wanted, and no company was awarded the contract. Starting the process from the beginning, Newman made another plea to HUD, asking for the inclusion of a schematic drawing. Again HUD said no. But everyone eventually learns to play the game around the edges in Yonkers, and for the second round of bids, Newman flirted with the rules. When the developers came to pick up their packages, they found a pile of schematic site plans next to the pile of packages. They were told they could either pick up the site plans with their bid packages, or not. Most of them did. This time, Newman received three proposals that were close matches to his vision.

In May of 1989, while Nick was deciding whether to run for reelection, a developer was hired. Deluxe Homes, Inc. was in far-off Berwick, Pennsylvania, where the prefabricated units could be put together with minimal interference from Yonkers protesters. HUD would pay $16.1 million to build the first 142 of the required 200 units of public housing. In October of 1989, while Nick was campaigning, Deluxe was completing thirty-five pages of neat white-on-blue construction plans, showing details of everything down to the towel rings. In December of 1989, days before Nick left office, the designs were submitted to HUD to make sure they were in compliance with federal requirements and state building codes. Nick was sent a copy of those plans, but the fine points of architectural blueprints were lost on him, so he never understood all that had been accomplished on his watch.

Oscar Newman, on the other hand, spent days scrutinizing every detail of the water-colored blueprints, sharply aware that he was holding the future—the city's future, his own professional future—in his hands. Years of reading these drawings meant that he could see a three-dimensional neighborhood on the flat, tinted pages. Each home in that neighborhood was slightly different from the one next to it, some with peaked roofs, some with bay windows. Each had an individual yard in back and space for a flower bed in front, allowing tenants to literally tend to what was theirs.

"Beautiful," Newman thought. "It had better work."

Billie's News (I)

Billie Rowan and John Santos were in the middle of breaking up when she told him she was pregnant.

They had been together for three months by then, and Billie had stopped working so she could be available whenever John wanted her. The routine of their lives was that it had no routine. They wouldn't make plans, for instance, and when John was ready to see her, he would stand outside her mother's building and summon her with a whistle, his trademark whistle, like a loud warbling bird. This man, this gentleman who had asked permission to kiss her, would never come to her door to get her. She would have to go to him. Then they would hang out—at Meeka's, on the sidewalks of Schlobohm, at the corner store.

More often, though, he would hang out with his friends, instead. He would be gone well past midnight, and Billie would wait for him, either at Meeka's or at his mother's, fixing her makeup, making herself her most attractive, knowing he would come home for the sex.

She believed that eventually she could wear him down, make him realize that she really cared about him. She did everything she could think of to keep him at home. When friends called, she wouldn't deliver the message, and when they came to the door she would tell them that he wasn't there. She turned up the music on the stereo to drown out their whistles from the street, but he left every night, anyway.

Before long, John felt trapped and confined by her efforts. She was nice. He liked her, maybe even loved her, but he didn't like the way it felt, this wanting to be with only one person. In early autumn he decided to end the relationship, and, as was his way, he tried to make her leave him first so it wouldn't be his fault.

"I'm nothing but a bum," he said, his voice as smooth and soft as his skin, hoping to sweet-talk his way to freedom. "I'm not good enough for you. Why don't you just forget about me?"

In answer, Billie spat her news at him. It was her way of shutting him up, of hurting him back. It was also her gamble that she could keep him.

"I'm pregnant," she said, her huge gold hoops shaking furiously in her ears as she spoke. "And I'm going to get rid of it."

Billie waited for John to say what she wanted him to say. When he didn't, she turned and stomped off.

John was not used to women walking out on him, and he did something he had never done before. He went after her. He followed Billie across Schlobohm and into her mother's building. For the first time in three months, he climbed the stairs and knocked.

"It's for you to decide," he told her, but if she wanted to have the baby he promised to "stick by it."

He also warned her that she shouldn't expect him to change.

"If this is your kind of test, to see where we stand or something, don't mess with me," he said. "If this is what you're doing to get me away from the streets, don't you understand, that's the only family I have."

Billie heard him, or said she did. But there was another message in his visit, far louder than his words. If a baby had the power to bring John Santos to her door, then, Billie Rowan decided, she definitely should have that baby.

Little Frankie

Alma Febles was pacing the American Airlines terminal at Kennedy Airport, looking out the window, though she knew the plane was not due for hours. She smoked her cigarettes, at a rate far heavier than the four to five packs a day she had been using in recent months. As she struck the match to light her tenth (maybe it was her eleventh), she made a deal with the heavens.

"God help me," she said aloud, placing her hands prayerfully over her red, tired eyes, "if Frankie gets off that plane I will not smoke one more cigarette again in my entire life."

About a year after Alma moved her children down to Santo Domingo, her second husband, Frankie's father, moved back down there, too. The gossip that drifted north to Alma said he had made a lot of money back in the United States. Alma did not know where the money came from, and she didn't want to know.

She did not hear much about the man for several months, until one summer evening when she called the peach house on Calle J-1 and was told that five-year-old Frankie wasn't there. His father had come for him, the maid told Alma. The man said he was his father, so she let Frankie go. No, she said, she didn't know when the boy was coming home. He didn't pack any clothes or anything, so he probably wouldn't be away too long.

For the first week, Alma felt concern, but not panic. "Maybe he just wants to spend some time with his son," she told herself, although she couldn't imagine what might cause this change of heart in a man who had rarely seen the boy during the past five years. "Maybe this is good. If I can't be there, maybe his father can be there."

She called the house every afternoon, casually asking for Frankie, swallowing hard when she learned he was not home. By the beginning of the second week she wanted to scream at the maid and tell her how irresponsible it had been to let Frankie go off with that man in the first place. But already this year, two young women had quit abruptly, walking out on the children when Alma was 1,550 miles away. So she checked her rising anger and had the same conversation with the maid each day: "Where is he?" "He's with his father." "Isn't he back?" "No, he isn't back yet."

After ten days, she realized Frankie wasn't coming back. She rooted out his father's phone number through the neighborhood grapevine, but decided not to call him. She suspected that the purpose of all this was to frighten or upset her, and if she spoke to him herself he would know he had succeeded. Added to that was the fact that all her calls to Santo Domingo were made collect. She would be humiliated if he accepted the charges, and more so if he did not.

Instead she told her maid, "You call his house and tell him that I called. Frankie's been there enough time. I want him back."

The next day, the maid had a message for Alma from her ex-husband. She read it as it had been delivered: "Frankie isn't coming back. Frankie stays with me."

"What did he say?" Alma asked, although she had heard every word.

"He said that Frankie's not coming back," the woman said more slowly and more loudly, as if Alma was having a problem with the phone line, not with the message itself. "He says if you want to discuss it with him, you should call him."

Close to hysteria, Alma dialed the international call from work. She would explain it to her boss later.

"Who gave you the authority?" she demanded when her ex answered the phone. "Why don't you bring Frankie back home."

"Frankie's my child," he said, then dug the knife into Alma's soul. "He's better off with me than with a maid who doesn't even know him," he said. "He's my child and he's going to stay with me."

Alma thought of all the nights she didn't sleep, of the heavy, crushing guilt, of the reasons that she brought the children to Santo Domingo and the reasons that she left them there. With one taunting comment, he had dismissed all that. He had made it sound like selfishness, like something she wanted to do, like a choice she had made. When she next spoke, her words were low and angry, almost a growl.

"I'm going to give you twenty-four hours to send him back home. This is my child. I haven't heard from you in a long time. You don't know the reasons Frankie's there and not here."

She took a deep breath. "If I call tomorrow and Frankie's not home," she said, "I'm gonna go there. I'm going to go over to your house, and I'm going to kill you and all of your family. The difference between you and me is that people think you're crazy. You're not crazy. I am."

She was speaking faster now. The volume and the pitch were rising. The growl became a screech. "Either you bring my child back today or I'm going to go there and kill you and all your family. The only person who is going to survive is Frankie, 'cause he's mine. I mean it."

Alma slammed down the phone and hugged her arms around herself in the backroom office. She was shaking uncontrollably and fighting the tears. She thought of how frightened Frankie must be, away from his brother and sister, with a father he didn't really know. He couldn't call Leyda or Virgilio and he couldn't call Alma. He didn't know the numbers, and he didn't know how to use a telephone. Then the thought struck her, clear and overwhelming. Frankie didn't belong in Santo Domingo. "He belongs at home," she said. "With me."

She found her boss, explained the phone call, and asked for a $400 loan, more than a week's salary. Then she called her ex-husband again and changed the specifics of her threat. "I'm going to send him a ticket," she said. It was late Friday afternoon. "You're going to put Frankie on a plane on Sunday. I want him to come home."

The next call was to a travel agent, a woman she knew well from all her trips back to the island over the past year. It would take until Monday to wire a ticket, the agent said, but she knew of someone who was leaving Saturday morning for Santo Domingo. Perhaps she could carry the ticket?

The arrangements were made and the only question was whether Alma's ultimatum would work. She sat by the telephone and tried to calm herself enough to think. What could she say to the man that would sufficiently frighten him? Did he really believe she would kill him? At that moment she felt as if she could, but she doubted that he understood that. He probably dismissed her threats as he had dismissed her feelings.

She made one last phone call that she couldn't afford. It was a hunch, a gamble, a hope that she, too, could hit a central nerve. "If you don't send Frankie," she said, trying to sound worldly and menacing, "I'm not going to go there and kill you. I'm going to call the American embassy and press charges to get custody of Frankie. You have the money, but Frankie's an American citizen. I'm going to put you in jail because you kidnapped Frankie," she said.

Now she smoked and prayed and hoped her threat had hit its mark. Frankie's plane was due to arrive at four o'clock. Alma was at Kennedy by two. When the hours finally passed, and the passengers began to disembark, she knelt on the carpet in the gate area and began to pray. Her prayers became sobs as a stream of unfamiliar faces came off the jetway. Her brother, who had come along to the airport, tried to quiet her. "He's not that crazy," he said. "He'll put him on the plane."

The parade of passengers stopped. The pilot came out, and the copilot, and there was still no sign of Frankie. The room started reeling and Alma put her head to her knees, trying not to faint.

"Mama," someone said, or maybe it was her imagination. "Mama."

She looked up and there was Frankie, two shades darker and two inches taller than when she'd seen him last, holding the hand of a stewardess.

Alma never smoked another cigarette again.

1990

Mayor Spallone

Mary Dorman felt a flash of personal triumph sitting in the audience at the Polish Community Center, waiting for Mayor Spallone's inauguration to begin. She had bought a new suit for the momentous occasion. Hank's swearing-in ceremony was open to the public, and there were a thousand people in the hall on this first Tuesday of 1990. The section where Mary was seated was by invitation only. As soon as she sat down, she carefully tucked the engraved card into her purse. It was a keeper.

Mary had worked hard so that Hank Spallone might be mayor. Just as the housing fight was her first experience as a protester, Hank's run for office was her first experience as a campaigner. She did all the ritual steps of a newcomer to the electoral dance: distributing flyers, attending rallies. This being Yonkers, she did some more unusual things, too. She became part of the group that followed Nick Wasicsko throughout the east side, rattling him at every stop.

This being Yonkers, it also didn't take long before the euphoria over Hank's victory began to sour. Like Nick two years earlier, Hank had campaigned with a legal appeal pending, and shortly after the election he had toned down his rhetoric.

"We will abide by the decision of the Supreme Court," he said the morning after election day, when asked about the pending court decision. "That is what law is about, that is what we are about. We've had our fight. We will get our decision and we'll work together to go forward."

Words like these, with their echo of earlier words from a previous mayor-elect, infuriated some of Spallone's core supporters. At a council meeting days before the inauguration, Jack O'Toole, the head of the Save Yonkers Federation, took the floor and attacked the man he had spent months working to elect. "The people elected you to fight and act," he said. "The people are getting upset. The natives are getting restless."

Mary was not yet one of those who were restless. She still believed in Hank Spallone, had believed in him completely since she first heard him speak in the days after the riotous meeting at Saunders High School. His was the voice that drew her to the cause. Over the year that followed, his had become the voice that represented the cause. And by the time he ran for mayor, the transposition was complete. To Mary Dorman, Hank Spallone *was* the cause.

She knew a lot about the Supreme Court appeal, because she made it her business to know a lot about everything that affected Spallone. The case of *Henry G. Spallone vs. United States of America and Yonkers Branch–National Association for the Advancement of Colored People*, she knew, raised the question of whether a legislator could be fined for not voting as a judge directed him to. The Constitution protected members of Congress from coercion and prosecution for their votes, a protection known as the "doctrine of legislative immunity." Over the years, lower appeals courts have extended that right to include local legislators, too. But until *Spallone vs. U.S.* the question had never made it to the Supreme Court.

Mary pored over the pages of analysis in the newspaper the day before the actual hearing and, though confused at first, managed to sort out the arguments in the case. Attorneys for the councilmen would argue that there had been less extreme ways to enforce the housing plan available to Judge Sand, like establishing an independent commission to override the council. The attorney for the government would argue that legislative immunity did not apply in this case because the legislators had already agreed to comply with the order and then backed out. The questions the justices were being asked to decide were these: Did Sand tamper dangerously with the separation of powers by telling the councilmen how to vote? Would a decision in favor of the councilmen mean chaos can reign and elected officials can break promises to obey court orders?

Mary wasn't clear where she stood on the subject of legislative immunity, but she was quite certain where she stood on the subject of Hank Spallone. Even if some of the others had reneged on their agreement, she thought, Hank should get his money back because he had refused to vote for the consent decree in the first place so he had never reneged on anything. The decision might not come for months, and now Hank was indisputably changing his tone, but Mary was not disillusioned. Her only disappointment was in how some of her Save Yonkers compatriots were acting. They were hearing "compliance" and "concession" when Hank was not saying either of those things. All he was saying was "wait and see." That approach was not a concession, Mary thought, if you are certain you will win.

Hank's talk of law and patience, she believed, was not moderation but growth. Now that he was the mayor, he was trying to act like the mayor. She had noticed that he had begun to talk about himself in the third person: "Mr. Spallone never supported that consent decree"; "Hank Spallone hasn't changed his position one iota." Many powerful people, she noticed, liked to do that. And he certainly seemed like a mayor as he was sworn in at the packed Polish Community Center. He spoke without a text, linking the future of Yonkers to the future of Eastern Europe, which was in the throes of transforming itself after the fall of Communism.

At the end of his speech, he presented the center with commemorative street signs. One read "Lech Walesa Drive," and the other read "Solidarity Square."

"Perhaps it will be the thing that binds this council and this city—for what it says is Solidarity—and I would hope that this represents our city," he said.

When the Supreme Court decision came down, eight days after the inauguration, it was welcome news. The justices overturned the councilmen's contempt fines, by a vote of 5 to 4. The majority opinion was narrowly written—it did not rule out contempt fines altogether, but ruled that Judge Sand had acted too quickly against the councilmen in this particular instance and should have allowed a "reasonable" time to see if crippling municipal fines forced them into compliance. The justices completely sidestepped the question of whether the fines violated free speech and legislative immunity.

Mary read every word of the analysis in the newspaper. All the articles said that while the decision was a victory for the councilmen, it would have no effect on the housing order itself, which had already been upheld on appeal. Even Chief Justice William Rehnquist, who wrote the majority opinion, was careful to say: "The issue before us is relatively narrow. There can be no question about the liability of the city of Yonkers for racial discrimination . . ." It did not sound to Mary like this was the opening that Hank had promised, but rather than question her faith in him, she turned her doubts onto herself. Maybe she was reading it wrong, she thought. Maybe this was something she couldn't understand.

She was reassured by the fact that Hank had seen the decision as something to celebrate. On hearing the news he had ordered a case of pink Korbel Brut champagne and a six-foot-long hero sandwich for an impromptu party at City Hall. "I don't think this is the end," he said, raising his champagne glass for a toast. "I think this is the beginning." And if Hank Spallone believed that, then Mary Dorman believed it, too.

John Goes to Jail (I)

Billie was in her fourth month of pregnancy, dreaming of happily ever after, when John was arrested. She tied a new silk scarf around her head, buttoned one of his old colorful shirts around her expanding middle, and went to see him in a foul-smelling visitors' room at Rikers Island, where he explained that none of this was his fault.

It all started several months earlier, he said, dropping his sexy, sweet-talking voice almost to a whisper. Soon after he and Billie had gotten together, he said, he went out one night with his good friend Stash. His purpose for the evening was to escape from Billie, who needed too much from him: "I needed to get away." He was the victim here. Somehow Billie was the villain.

He and Stash found their way south, to the Bronx, "like usual," he said, where "we was partying and we went to the clubs." At one of those clubs, he said, "Stash introduced me to another guy, who I really didn't know, but I trusted Stash, I trusted his judgment.

"Then we were coming back and it starts to rain. I say, 'We can take the train,' but the other guys don't want to. These girls come by in a car and Stash tells them to stop. So they did and we started talking and they said they could give us a lift."

Stash's no-name friend sat in front with two of the girls, while Stash and John sat in back with two others.

"We're all laughing and stuff. So they ask for our names and telephone numbers and I give them mine. Not my real name. Just Hot. But I give the real number."

Unbeknownst to him, he said, his friends did not do the same.

"Then, a little bit later," John continued, warming up to his story, "Stash's friend, he tries to rob one of the girls and they're all screaming. I'm like 'what's going on here?' We all took off and I thought that was the end of it. But I guess one of them went to the cops and I'm the only one they could find, cause I'm the only one whose real number they had. Now they're charging me with Robbery Two."

His excuses were so earnest, so detailed, that even he seemed to believe them. His voice was so confident, so smooth, that Billie chose to believe his story, too.

John plea-bargained for a one-year sentence, of which he would serve eight months. He told Billie that her visit to him in jail made him realize that they were meant to be a couple.

"My friends turned on me, the cops scared me, and you believed me," he said.

Billie promised she would wait for him. John promised he would change.

134   *Show Me a Hero*

To March or Not to March

When Norma O'Neal and Pat Williams argue, they do so in the clipped shorthand reserved only for friends who have known each other for years. Pat is Norma's best friend. They met in 1983, when they were both working at the Lillian Vernon warehouse, and Norma regularly heard "Pat Williams" being paged over the intercom. One day Norma happened to meet the woman whose name was so familiar. "Oh, you're Pat Williams," Norma said, deadpan. "I've heard a lot about you."

A few others in Norma's circle would describe themselves as her best friend, but failing eyesight is a profound measure of friendship, and in the months after Norma lost her vision she learned who her truest friends were. There were her children, of course, along with Phyllis Pearl, who came over to read the mail every afternoon. Pat Williams was there to do almost everything else. When Norma had no choice but to quit her job, Pat helped her apply for disability. When the disability application was denied, Pat walked the three miles from her own house to Schlobohm, to help Norma decipher the denial and fill out the application again. When Norma's income dropped from the $335 a *week* she earned as a night health aide, to the $189 a *month* she received on welfare, Pat always seemed to be around with extra groceries, or extra cash. Norma protested, but Pat didn't listen. She figured Norma would do the same for her.

This loyalty, this connection, gave Pat the right to speak her mind. And what was on her mind one January morning was the upcoming housing march. She had heard at church that a pro-housing protest—"a black people's march"—was planned on the east side. Pat was going, and she wanted Norma to come along too.

"It's time people here fought their own fight instead of letting the courts and the lawyers do it all," Pat said. "How come the only people talking about this are white? How come all the faces you see on the news about this are white? They don't want us living over there, well, they don't know us. They've never seen us. And whose fault is that? It will be your fault if you just stay over here and do nothing."

Norma shook her head, then pushed an errant strand of steel gray hair from her face. "It won't make anyone want anyone, it'll just make it worse. Just leave things alone."

"You're afraid," Pat said. It was part observation, part accusation.

"Afraid of making trouble that doesn't need to be made."

"Well I don't scare easily," Pat said. "We should let people see we're the same as them. That we want what they want."

"They'll see that we want what they *have*," said Norma. "They'll see what they want to see."

The conversation in Norma's living room was a small-scale version of one going on in much of the minority community in Yonkers during the weeks since Hank Spallone became mayor. The question at the center of those conversations was phrased with varying degrees of political correctness, but the heart of the issue was this: Where were the blacks? Where were all the people of color? For years, Yonkers had been convulsed with protests, but they were almost all protests *against* the housing. City council meetings were filled with angry faces, but nearly all of those faces were *white*.

Their absence was part of a deliberate strategy. From the first days of the court case, the NAACP had decided to take what it considered the high road, urging its members to stay quiet and work the courts, not the streets. It would not help the cause, they believed, to have angry black people confronting angry white people on the news every night. The strategy worked in that it did prevent direct confrontation. But it was a success with side effects, the supporters of the housing being so quiet that they seemed not to exist. Nick cursed them silently at meetings, feeling he had been left out there alone to fight someone else's battle. Mary, in turn, saw their absence as evidence that minority residents of the west side agreed with her and did not want the new housing, either.

Over the years, there were rumbles of complaint on the west side, from people who argued that it was demeaning to ask blacks to contain their anger so that white people wouldn't be frightened. But those rumbles were kept in check, and the strategy of restraint was held in place as long as there was someone else who seemed to be fighting the fight for them. But by January of 1990, there was no one else. Nick Wasicsko, whose main message had been compliance, had been voted out of office, replaced by the defiant Hank Spallone. For the first time, an appeals court—the Supreme Court—had turned against the judge. Public sentiment is a fluid, unpredictable thing, and what is unheard-of one day may be unstoppable the next. Soon after the Supreme Court ruling there was talk on the west side of marches and sit-ins. It was contagious talk. Talk like there had never been before.

Pat Williams went to the Messiah Baptist church on Sunday, and listened as the Reverend Darryl George invited his four-hundred-member congregation to march on the east side. The route, he said, was a secret, because others might try to stop it. It was time, he said, "to bring down the wall of racism in Yonkers." The march was just the beginning of a new visibility for "people of color and conscience," who would no longer remain passive. "Previously we have been silent and done nothing," he said. "We've allowed the court to speak for us. Now we're saying there's a higher court—a moral court. Enough is enough. This is a new beginning."

The most controversial part of George's announcement was not the march, but who he had invited along on the march. The Reverend Al Sharpton and the lawyer Alton Mattox would be there, he said, and they would bring busloads of supporters from outside Yonkers. They would also bring outside attention, because controversy and publicity followed the two men everywhere. Sharpton and Mattox were both advisers to Tawana Brawley, the black teenager whose claims that she had been sexually assaulted by a group of white men made international headlines and was later found by a grand jury to have been a hoax. The New York state attorney general Robert Abrams called Sharpton "deplorable, disgraceful, reprehensible, irresponsible," but George saw their reputations, their visibility, as part of their value to the cause.

"We have been catching hell," he said. "Now we will raise hell."

Said Sharpton, who held a news conference to spread the word: "This ain't a one-night stand, this is a marriage, and we're going to find the baddest honeymoon suite on the east side and engage in social intercourse."

The announcement of the march brought the conversation into the open throughout the minority communities of Yonkers. Fighting back had been something that no one would talk about. Now it was what everyone was talking about. The debate became loud and public, urgent and everywhere, and the divisions in the community were following familiar faultlines.

"It goes back to the classic case of Malcolm X saying 'You hit me and I'll hit you back,' while King said, 'You hit me and I'll turn the other cheek,' " said Herman Keith, a Westchester County legislator and the first black elected official in Yonkers.

Norma agreed with Martin Luther King. Pat sided with Malcolm X. Pat joined the march. Norma stayed home.

There were nearly four hundred people, mostly blacks and Hispanics, gathered outside the Messiah Baptist Church early on Saturday morning. At the appointed hour, the milling crowd coalesced into a parade, with Sharpton, George, and Mattox in the lead. It was more a stroll than a walk, and there was none of the drama and violence that marked decades of other civil rights marches, none of the water cannons of Selma, or the attack dogs of Birmingham. Nothing like all those scenes engraved in Pat's mind since childhood. In fact, the one hundred police officers in full riot gear far outnumbered the bystanders along the route. It was as if east Yonkers had chosen to ignore them completely.

Two hours later, the marchers neared School 4 on Trenchard Street, a trip of 3.4 miles. Although the destination was supposed to be a secret, School 4 was the obvious choice for this rally. The mammoth brick building, once proud, now boarded up and crumbling, had long been the symbolic heart of the anti-housing fight. It was already slated for demolition when Judge Sand issued his order, and Oscar Newman made it one of the first sites on his list for the new townhouses. The neighborhood fought back fiercely, full of new love for the weed-infested, graffiti-covered structure, insisting they would not be a true neighborhood without it. They conveniently ignored the fact that it was ugly—built, in the architectural style of the industrial revolution, to look like a factory.

They had it placed on the National Register of Historic Places, only to learn that that did not automatically save it from destruction. They drew up plans that would transform it into a community recreation center. Local protesters even cut the lawn and held a birthday party for the 104-year-old building, complete with ice cream and cake.

So what better place to make a pro-housing statement than at School 4? As the marchers neared the doomed building, their energy and their enthusiasm increased. "Guess what?" they chanted, gleefully. "We're moving in."

"Niggers, get out," someone shouted from the anonymity of an office building window, one of the first reactions the marchers had heard all day.

"We don't want you here," said another voice from a storefront doorway.

And, as the group turned left onto Trenchard Street and into the schoolyard, Pat clearly heard someone shout, "Go back to your own neighborhood."

Pat did go back to her neighborhood, on one of the rented yellow school buses that were waiting to drive the marchers home to the west side. That evening, she sat in Norma's living room telling her everything that happened during the day. "You should have been there," Pat said. "We showed them we wouldn't be kicked around."

"Did you change any minds?" Norma asked.

"Probably not," Pat said.

"When those buildings are built, black folks have to move into them," Norma said. "You've just made it harder for them to do that. That's all."

Doreen's Father Finds Out

Jaron James was an excited two-year-old, tugging his grandfather's hand as they walked along the glass-strewn path toward Building Two at Schlobohm. Doreen stayed several paces behind them, marveling, as she so often did, at the untainted joy that her son felt at even the simplest moments in his life. She'd seen photographs of herself with that same gleeful grin, and she wondered when she'd lost that smile, and when Jaron would lose his.

Of all his favorite things, and there were many, visits from his grandfather topped the list. Warren James visited Schlobohm as often as he could. He said he was coming just to see Jaron, but Doreen knew he was still taking care of her, as well. He never lectured her on this life that she had chosen and never wondered aloud whether this independence of hers was all she'd expected it to be. He just brought his gifts, and his hugs. As he headed home after each visit, he would say, "You know where to find us if you need us," or "Our door is always open."

Doreen followed Warren and Jaron through the battered front door of her building, then caught up with them as her father was lifting her son so he could push the button for the temperamental elevator. As he touched back down on the ground, something caught Jaron's ever-eager eye, and he reached over to pick up a broken crack vial from the concrete floor.

"No, Jaron, hot," Doreen yelled. He knew from experience with the Schlobohm radiators that "hot" was something he should not touch. She grabbed the boy's forearm and shook it forcefully, until the vial fell from his chubby hand, shattering at his feet. As it did, Doreen opened his palm and, using the only piece of fabric she could find, wiped his hand with the hem of her shirt, rubbing until the child began to cry.

"I'm sorry, Mommy's sorry," she said, knowing she was trying to clean away more than the taint of the vial.

The elevator doors opened and she guided Jaron inside.

"Filthy junkies, leaving their crap where decent people try to live," she said as her father stepped in next to her. "Why do they need to be doing their shit around here?"

Warren James said nothing as the car lurched upward. Then, as it reached the seventh floor, Doreen's floor, he said, "People talking about what other people are doing. And they're doing the same thing." He spoke quietly, almost a whisper, but his words had the force of an explosion.

Show Me a Hero

There was no more mention of drugs that afternoon. Warren's embrace was stiff as he hugged his daughter good-bye. "You know where to find us if you need us," he said.

Doreen felt her parents' disappointment in that hug. In the weeks that followed, although they still sent packages for Jaron, their visits became few and brief. She was lonely over the next few months. Her parents no longer trusted her. She, in turn, no longer trusted her sisters, because she was certain that one of them had squealed.

The sadness that already swallowed all her days grew deeper, and she needed more drugs to make it go away. Though her craving was greater, her ability to pay was not, since no one in her family would lend her money anymore. She borrowed from friends when she could, but mostly she "borrowed" from Jaron. One by one she broke her rules, deconstructing her imaginary fence that kept her from becoming one of "them." Sometimes there was no milk in the house, and Jaron drank water. Sometimes she was not sure if she had remembered to feed him at all. He was not always asleep when she smoked. If he interrupted her, she shushed him, then sent him back to bed.

Every day, every moment, became part of a rapidly descending spiral. When she was high, she was not high enough; it did not feel as pure or as perfect as it had before. When she wasn't high, she was sick. Nauseous, exhausted, and profoundly depressed, she moved even more slowly than usual.

One night, the worst night, she had smoked everything she had and still needed more. She ransacked her own few drawers, looking for money or a forgotten vial. Even a trace of crack dust mixed with gritty lint would do. As she searched, she thought of other ways she might pay for more drugs. She couldn't steal. She wasn't that desperate yet. She knew the dealers downstairs sometimes traded drugs for sex. Could she do that? Her body, already numb and deadened, was just something to escape from. Maybe she could.

Just then she came upon the tiny gold cross in Jaron's room, the one she had exchanged for the engagement ring she never wore. It was the only thing of value in the house. She held it up by its chain and watched as it swayed slightly from side to side. What would it be worth? Ten vials? Fifteen vials? More? Then, with a life-changing snap, she let the necklace drop from her fingers, back into the drawer.

She had hit rock bottom. Crying and shaking, she went to the phone and called her parents.

"I need help," she said, very quietly. "I'm sick and tired of being sick and tired. Mommy, please help me."

Her parents drove over from New Jersey and brought their daughter home.

Alma Brings the Children Home

By the spring of 1990, Alma realized it was time to bring her children back to Schlobohm. Just as there was no one moment when she had decided to flee Yonkers in the first place, there was no single event that led to this decision, either. Instead it was the feeling that, as the months continued to pass, Virgilio and Leyda seemed farther and farther away.

She was not there when Leyda was bitten by a neighbor's dog, then hid the bite from everyone for a week until the wound turned angry and red and infected. "Don't tell your mom," the neighbor said, and Leyda didn't, fearing that Alma would be angry. Finally a family friend noticed and Leyda went to the hospital for antibiotics.

Nor was she there when Virgilio was helping a pal tinker with the old truck that seemed to be perched permanently on blocks in front of his house. One day, in a rare attempt to start the rolling junk heap, Virgilio and a group of friends tried to push it, and one of the right wheels rolled over Virgilio's left foot. He slid a good distance with the wheel on top of his instep, and this time there was no wait before he went to the hospital. When he told Alma about the accident, she questioned the sense of pushing trucks that don't work.

"Everyone's always getting hurt over here," he answered. "All there is to do for fun is bad things."

What troubled Alma more than the growing recklessness of her children was their growing fear. Over time they became afraid of the house, certain that it was haunted by the ghost of an old man who died there one night while rocking in his rocking chair. There were several rocking chairs in Alma's house on Calle J-1, and Virgilio swore that they often started to rock on their own. One night, as he was getting undressed for bed, "the windows started closing by themselves," he told Alma. "I had my pants down to my knees and I just ran out of the house. I had my shirt on, and my underwear. People were looking at me." He ran to his grandmother's house, where he spent the night.

Alma believed that Virgilio was not just telling stories—he really saw these things. Maybe his mind was playing tricks on him because he wanted to leave. Maybe the house really was haunted, and the eerie happenings were a sign that it was time for him to leave. But if the children were going to be in danger where they lived, and if they were going to be afraid of where they lived, then they might as well be in danger and afraid closer to her. Increasingly often during her sleepless hours in the middle of the night Alma would think of the years when she was still in Santo Domingo, waiting to join her mother in the United States. "I've been blaming my mother for so long for leaving me behind," she decided. "I can't do the same thing. We are a family. We're four. We have to be together."

The family of four moved back to Yonkers in May of 1990, after Leyda and Virgilio finished their school semesters. Alma, exhausted from three years of worry and guilt, slept for the better part of three days. While she slept, the children made themselves hamburgers, which were an unaffordable luxury on the island, and took long bubbly baths, because the peach house only had a shower. They elbowed each other for space in the small apartment, squabbling the way only siblings can, readjusting to being together. By the time Alma awoke, they were complaining that they wanted to go "back home."

But Alma knew what her children couldn't—there was no

"back home." Many things had become clearer to her over the years since she first moved her family to Santo Domingo, and the hardest to accept was that she really didn't have a home. For a long time she had believed that when life became unbearable in Yonkers, she could always escape into her past, back to the island of her childhood. But she had tried that, and she had failed. The dream had evaporated at her touch. Santo Domingo was not the answer to her problem. Did that mean that there was no answer?

No Place for a Baby

John Billie Santos III was just a few weeks old when Billie Rowan brought him to Rikers Island to meet his father. Billie's mother tried to talk her out of the visit, asking "Why are you bringing a baby to that disgusting place?" But Billie couldn't wait to present her son to her man.

So she took two buses to the subway, then took the subway to the Queens Plaza station. She waited in the cold for the bright orange bus to Rikers, then spilled the contents of her bag and her pockets onto a table in the huge, drab waiting room. Once the guards determined that she was not carrying contraband, she was allowed to board another bus, a blue one, labeled CIFM. That took her to the Correctional Institute for Men, one of ten separate jails on the island, and the one where John was doing his time.

The entire trip took more than three hours, and by the time she found a seat in the windowless communal visiting room, she was almost as cranky as her baby. Many long minutes passed before John appeared, and she tried to examine her makeup in the glare from a barred window, while giving herself a silent lecture to keep her feelings to herself. She had to be the way John wanted her to be.

Their relationship during the months he had been in prison was far better than it had been when he was at home. They wrote letters almost daily, long, romantic professions of love, and John's

Show Me a Hero

During the months Doreen had spent back home in New Jersey, her sisters also re-entered her life. Barbara, who was closest in age to Doreen, had taken the role of friend and confidante. Sheila, the oldest, was like a third parent, there to point out where Doreen had gone wrong, and always eager to step in and make it right. It took a long time before Warren and Pearl James could trust Doreen, and one of their first steps toward that goal was allowing her to spend time back in Yonkers with Sheila. One of Sheila's many plans for Doreen's life included this meeting, of the Resident Empowerment Association Developing Yonkers, known as READY.

Sheila, who had always been more energetic than Doreen, was one of the founders of READY. When the rest of the James family had moved out of Yonkers twelve years earlier, Sheila had been lucky enough to qualify for an apartment in the Dunbar Houses, the only public-housing project in Runyon Heights, the black middle-class neighborhood on the east side. One of her neighbors there was Sadie Young Jefferson, president of the Dunbar tenant council. A stern, dynamic, determined woman, who was partial to no-nonsense dresses and sensible shoes, Sadie raised seven children in Yonkers public housing, and she knew well that Dunbar was the best. But instead of counting her blessings and crossing her fingers, she decided that residents of the other projects deserved housing as good as hers. "If this can be maintained this way, then all of them should be maintained in the same way," she said.

Sadie had been unimpressed and angered by the 1988 battle to bring public housing to the east side. Angry because "they say they're not prejudiced. Wrong. They're prejudiced." And unimpressed because she did not think that blacks should only consider their homes acceptable if they were near the homes of whites. The solution, she thought, was not to move people across town where they weren't wanted. The solution would be to give them power on their own side of town.

"If we're going to live plantation style," she preached to Sheila, "then we can run our *own* plantation."

During the previous year, while Doreen was losing herself to crack, Sheila was immersing herself in the ways of public housing and in the gospel of Sadie Young Jefferson. She traveled to Wash-

Show Me a Hero

words had the same overwhelming effect on paper as they had in person. After her sonogram, Billie spilled the beans that the baby was a boy. At first John was angry—he had wanted it to be a surprise—but soon he was proud, and he now had a reason to "settle down, go back to school, go to college. I want to devote myself to my family."

It was Billie's idea to give the baby both their names, a symbol of the fact that they were forever connected because of him. John argued that carrying the name of his own father had been a burden, one he didn't want to place on his son, but he eventually agreed.

Finally John was escorted into the visiting room, looking as she pictured him when she read his letters. He was dressed in his prison-issue work pants and work shirt. He had a scar on his cheek, a badge earned during a knife fight shortly after he arrived. The rules said she could not hug him, and she could not hand him anything—except their son.

John lifted Johnny from Billie's arms, and gazed at him. Billie tried to concentrate on that gaze, and to ignore the other families, the screaming children, the guards by the doors, and the clock on the wall.

When their hour was over, Billie bundled up the baby and got back on the blue bus. She made her whole complicated trip in reverse, arriving at Schlobohm near dinnertime. The visit had been draining, but not depressing. Eight months, she reasoned, was not a long time. John obviously loved his son, meaning he must love her, too. He would be home soon, and her life could take the shape she had originally planned.

Doreen's First Meeting

Doreen kept her handbag in her lap and eyes on the door while waiting for the meeting to begin. Sh here in this over-air-conditioned community room only be she had promised Sheila she would come.

The Explosion

ington, D.C. with Sadie, to the massive public information library in the headquarters of HUD, and they emerged twelve hours later with suitcases full of information on tenants' rights. With Sadie she learned how to calculate the rent they owed to Municipal Housing—30 percent of their monthly household income, less certain complicated deductions—and found that each had been receiving a rent bill that was wrong. They talked of tenant patrols, and on-site day care, and in-house screening committees that would keep the undesirables out in the first place.

Sadie, whose many careers had included grant-writing for social service programs, applied for and received private money to help fund her grand dreams. The National Center for Neighborhood Enterprises gave READY $5,000, which it used to hire lawyers and incorporate itself. Then, a philanthropic group that funds nascent causes provided $100,000 for office space and tenant training programs, and READY became a reality.

Doreen found herself in one of those offices attending one of those programs because she was trying to prove to her parents that she could be trustworthy and responsible. If she spent more time with Sheila, the "mature one," then maybe her sister's internal compass would guide her, as well. The meetings were a means to an end, a way to gain the confidence of her family. No one was more surprised than Doreen when she began to look forward to Sadie's teachings, and to gain confidence in herself.

Under Sadie's watch, these sessions were rallies more than lessons, about rebuilding yourself as much as rebuilding public housing. She did not lecture at the front of the room, she chanted, and as the event took on the character of a revival meeting, the audience began to call out in agreement as she spoke.

"They say we are 'tenants,'" Sadie declared. "We are not tenants, we are *residents*, a *community*."

"Amen, sister," someone said.

"Calling the projects 'projects,'" Sadie went on, "I recall projects being science projects. We are not a *project*. We are, I would think, a complex or a development."

"You say it, girl."

"Low income," she shouted, "does not mean low class!"

"Amen. Amen. Amen."

"They think that all the people in public housing are low, that all we want to do is lay around and smoke drugs," Sadie said. Her voice became low and angry. "I live in public housing. I'm nothing like they're describing. People in public housing are decent, educated, talented, everything that everybody else is — we just happen to make less money so we need lower rent."

It was a most unusual kind of twelve-step program. Sitting in her uncomfortable folding chair, meeting after meeting, Doreen wanted to be everything Sadie said she could be. Soon afterward, she went to her parents and said she was ready to take control of her own life again. She wanted to move back into Schlobohm.

1988 Redux

Slowly, very slowly, a proud house was emerging from the whirlwind of renovation at 175 Yonkers Avenue.

When Nick and Nay first bought the house, they knew it needed "some work." After they moved in, they realized there wasn't a single part of the house that didn't need work. The cost of a professional contractor was out of the question, and Nick's only knowledge of construction was that he "knew enough not to pick up a hammer," so most of the overhaul was done by Nick's brother, Michael, who was an electrician by trade and had spent a summer between high school and college working as a carpenter. He had learned a lot during that summer, he assured Nick, and his most deeply ingrained lesson was "it's too easy to hurt yourself doing this," which is why he switched to electrical work, instead. But the one summer of experience, along with many nights watching *This Old House* on PBS, made him certain he could handle the job.

Nick and Nay spent their first weeks as homeowners living in their dining room, while Michael knocked down a circa-1960s wall that had been erected down the center of the living room. Together, Nick, Nay, Michael, and Michael's girlfriend, Lisa, spent endless evenings ripping ugly linoleum off the living room floors and exposing the wood underneath. There was a gap in the floor where the dividing wall had been, so Lisa learned how to splice new pieces of oak to match the ones that had been there since 1890.

When the living room was finished, Nick and Nay moved into that larger space, and Michael moved on to the second floor, where he knocked down more walls, added insulation, hired a friend to put up new sheetrock, rewired the entire electrical system, and retiled the hall bathroom. Now Nick and Nay were able to expand their living space to include an actual bedroom. They had plans for a master bath, but that would have to wait.

The third floor was next, and Michael and Nick turned it into an apartment for their mother, with a bedroom, a living room, a bathroom, and a small kitchen. Increasingly skilled and confident, Michael made all the cabinets himself. While pounding a sledgehammer through ancient plaster, Nick found a sepia-toned picture of the first owner of the house, along with a photo of the building itself back when it was part of a working farm. The link to the past made him feel all the more attached to his home. He spent hours in the reference room of the local library, poring over books of historic Yonkers houses, learning more of the erratic history of his city at the same time.

He was able to do these things because he really wasn't doing much of anything else. The mortgage needed to be paid, so he was working part-time at John Jay College in Manhattan, teaching a course on the workings of local government. He also hosted a radio program on local WFAS-FM every Tuesday at 1:00 P.M., called *Nick Wasicsko, Attorney at Law*. He did these things despite his suspicions that he was the wrong man for each job. The only time he had spent in a courtroom recently was when he sat in the audience while the Supreme Court heard arguments in *Spallone vs. United States*. And his real expertise was not how government worked, but how it *didn't* work.

Of course, government wasn't working particularly smoothly for those who succeeded Nick in office, either. Hank Spallone was looking less like a street-smart operator and more like one of those hapless cartoon characters, the kind that frantically throws trash cans and old chairs into the path of the oncoming monster, but still the monster keeps coming. The new federal appeal Spallone had promised during his campaign was filed; in fact, several of them were, but they barely slowed the beast, as the courts refused to hear them. Then Spallone vowed that the council would not vote to transfer title to the five building sites to the developer. Judge Sand, who had learned a lot during August of 1988, didn't bother to wait for the council to vote, but simply ordered Neil DeLuca, still "interim" city manager, to release the land. The next thing Spallone grabbed for was the building permit for the housing. The builder had been erroneously issued a "multifamily" permit, which carried stricter construction requirements than the correct "single-family" one. Spallone announced that the proper permit would not be reissued until land surveys and other studies were done. Sand shrugged with annoyance, then ordered that DeLuca reissue the permit. DeLuca complied. No one bothered to consult the mayor.

Within a year of his landslide election, Spallone was openly feuding with DeLuca and with the other members of the council, including those who were theoretically his allies. He was "incompetent," they said, "an embarrassment," "unable to work with anyone." He was also under attack from those who elected him in the first place. The distrust that had sprouted shortly after Spallone's election was more deeply rooted now, and Save Yonkers had publicly renounced its former hero. Spallone ejected Save Yonkers members from City Council meetings. Save Yonkers took out a half-page ad in the *Herald Statesman* accusing Spallone of "selling out." After one particularly nasty council meeting, the mayor needed a police escort to leave City Hall, and things looked like 1988 all over again.

"We will not stop attacking him," warned Jack O'Toole, the founder and head of Save Yonkers. "Spallone, as far as we're concerned, will not be reelected mayor. The man is finished."

Not surprisingly, Spallone began feeling trapped and besieged. "I'm not the only representative in this town," he yelled back at Save Yonkers members. "Just maybe I need a little more support."

Things got so bad that Nick actually felt sorry for his longtime nemesis. The sympathy was coupled with bemusement at the fact

Show Me a Hero

that while Nick could not *get* the housing built when he was mayor, Spallone could not *keep* the housing from being built. The inability of any mayor to accomplish much of anything, Nick knew, was a function of the way the government of Yonkers worked. The real power — the power to hire, fire, and spend money — still lay mostly with the city manager, except that he was appointed by, and could therefore be dismissed by, the members of the City Council. The end result was that no one was ever really in charge in Yonkers.

Ironically, Nick's only major victory during his punishing term in office was to change the governing structure of Yonkers. The frustration and paralysis caused by the system had led him to appoint a Charter Revision Committee during his final year. The group proposed eliminating the city manager form of government and replacing it with a "strong mayor" system, a proposal that had been made by several other commissions over time, but that had never been approved by the voters. Under this incarnation of the plan, the job of city manager would be eliminated entirely, and the mayor would assume the role and the salary that had been the city manager's. In addition, a new position of City Council president would be created to replace the job that had been done by the mayor.

The proposal was on the ballot in November 1989, and while Nick Wasicsko was defeated, his strong mayor plan was approved. Spallone would be the last mayor to have a title but no clout. The strong mayor system would go into effect in January 1992, meaning the city's first strong mayor would be elected in November 1991.

Hank Spallone clearly wanted to win that all-important election. Just as clearly, his chance was slipping away. In September of 1990, near the height of his arguments with Save Yonkers, he announced that he would run for reelection in one year and two months. "I'm coming out, I'm running," he said to an audience of one hundred still-ardent supporters who had gathered at the Italian City Club. They were defectors from Save Yonkers, and they had formed their own smaller, but rabidly loyal group, called Concerned Citizens. Mary Dorman, still a fan of Spallone's, was a member.

"Those people who think I'm such an easy turkey, come on

then," he shouted, as the Concerned Citizens gave him a standing ovation. "I'll be campaigning tonight."

If the early declaration was supposed to scare off challengers, it did not. To the contrary, it made Spallone look vulnerable. Other Yonkers politicians began thinking that they, too, would like to be the first strong mayor. By the end of the year the list of rumored candidates was nearing a dozen, and the talk at the house on the hill started to be less about remodeling and more about politics. "I'm a mayor in exile," Nick would joke, increasingly often.

He did not make a definite decision. He was still too bruised and unsteady for that. But he took deep pride in the fact that the strong mayor plan was developed on his watch, and he liked flirting with the idea of running again. He also liked the fact that others were watching him closely while he did. During his time out of office, he had felt as if he were a ghost in his own city—a politician without a title is a man who does not exist. Politics, he was learning, had the power to break his heart, but it also gave it the power to beat.

As the renovations progressed on their house, Nick and Nay each found a favorite spot, one they would seek out when they needed solace or silence. For Nay, it was the mirrored exercise room adjacent to the master bedroom and next to what would one day be the master bath. For Nick, it was the living room in his mother's third-floor apartment. Every morning, after Nay left for work, he would take his cup of coffee and his three newspapers, then climb the stairs to the spot where he most liked to think and to read. What he found most appealing about the room was the view. He could sit and sip his coffee and stare across town at the unobstructed spires of City Hall.

Billie's News (II)

John Santos was released from prison on September 11, 1990, eight months less one day after he had been arrested. He came home to Schlobohm and tried, for a while, to keep

Show Me a Hero

his promise to Billie. Trying hard to change, he worked two jobs, at a nearby grocery and at a men's clothing store.

Billie had moved out of her mother's apartment by then, and into Building Four, near Meeka and Mambo. John's name was not on Billie's lease. Officially, he still lived with his mother in Building One, but that was just a technicality. He and Billie talked about making their living arrangement permanent, just as they talked about getting married, but they never got around to doing either of those things. Billie refused to marry John until they had the money to do it right. She thought a white dress might look foolish, but she wanted something new and nice to wear, and she definitely wanted wedding rings. She had seen some in Getty Square for $109, and was determined to have them.

So money was the reason there was no wedding, or, maybe, there was another reason, too. The adventure Billie thought she would find with John had not turned out to be so exciting after all. He went to jail, she waited for him, and now they had this infant who kept them up at night and inside during the day. If she wanted humdrum and routine, she would have stayed in high school or kept her job bathing mentally handicapped children.

Whatever her frustrations, Billie had to admit that John was good with their boy. He was fiercely attached to little Johnny, willingly getting up to feed him in the middle of the night. John and Billie fought a lot, "regular fights about the usual stuff," she described them, and often during those bouts Billie would storm out in anger and head for her mother's. "Go ahead and leave," John would scream after her. "The baby stays here with me."

Between the fights they got along, and John soon decided that he wanted another baby.

"Let's have a little girl," he cooed.

Billie had her doubts, but she agreed. John could be very persuasive. When she told him she was pregnant, he promised, not for the first time, to stop hanging out and using drugs. ("I was sniffing a lot of coke," he explained. "I did crack, too. Not freebase, we just used to mix it with other drugs, so I never considered myself really doing it.")

Billie tried to feel happy, but found herself crying, instead. Near the end of her third month, she told John, "One is enough. I didn't even want that one."

He was furious. "What are you? Crazy?" he screamed. "What's wrong with you—are you delirious?" His eyes became wild. It was the first time Billie was ever afraid of him.

"You're gonna have this baby," he said, "even if I'm going to have to lock you up in this closet and feed you under the door. You WILL have this baby."

John never did lock Billie up. He did something even more effective. When she walked into her living room the following day, she found him lying ill on the floor, holding an empty bottle of Tylenol pills.

At first, she didn't believe him.

"I need to go to the emergency room," he said, his speech slurred.

"You're faking," she said. "I'm going to my mother's house. See you later."

When she did see him next, it was in the emergency room. "I'm sorry, I didn't think you took the pills," she said, sobbing.

He wiped away her tears.

"I want you to have the baby," he said.

She promised she would.

Not until years later would he admit that he *had* been faking. He never actually swallowed any pills.

1991

Breaking Ground

The phrase "idle gossip" does not apply in Yonkers. Gossip is not idle here, it is purposeful and serious, aggressive and active. For years, the explosive force of gossip was enough to bring hundreds of people to City Hall. Someone would hear that something was happening, and they would phone people who would phone more people until a crowd had gathered, seemingly out of nowhere.

Now, in the spring of 1991, gossip sent many of those same people into their cars to cruise the Yonkers streets. Rumor was that ground would be broken at any moment on the new housing, though the developer, anticipating protests, was not saying exactly when. There would be no announcement, and there certainly would not be a groundbreaking ceremony. The only way to know —to be one of the first to know—was to go out and look.

Mary's surveillance method was one of regular detours. She never set out to check on the housing, but whenever she was in the car for another reason she was likely to swing past one or more of the sites for a quick peek. Day after day, the square of land at Central Park Avenue and Clark Street looked exactly the same, a barricaded asphalt parking lot, one that used to be part of the Yonkers Raceway, with small, sweet homes all around, much like Mary's own home a few blocks away. Night after night, nothing changed at the School 4 building, either. It was still a solid, seemingly unmovable building, standing between Trenchard Street and Gaffney Place, where it had been for 107 years.

Nick's visits to the sites were more purposeful. The housing was not a side trip for him, but a destination. Wandering the city had long been a hobby of his. Back when he was mayor, he kept a

155

police scanner at home, and if word came of something exciting, he would strap on his ankle holster and be out the door, usually taking Nay along for the ride. They went to fires at two o'clock in the morning and auto accidents in the middle of dinner. They saw broken water mains, flooded streets, and downed power lines. After visiting a scene, they would rarely head home, but would drive the streets for a while, exploring.

When Nick left office, the police scanner disappeared, but the drives became more frequent. He would take the wheel almost every night after dinner, and, because he had agreed not to smoke his stogies in the house, he called the trips "cigar runs." Driving and puffing, he unwound on the side streets that he had come to know by heart. Sometimes he went with Nay, or with a friend, but often he went on his own. As rumors of the groundbreaking grew louder, the cigar runs were no longer aimless. He set out each night wondering if it would be *the* night, if all the years of talk would finally take tangible form. For weeks, there was nothing. The empty lot on Helena Avenue was still an empty lot, surrounded by modest homes. The giant boulders remained undisturbed on Midland Avenue, across the street from a condominium complex and around the corner from Sarah Lawrence College. The ducks continued to swim in the pond across from Shoreview Drive.

Then, early on the morning of April 12, 1991, the construction began. Once it did, it seemed absurd to have thought that anyone would have had to search for it. With a grinding roar, the housing announced its presence on Clark Street, as workers ground the asphalt parking lot into dirt. One of the bulldozers had a set of menacing shark jaws painted on the front. Word spread with its usual speed, and soon a crowd of onlookers had gathered to watch.

"It's a dark day for Yonkers," Mayor Spallone said. "I really do think it's a tragedy."

Naturally, there were protests. Two hundred demonstrators gathered at the site on Saturday, as they would every Saturday for the next few months. They spent ninety minutes marching in front of the towering heaps of dirt that filled the battered parking lot. Passing cars blared their horns in support. The marchers carried effigies of Judge Sand, of NAACP lawyer Michael Sussman, and of the U.S. secretary of housing, Jack Kemp. They treated those stuffed symbols much as the bulldozers had treated the asphalt. One woman kicked the Sussman effigy in the leg. Another woman jabbed an American flag into it.

The marches did nothing to stop the construction. Deluxe Homes, Inc. was run by Don Meske, a man whose hobby was big game hunting, and whose wall trophies included a Canadian mountain lion and an African horned white rhino. The protests, he said, were an annoyance, not a threat. "When you're facing an elephant that weighs twelve thousand pounds," he said, "*then* you've got something to be scared of."

Mary did not join any of the weekly marches. They were organized by Save Yonkers, the group she had been part of until it turned its back on Hank Spallone, and she felt awkward and unwanted among her former friends. She did follow the marches from the sidelines, however, reading the newspaper and glimpsing the action up close as she *happened* to drive past. Viewed through her new lens, the protests looked different than they had from the inside. She did not see warriors committed to a cause. She saw foot soldiers flailing away at the air, at the nothingness, not realizing that this was a fight they could not win. Had things changed, she wondered, or had they always looked that way?

At one of the protests, a Save Yonkers member said: "We have to show we're still organized. Right now it doesn't look too good, but you got to fight down to the wire. It's never too late."

But you're not organized, Mary thought. And it is too late.

Kenneth Jenkins, NAACP branch president, responded to the protests, saying: "I understand fighting, but the patient's dead. Quite frankly, I think the people of Yonkers are tired of this."

Mary realized that she was tired of it. Bone tired.

Weeks passed, and concrete foundations emerged at four of the sites: twenty-four at Clark Street, twenty-eight at Midland Avenue, fourteen at Helena Avenue, forty-eight at Shoreview Drive. While they were being poured, workers quietly removed the asbestos from inside School 4. When that messy job was finished, a messier one began—a bulldozer with a battering ram plowed into the two-story brick building and began tearing it apart. The demolition started with the auditorium, and soon hundreds of seats were piled in the school parking lot. The dozer's steel jaws continued to devour the massive structure, ripping out the walls, the roof, the innards and depositing the tangle of brick, metal, and wood onto the weed-filled former playground. The growl of the machine was joined by the hiss of water hoses, which sprayed constantly to keep down the clouds of dust.

Again a crowd gathered, and again there was talk of continuing the fight. When Mary drove to the shell of the school, however, she didn't see anything left to fight for. All she saw was the final casualty of a lost cause, a sight so painful that her first reaction was to close her eyes. She quickly opened them again, then stared at the rubble for a long time, thinking of all the reasons she opposed what was happening and all that she had done in the futile attempt to stop it.

When she finally walked back to her car, it was with the mixture of regret and resignation. The fight was over—she was as certain of that fact as she was sorry about it. It had suffused her world, and now it was gone. Mary Dorman was no longer fighting the housing.

Doreen the Candidate

Doreen James heard the swish of the envelope as it was slipped under her door. That is how messages from Municipal Housing are delivered at Schlobohm, door-to-door, not by mailman. The only letters that seemed to come in the mail were "letters in demand," when back rent was owed, or warnings that the marshal was coming to carry out an eviction order. Doreen assumed the process was designed to save the cost of several hundred stamps every time Municipal Housing had something to say. But there was an eerie quality to the system. In her two years at Schlobohm, she had never actually seen whoever it was that distributed the mail.

Show Me a Hero

This piece of paper was sent to inform all interested tenants that candidates were being sought for the tenant council. Because she had spent so many mornings with Sadie Young Jefferson, Doreen knew about the council. More specifically, she knew that Sadie was frustrated with it.

The group had been founded in 1971, during a point in the history of public-housing policy when the idea of self-governance was very much in vogue. The influence of that approach has waxed and waned in the years since. Proponents, like Sadie, see it as democracy in its purest form. Critics say it is foolish to take people who have made a mess of their lives and allow them to manage other people's lives too.

In Yonkers in 1991, the tenant council consisted of three representatives from each housing site who met once a month at the housing office on Central Avenue. Sadie had told Doreen that, on paper, the council had broad power, with the authority to allocate certain funds and request and approve certain categories of policy changes. But in practice, Sadie explained, the council worked against the needs of the young, single, African-American and Hispanic women who were the overwhelming majority of public-housing residents.

The problem, Doreen learned, was that there were more public-housing sites for senior citizens (seven) than there were public housing sites for families (five). The size of the site did not affect the number of delegates to the council, so the senior citizens, most of whom were white, had a de facto majority of 21 to 15. Add to that the fact that the senior citizens, with more extra time, perhaps, or more interest, were more vocal and involved, while the family housing delegates tended to be less committed or insistent.

READY could not change the number of delegates, but it could change the clout of those delegates by selecting and training candidates to the council. Which is why Doreen carefully read, then reread, the letter. For months, Sadie had been telling her that she was "ready to fly," to become a leader in her chosen home. Doreen inhaled the praise like a new kind of drug, but away from Sadie she had her doubts.

That night, Sheila came to visit Doreen, armed to persuade.

"You give me all that talk about being independent and being in charge," she said, holding the self-nomination form out toward her sister. "Here. Be in charge."

Doreen waited several days before signing her name. Even after she dropped the paper in the designated box at the Municipal Housing office, she was not certain that this was an election she wanted to win.

Reelection Redux

Every major turn in Nick Wasicsko's adult life had been linked in time with politics. He lost his father to leukemia shortly before he was first elected to the City Council. He was sworn in as a lawyer during his first campaign for mayor. He met Nay Noe because he ran for mayor, and he fell in love with her during the months of political siege. He bought his first house as he fought to remain the mayor, and he proposed to Nay in that house shortly after his losing to Hank Spallone. Even his proposal carried political overtones. "You're the only one who's really stood by me," he said.

In keeping with that life pattern, politics was everywhere in the spring of 1991 as the preparations for his wedding melded with preparations for his possible run for City Hall. He was certain that he wanted to marry Nay. He was less certain about whether he wanted to enter the race for mayor. To do so would mean a tough primary against Terrence M. Zaleski, a Democratic state assemblyman with much the same constituency as Nick, but none of the historical baggage. If he lost the primary to Zaleski, or to the other Democratic candidate, restaurateur James J. Mannion, would that seal his political fate? Would two losses complete the agonizing transformation from twenty-eight-year-old prodigy to thirty-two-year-old has-been?

The doubts and second-guessing were new to Nick, confining

him like an ill-fitting suit that chafed and bound. In each of his three other races, even the last, disastrous one against Hank Spallone, he was positive that running was what he should do, what he wanted to do. Polls, gossip, conventional wisdom, none of those had stopped him before. Now they had him paralyzed.

Some days he talked of the strong mayor job as rightfully his, a place in local history for which he had already paid with anguish and sweat. Other days he fumed that the timing was all wrong, that the wounds were too fresh and his city was not yet in a forgiving mood. He wrestled with these pros and cons while also wrestling with the wording on the formal wedding invitations, the location of the ceremony and reception, the style of the two pristine gold bands. Finally, fitfully, all of the talking turned itself into a plan. He had learned that he was one of four finalists for the 1991 John F. Kennedy Profile in Courage Award. A prestigious honor, one accompanied by a $25,000 check, it is given every year to a public official "noted for taking a principled stand on an issue in the face of political and public opposition." Although that was not what many in Yonkers seemed to think he had done, it was what Nick himself thought he had done, and he seized upon the nomination as some sort of sign. If he won, he decided, he would run for mayor, and he would make his announcement on the heels of receiving the award. A year earlier, Jackie Kennedy Onassis herself presented the coveted statuette to the winner. What more could Yonkers want from him than that?

Nay wanted him to run for mayor, and she supported the Profile in Courage game plan. Nick began spreading the word that he would enter the race, and started to search around for a campaign team. One of the first people he called was Jim Surdoval, who had launched his political consulting career as an adviser to Nick, and who was now an entrenched Yonkers "player." Nick assumed Jim would welcome his news.

"I'm sorry," Jim said. "I'm committed to Terry Zaleski."

Not only was he supporting Zaleski, he told Nick, but he and a group of other Democrats had actively recruited Terry Zaleski and encouraged him to run.

"He's the highest-ranking Democrat in Yonkers," Jim explained. "He has an east side district, so he can carry the east side. He's pro-compliance on housing, but he's not identified with it, like you are; he doesn't have that negative."

"He's not identified with it," Nick snapped, "because he hid up in Albany in '88. He stayed as far away from the housing as he could."

"Right," agreed Jim. "So now he doesn't have that negative. He's a clean slate. It's the first strong mayor. We need the Democrat with the best shot."

Nick, dizzy with surprise, tried to focus, to find some way to bring his former adviser back around to his side.

"It doesn't have to be a negative," he said. "I took a courageous stand, and I was a hero. I was the only one in the goddamn city who did the right thing."

Jim sighed before he answered. "'Courage' isn't the kind of word you use to describe yourself, Nick, even if we both know it's true. That only works if other people are saying it.

"Don't try to make a comeback as mayor," Jim continued, giving the advice he knew would most help Zaleski. "They're not ready for you as mayor. Run for council, instead. We'll support you in that."

Soon after his talk with Jim Surdoval, Nick learned that the Profile in Courage Award, the linchpin in his plan, would be presented to someone else. His mind, his emotions, his life were all in chaos. The two subjects, the wedding and the mayoral race, became ever more enmeshed at 175 Yonkers Avenue—hors d'oeuvres and nominating petitions, table settings and campaign slogans, the beginning of their life together and the crossroads in Nick's political life. Nick and Nay squabbled and talked past each other, two people who were in love but also in turmoil. Nay admitted to Nick her relief that he did not win the award, because it would be presented during their honeymoon. What Nick heard was that she had not wanted him to win.

In the end, Nick decided to run for mayor anyway, more out of confusion than resolve. He scheduled his announcement for May 8 because it was National Law Day and he had, above all, complied with the law.

Show Me a Hero

As that day approached, however, he started receiving telephone calls from people he assumed would support him. "I thought you should know," they said, "I'm behind Terry Zaleski." They explained, as Jim Surdoval had, that Zaleski had a better chance because he was a "clean slate." They even used many of the same phrases that Surdoval had used. The only thing they didn't say was something Nick quickly figured out—that Surdoval had asked all of them to call.

At the last moment, Nick abruptly changed his announcement to May 13, his thirty-third birthday, giving him another weekend to think. He asked Jim to set up a "face-to-face" with Terry Zaleski, and he spent much of that weekend at Zaleski's house, listening as Zaleski tried to talk him out of the race. Nay came, too, and while Nick listened to Terry in the living room, Nay heard most of the same things from Terry's wife, Lynn, out in the kitchen.

"You don't want this now," the Zaleskis said. "You're getting married, you don't need this." There was much talk of a divided primary that would give Mannion the nomination and Spallone the election. There was mention of Nick being appointed deputy mayor once Zaleski was elected.

Nick had asked his fiancée to come along because he had come to rely on her sense of people. Over the years he had realized that what he first saw as shyness was really insight. Nay would stand quietly to one side at a political event, seemingly overwhelmed, but later, when they would dish the dirt after the party, she would have noticed things that had gone right past Nick. He also asked her to come with him to the Zaleskis' because he feared Terry would have some of his political advisers there, Jim Surdoval in particular, and Nick wanted to bring a team along, too. But the harsh reality was, he didn't have a team. Nay was the only person who was completely on his side.

When they left the marathon meeting, Nay was full of advice. "He's a weasel," she said, of Zaleski. She did not buy Terry's arguments or believe his promises. "Where was he while you were being crucified over the housing? He was up in Albany, and he didn't even pick up the phone once to tell you to hang in there."

Having asked Nay's advice on the eve of their wedding, he

rejected it. He held his press conference as scheduled on May 13, but it was a very different event than the one he had originally planned. He and Terry Zaleski stood side by side in the driveway of Nick's house as Nick announced that he would not run for mayor, but would give his support to Zaleski, instead.

It was a political and personal sacrifice, Nick said, made for the good of the party.

"This was not an easy decision for me," he said. "I was torn between what I felt I was entitled to do and what was helpful. I've been agonizing for months that this split could weaken the general effort. The thing that matters is getting Spallone and the Republicans out of government."

The knot of reporters in the driveway didn't really believe those were his reasons, and neither did Nay. She spent the next few days arranging their rehearsal dinner and arguing politics with him. "He'll never make you deputy," she said. "If he really thought you weren't a threat, why did he work so hard to get you out? If you're afraid of another race in this town, then admit it. Don't pretend you're doing this for the party."

On May 16, Nick made another announcement. He would run for the City Council seat from the Second District, the one that had been held by Peter Chema, who would be giving it up to face Hank Spallone and Angelo Martinelli in the Republican primary.

"I want to see Terry elected," he said, "but I also want to see him effective, and nobody knows better than I that an obstructionist City Council can detract from a mayor's effectiveness."

Two days later, at noon, Nick Wasicsko married Nay Noe at the church where his own parents had wed. Nick had promised his bride that this would not be a political event, but that was not the way his life worked, and it was not a promise he could keep. An article in the *Herald Statesman* mentioned that the "wedding ceremony is open to the public at the church, 239 Nepperhan Ave." A Cablevision crew came to cover the event, a fact that made Nay more nervous than the idea of actually getting married. Neither Terry Zaleski nor Hank Spallone was invited, but Nay noticed them seated in the pews as she walked down the aisle. The recep-

Show Me a Hero

tion, at a country club in the nearby village of New Rochelle, included a sit-down dinner for 150.

Three days after that party, the Wasicskos left for a two-week honeymoon in Spain and Morocco, where they discussed politics much of the time. While they were gone, the John F. Kennedy Library Foundation in Boston announced that Nicholas C. Wasicsko was one of three runners-up out of one thousand nominees for the Profile in Courage Award. The winner was Charles Longstreet Weltner, a former Georgia congressman who was recognized for refusing to run for reelection in 1966 on the same ticket as an advocate of racial segregation.

In a statement accompanying the announcement, the foundation said of Nick:

"Although he came to the office of mayor with only two years' experience as an elected official, Wasicsko distinguished himself as a man of conscience under fire. He summoned the courage to uphold the rule of law and demonstrated extraordinary leadership for the people of his divided city."

Someone else had finally said it about him.

The Townhouses Appear

In July, the first of the townhouses arrived in Yonkers. It was driven to Clark Street on the back of a flatbed truck, and it had the eerie disembodied look that all prefabricated buildings have when they are still in transit.

Oscar Newman had never considered using anything but prefab units for what were, in so many ways, *his* townhouses. Not only were they less expensive, but, equally important given their history in Yonkers, their creation was less public. Only the brick veneer would be laid at the site, meaning there would be less cause for protest and fewer targets for vandalism. Nearly everything would be done three hours away, in the working-class town of

Berwick, Pennsylvania. Once coal-mining country, the region had adapted to its own inevitable realities by becoming the hub of modular home construction in the northeast.

The two huge dusty factory buildings that housed Deluxe Homes, Inc. were once part of a railroad car manufacturing plant that had closed its doors thirty years earlier. The Yonkers townhouses began in those buildings, as steel coils were transformed, amid a grinding shower of sparks, into the wall studs and trusses that would support the buildings. These beams were then sent next door and placed on a 1,200-foot assembly line, the length of four football fields.

There, welders molded the studs and trusses, creating wall, floor, ceiling, and roof frames. The frames were placed in the carts that ran along the vestigial railroad tracks, and the carts continued on their way, from one work station to the next. Plumbing, gas, electric, and drainage lines were added. Window frames were installed. Plywood floors and plasterboard walls and ceilings were glued and bolted on. A complete bathroom, made in another part of the building, was loaded in.

Eventually the frames, each one a separate room, were attached to form a larger, single-story box. A roof was attached. Insulation was installed, along with windows, doors, lighting, bathroom fixtures, kitchen cabinets and counters, doorknobs, and floor tiles. Near the end of the line, workers on stilts taped and spackled seams in the ceilings and walls. Finally, each half of the two-piece duplex was wrapped in plastic and hoisted onto a trailer for the trip to Yonkers. Every townhouse arrived as a done deal, a fait accompli. Not only were the units made out of sight, they were installed quickly. The one that arrived at Clark Street on July 9 was bolted onto its foundation that same day. After that, the completion rate was two or three a day. Within a week, the outline of a nascent neighborhood was clearly drawn on Clark Street. Although Oscar Newman's hard-won brick veneer, cream-colored paint, and higher-quality landscaping would not be added until later, the peaked roofs and bay windows were already visible, and the neighbors grudgingly agreed that the housing looked "pretty good."

There were a few attempts to rekindle the old fight. Someone—

Show Me a Hero

mischievous kids, the FBI decided—painted "No Nigger" and "KKK" on one of the newly installed buildings, and broke the windows of two others. Around the same time, the City Council tried its own form of vandalism, briefly threatening to withhold a sewer permit for the Clark Street site. HUD presented its own last-minute roadblocks, skirmishing with Oscar Newman about everything from the gauge of the tubing on the backyard fences to the location of the outdoor trash cans.

He lost the fight over the fences. He had envisioned a wrought-iron look to separate the individual yards, but HUD would not pay for even the faux version of wrought iron, so he was forced to settle for galvanized iron chain-link instead. He had more success with the trash cans. The agency wanted communal trash cans—a big Dumpster shared by several families. It was the least expensive type of container, and the kind that had always been used at housing projects. Newman wanted each townhouse to have its own in-ground trash can, which fit in a metal sheath set next to the walk leading up to each home. It would make tenants take responsibility for their garbage, he argued, if they could not pile it on an anonymous heap somewhere. In the end, Peter Smith took Newman's side and cleared the way for the individual containers, but he did so with a look that said, "It's on your head if this doesn't work."

The nearer the housing came to completion, the more often Newman heard that message: these townhouses were his idea; their failure would be his, as well. There is nothing more nerve-wracking than being inches from a lifelong goal. Everything Newman had learned over thirty years was built into the housing. So it was with a mix of pride and jitters that Newman took Judge Sand to visit the sites one dreary, chilly afternoon.

Sand said some complimentary things, but mostly he was quiet. Newman could not decide if the judge was displeased, or simply overwhelmed by the physical embodiment of more than a decade of work. But when they walked into the backyards and Sand stared disapprovingly at the chain-link fencing, Newman did not have to wonder what the Judge was thinking.

"They look like pigsties," Sand said. "Is it really necessary to have the fencing?"

Newman took a deep breath and explained how fencing, even the ugliest fencing, was better than none at all. "The rear yards will take on a very different character once they're occupied," he said. And without the fencing, he continued, there would be "no sense of ownership, no feeling of responsibility." The area would become one huge yard, he said, that everyone would neglect and, eventually, no one would use.

Sand shook his head in answer.

"I hope you know what you're doing" was all he said.

The Election of 1991

Henry Spallone never made it onto the strong mayor ballot. His primary campaign was a study in confusion, with a $38,000 debt that he temporarily repaid with a personal loan. Peter Chema won the Republican primary, leading Angelo Martinelli by one hundred votes. Spallone was a distant third. In a bizarre turn, Judge Leonard Sand, a lifelong Democrat, received one write-in vote.

Rejected by the Republicans, Spallone tried to run as an independent, but Chema challenged his designating petitions. Fifteen hundred signatures were necessary to qualify for the independent line. A total of 2,150 people had signed Spallone's petitions, but Chema proved that 675 of those were invalid under the state's complex and arcane election law, leaving Spallone twenty-five signatures short of a second chance. Spallone appealed the decision of the Board of Elections, and proved to the State Supreme Court that some of the disallowed signatures were actually valid, but there were not enough of those to qualify.

Mary Dorman was in the courtroom when Spallone, the fight gone out of him, accepted the decision. It was over, he said, he would not appeal. She was furious that he was walking away from a fight—he who had taught her how to fight in the first place. And she was embarrassed for him. Here was a man whose career was based on his defiance of a court order. Now that same career was ended by compliance with a court order.

Outside the courthouse, Spallone vowed that this was the end of his *campaign*, not the end of his *career*. He would be back, he said. But hadn't he also promised that he would never permit low-income housing in Mary's neighborhood? When ground was broken on the townhouses, she had stopped believing in the fight, not the man. With this withdrawal from the race, she could no longer believe in the man, either. Politics was now a habit for her, and there would be unfillable hours if it was gone, so she spent the remaining month of the campaign halfheartedly working for Angelo Martinelli, who had not been disqualified from the independent ballot. She did not really believe in Martinelli, but for the moment that didn't matter. Working for him distracted her from the fact that she would now need something new to believe in.

Terry Zaleski received only 36 percent of the vote on Election Day, but that was enough to become the first strong mayor of Yonkers. As usual, the election results showed a divided city, with five of six precincts on the west side voting for Zaleski, the candidate with the most moderate position on desegregation, and five of six precincts on the east side voting for Chema, the strongest desegregation opponent in the race. Also as usual, more voters went to the polls on the east side than on the west side. The only reason Zaleski won was because Martinelli took a crucial east side district from Peter Chema.

Despite the slim margin, despite the lasting divisions, Zaleski declared victory with the same confidence that every politician feels on election night. "This has truly been a campaign for the future of the city of Yonkers," he declared just after 11:00 P.M.

While Zaleski was celebrating, Nick Wasicsko was home, stunned at the direction his own Second District race was taking. Because he had won the Democratic primary by a 3-to-1 margin, and because this was a heavily Democratic district, Nick had expected a fairly easy win in the general election. Instead, the early results showed him losing to his opponent, Edward Magilton, a political first-timer whose day job was as an operations specialist in the city Department of Public Works. At 10:30 P.M., Magilton led

Wasicsko by 150 votes. Over the next hour or so, the race began to tighten, and with 97 percent of the votes counted, Magilton's lead was down to 40 votes. At midnight, Nick obtained a court order to impound the voting machines for a recount. He went to bed at 2:30 in the morning, wondering whether he should have conceded the race when there was no one awake to hear him.

Morning brought the news that more of the votes had been counted, and in one precinct he led 137 to 60, enough to move him from 40 votes behind to 30 votes ahead. By the time he dressed and left the house, all the remaining precincts had been counted, and he was trailing again—by two votes.

It was several days before the recount, and he spent that time becoming increasingly certain that his political career was over. "I blew it," he said. "What am I going to do now?"

He was despondent. He spent hours sitting by the phone. There were some calls telling him to "hang in there" or "it will all work out," but there were not as many as he thought there should be and, more important, not one was from Terry Zaleski. "I sacrificed it all for that guy," he said. "He can't pick up the phone?" Eventually, Zaleski did call. What Nick never knew was that Nay, frightened by her husband's growing depression, had contacted Jim Surdoval, demanding that Zaleski talk to Nick.

The recount of all the voting machines gave Nick a sixteen-vote lead. Another few days passed while the absentee ballots were tallied. Nick gained another ten votes. The final count was 3,006 for Wasicsko and 2,980 for Magilton. Nick was a City Council member again, by a margin of twenty-six votes.

Show Me a Hero

Part Two

The Rebuilding

1 9 9 2

The Lottery

By twos and threes, with fingers crossed and lucky charms palmed, hundreds of people stepped from the darkness of School Street and into the bright, warm gym. As they entered the crowded room, they squinted in the fluorescent lights, then scanned the endless rows of folding chairs in the slim chance of finding a seat.

They had not expected that there would be a crowd. The thunderstorm alone should have been enough to keep everyone at home, especially at a place like School Street. No one goes out at night on School Street, just as no one goes out at night in any of the other housing projects in Yonkers—not if they can help it.

But what was being offered in the gym on this night was a powerful draw, so the room was filled, and the crowd was still coming. Six police officers were positioned along one wall, appearing to expect trouble. While the children ran through the aisles, staging sword fights with closed umbrellas, their parents were distracted by the battered metal and Plexiglas drum on the stage at the front of the gym. It was, literally, a bingo drum. Peter Smith, the head of the Municipal Housing Authority, had borrowed it from the Polish Community Center, two long blocks away.

Standing on the stage, feeding 220 names into the bingo drum, Smith was unnerved by all the eyes upon him and sobered by how fitting this contraption was to his task. It was a toy, and he was using it to play with people's lives. He knew he could not use a computer. The people in this room, justifiably suspicious of anything they could not see, would have no faith in a computer lottery. But still, the symbolism of the bingo drum weighed heavy on him. Wasn't this in keeping with the capricious nature of the entire housing case, which had been brought because some lawyers somewhere had chosen to concentrate on Yonkers? Didn't it reflect the random, inadequate nature of the solution: five thousand residents of public housing in the city, and, after all the years of turmoil, a first round of only seventy-one townhouses? And, certainly, there could be no more perfect way to symbolize the two-steps-behind-the-times feel of Yonkers. Any other city, Peter thought, would have figured out a way to avoid such a circus. Other cities would never have gotten themselves into this mess in the first place.

To Norma O'Neal, it did not feel like a circus. From where she sat, up in the front row, this was a celebration. Tucked in her handbag, which she held tightly on her lap, were two letters from Municipal Housing. She could not read the letters, but she knew what they said because her friend Pat Williams had read them aloud to her so many times. By now Norma knew the words by heart, and she expected them to change her life.

The first of the envelopes had been slipped under her door one January morning, looking just like every form letter from Municipal Housing, and Pat had opened it without any particular sense of anticipation. But from the first word, it did not sound to Norma like any other letter she had ever received. It did not begin "Dear tenant," like most of the others, or "Dear Miss O'Neal," like the few more worrisome ones. Instead it began:

> *Bulletin.*
> *To: All Residents of Public Housing in the City of Yonkers*
>   *With the approval of the Federal Court, tenant selection for the new units of public housing constructed in East Yonkers will be open to current residents of public housing in the City of Yonkers.*
>   *142 Units of public housing will be completed some time near the end of this year. Under the procedure approved by Judge Sand, tenants will be selected on the basis of an open lottery.*

Show Me a Hero

> *The Authority is requesting that tenants who are interested in moving to the housing indicate their interest by filling out the form below. If you need assistance, the rent office will help you complete the form.*
>
> *Residents selected for the new units must have a good rent-paying record with the Authority, their apartments must be kept in a clean, sanitary condition, and they must have no outstanding lease violations pending with the Authority.*

The form was due in two weeks. Norma spent those weeks angling for a townhouse. The letter said the rent office would help her fill out the form, but the kind of help she needed was more direct and heavyhanded than that. The letter talked about a lottery, and she didn't want to put her trust in a lottery. She had lived with the burden of blindness for three years now. She had lost her job to it and also lost her freedom to it. It was time it did her some good.

She had heard that Peter Smith was a "nice man" who "sometimes could help" and she tried to reach him by telephone. When that didn't work, she learned that he would be at an appointment in Schlobohm one afternoon, and she waited near the door for him.

"Mr. Smith," she called out, when she saw the hazy shape of a balding white man in a suit and tie. He stopped. She held up the envelope like a ticket of admission. "I would like to speak to you."

Smith came closer, and Norma could almost see his face. "I'm legally blind," she said. "I can't see. I'm scared to go in and out of the apartment. Can you help me with this?" She unfolded the letter and handed it to him.

Smith glanced at the piece of paper, then looked much more closely at Norma.

"There are handicapped units at each site," he said, "for those who qualify. Do you require home assistance?"

"It's hard to get home care here," she said, then, fearing that would somehow disqualify her, she added, "I go every week to Guild for the Blind."

"When did you start going there?"

"Two years ago next March."

"Have one of the ladies there write me a letter," Smith said. "I'll see what I can do."

What he did was sign the second letter, which had arrived—by proper mail this time—several days before this lottery.

"You have been selected for an opportunity to move into the new housing and have been assigned a handicapped apartment," it said. "Congratulations to you and your family. Very Truly Yours, Peter Smith."

With a mixture of guilt and defiance, Doreen James found an aisle seat near the middle of the room. She peeled off her raincoat, helped Jaron out of his, shook the water off of each, and settled her little boy on her ample lap. She still wasn't certain she should be here.

By the time she'd received the application for the townhouse lottery, Doreen had been a member of the tenant council for several months. She showed the letter to Sheila, who argued that she should throw it away.

"You need to stay here and finish what you started," said Sheila, who had persuaded Doreen to run for the council in the first place. "Nothing will ever happen if the best people leave."

Doreen shrugged her slow sigh of a shrug. She didn't believe she had "started" much of anything. She took minimal pride in her election, because she was the only candidate for her position and few Schlobohm tenants even voted. Dutifully, she held weekly meetings for the residents, but it was a rare evening when more than three people came. Those who did come spent the hour complaining. Guided by Sadie, Doreen had grand plans: tenant security patrols, cooperative maintenance schedules, a resident-run day-care center. But the tenants, she told Sheila, "didn't want to talk about nothing but how their sink needs to be done, or their closet door hasn't been fixed and how they called and called and nothing happened." So Doreen spent the meetings making lists of names, apartment numbers, and needed repairs, and forwarding them to Peter Smith at the Municipal Housing office.

Soon after her election, she was appointed to the council's Steering Committee for Comprehensive Grants, which has the power to decide how large amounts of grant money from HUD could best be spent. This, too, sounded more promising than Doreen found it to be. She had countless ideas for how money could be used at Schlobohm: "We need security. We need fences for children in the playground. We need roof doors, front doors, back doors." She typed these suggestions up, too, and sent them off to Central Avenue. Usually, nothing happened. A few of her requests were granted, the new doors for instance, and she found that even more disheartening than the silence, because it took no more than a few weeks before all those new doors were scarred or broken in some way. Each small action she might take seemed so insignificant against the overwhelming whole that she wondered why she even bothered.

"Nothing makes you feel good?" Sheila asked.

Doreen rubbed her tired temples and thought before she spoke. "Yes," she said, "there was one time, when a woman who I didn't know came over to me and said thank you for her new door."

Realizing she was on the losing end of the argument, Sheila changed her approach. The townhouses, she worried aloud, were a setup, a seductive trap, a charade that was intended to fail.

"They built them fast, so they'll fall apart fast," Sheila said. "Then they can point and say, 'Told you so. Those black folks can't take care of their things.' You know what Sadie calls them? She calls them 'cardboard houses.' They have to do this, so they're doing it, but that don't mean they have to want to make it work."

Grass may not grow in the cramped destitution of Schlobohm, but rumor and conspiracy theory find fertile ground, and this was an accusation that Doreen had heard before. She had long since learned to ignore such talk, also with a shrug—one that didn't quite say "nonsense," but rather "I'll wait and see."

She shrugged her shrug at Sheila, who stopped and altered course yet again. Leaning forward in her chair, her hands folded on the table in front of her, her tone became urgent.

"You'll get yourself killed over there," she said.

Sheila ripped up the application that night, then crumpled the pieces into a ball and threw them away. The next morning, Doreen walked into her building at Schlobohm and learned that some kid—they never did catch him—set a paint can on fire in the elevator and blew the inside of the car apart. There was a huge hole in the floor, the buttons were melted, and the entire elevator (there was only one in each building) had to be rebuilt.

Doreen steered Jaron toward the acrid stairwell. The three-year-old boy was too heavy to carry up the seven flights, but too young to keep his hands off the urine-coated banister. As Doreen struggled toward the top floor, wheezing from exertion and anger, the muck on the stairs became a flood. The new door to the roof, she realized, was broken, and water from outside was gushing down the steps like a river. Somewhere on that staircase she decided she could no longer be a Schlobohm representative because she could no longer bear to live in Schlobohm. She walked back down to the main office, asked for another application, and filled it out.

In the weeks since then, she and Sheila had carefully avoided all talk of the new housing. Instead, Doreen replayed and revised their last conversation continually in her head, repeating Sheila's words, then silently arguing back with her own. Maybe she did have an obligation to the "cause," she thought, but couldn't she become a representative on the other side of town? And maybe the townhouses *were* destined to fail, she agreed, but for the moment they were better than Schlobohm.

The only part of the quarrel that she did not revisit during these silent arguments was Sheila's warning: "You'll get yourself killed over there." Then, as now, she had no rebuttal. Sitting here at the lottery, watching the bingo drum, she still worried that her sister might be right.

By the time Alma Febles and her family arrived, the only vacant seats were in the back, and there were not enough of them for Alma, her sister Dulce, Alma's three children, and Dulce's two. Dulce's grown daughters took Frankie and Virgilio to stand near the rear wall, and Leyda sat between her mother and her aunt.

Alma had been surprised that her sister had applied to be here tonight. This move was something parents do for their children,

Show Me a Hero

Alma thought, and Dulce's daughters were no longer children. They had made it into their teens, out of school, into jobs, out of danger. They did all that without getting injured, or pregnant, or worse. For Virgilio, Leyda, and Frankie, there were years of land mines ahead. Not only that, Alma had learned English during her years at Schlobohm while Dulce had not. Who would her sister talk to on the east side?

Alma never asked Dulce why she had entered the lottery. She feared that if she voiced the question, her sister would hear her anger. In the weeks since they sent in their applications, the two women talked only about how they would decorate their apartments, the parties they would have there, the flowers they would plant in the backyards. They never talked about what would happen if only one was given the chance to move.

Instead they sat, with noise all around but silence between them. Leyda rubbed the statue of the Blessed Virgin that she had tucked in her pocket. With equal fervor, Alma fingered the glossy pages of the housewares catalog she carried in her purse.

When the letter for the housing lottery arrived, Alma had recently started a new job, talking to Spanish-speaking clients over the phone at the personal injury law firm of Fitzgerald & Fitzgerald. The seven dollars an hour pleased her, but what she truly relished was the freedom. Now that the children were all older and in school, she could take a job that got her away from Schlobohm every day, and into another world. A world where people took walks at lunchtime, wore new clothes, owned cars, and decorated their windows with curtains and potted plants.

The lottery, coming on the heels of the new job, seemed like an omen to Alma. First, work had granted her a daily pass into the world beyond the projects; next, the mail had brought her this permanent plan of escape. Ever since the letter arrived she had been feeling oddly lucky. For the first time in years she began dreaming, and once begun, the dreams were too delicious to stop. She knew she shouldn't get the children's hopes up, and she tried to remind them often that there were so few townhouses and so many eligible people, but she was incapable of keeping her own expectations in check. She had forgotten how good hope felt.

One afternoon, she arrived home carrying a large, heavy box. "What's that?" Leyda asked, as Alma put the box down on the worn counter, then opened the silverware drawer and began to set the table.

"New pots," Alma answered. "Three of them, metal ones, heavy iron, very good quality, in three different sizes. I bought them from a woman at work who sells through a catalog. They cost one hundred and fifty dollars, but I can pay her thirteen dollars a week."

"We need new pots," Leyda said, banging the dented aluminum one on the stove with a ladle for emphasis.

"We need new everything," said Alma, rummaging through the drawer in search of spoons, which were always in mysteriously short supply in her kitchen. She suspected Frankie threw them away so he would not have to wash them. "But these aren't for now. I'm not opening them yet. They're for the new apartment."

From then on, the houseware catalogs were Alma's obsession. She could not keep herself away from the glossy, self-indulgent pages. Each photo showed life as Alma wanted it to be—contented people in cheerful settings using an array of gadgets and items designed to make life orderly and under control. Most of the items she sent for—including the pots—were more than she could really afford, but the townhouse that was fated to be hers would need to be fully stocked. Dreams do not come cheap.

So she ordered the pieces of her fantasy, and carefully stored the unopened boxes in a closet when they arrived.

"What's the point of a pot if you can't cook in it?" Leyda would ask.

"They're too good for this place, I can't explain it," Alma would say.

"Just like us?" Leyda asked. Alma didn't answer.

Billie Rowan arrived at the School Street gym at the last minute, so she stood near the doorway, leaning her shoulder against the wall, not bothering to search for a seat. She felt airy and untethered as she looked around at the crowd. Her mood was so light that the simple act of closing her umbrella made her smile. Because of the storm, her mother had agreed to keep the children for a few hours, and Billie was blissfully alone. It was an occasion so rare that it was worth celebrating, so Billie had taken the time to fix herself up, something else she had not done in months. Why put on the makeup and jewelry, she'd decided, when there's no one around to notice? But tonight, she even took off the ratty kerchief that had covered her cornrows lately. She was almost certain that no one could see the spots where stress had thinned her hair.

She was stressed because John was in prison again—to no one's surprise but her own. He had pulled a knife on a couple whom he may or may not have been trying to rob, and had been sentenced to eighteen months at the Cayuga Correctional Facility, which was a five-hour bus ride from Yonkers. He had been there when their daughter, Shanda May Santos, was born, and this time Billie did not rush her baby to a prison waiting room as she had done with Johnny. If John had cared so much about seeing his daughter, she thought, then he would have found a way to stay out of trouble.

She was angry at John, but she was not through with him. To the contrary, he filled nearly all her thoughts. When John comes home, she promised herself, I can go into the bathroom alone. When John comes home, I can take a shower with the door closed. So many sentences in her head seemed to start "When John comes home . . ." When John comes home, they would have a real life. They would be a family. The children would behave. The house would be clean. She would learn to cook. He would get a job. Nothing would be like it was before. Nothing would be like it was now.

She tried to keep the thoughts positive, but the pinpricks of reality kept intruding. In the three years that John and Billie had been together, the amount of time he had actually been home totaled less than six months. He had never spent her birthday with her. He barely knew his son, he did not know his daughter, and Billie wondered how much she and John knew each other. She did not have a single photograph of the man that was not taken in prison.

In one of John's most recent letters, he had redefined his aimlessness as fate. It was fate that sent him to prison, and fate would take care of him when he came out. Shortly after he'd sent that letter, Billie had filled out the application for the lottery. She was trusting those same fates to pick her name out of the bingo drum, and to hand her a new life, a new start. She believed this fantasy that he could do right as fiercely as she believed his years of assurances that he had never really done anything wrong.

When Peter Smith walked to the microphone, shortly before eight o'clock, the crowd became relatively silent. A baby began to cry, and his mother quickly slid a pacifier into his mouth. There were a few sneezes, some throat-clearing, and more than a handful of fidgety children, but overall it was quiet enough to hear a bingo drum spin.

Smith wasted little time introducing himself before he picked the first folded paper out of the drum. "Number one, Delphina Paige." Out in the audience, the owner of that name jumped up and did a little dance at her seat. Name after name was picked from the seemingly bottomless drum, and each was met by cheers or tears or a fist pumped in the air in a victory salute.

"Number nine, Doreen James." Doreen buried her face in her hands so Jaron would not see her cry.

"Number forty-three, Billie Rowan." Billie grinned at no one in particular for a few minutes, then gleefully ran home in the rain.

As the barrel spun, the noise level in the room rose, and Smith found himself shouting into the microphone. Alma barely heard him call her sister's name. "Number seventy-one, Dulce Manzueta." That meant Alma's nieces were going. Her grown nieces who already had jobs and apartments of their own, and didn't have to spend every afternoon locked away at home. Alma gave her sister what she hoped was a joyful smile, then reached for her own daughter's hand.

Just then, Smith stopped the drum from spinning. He held up his hands, asking for quiet. "The first seventy-one names have been chosen," he said. "There are only seventy-one apartments right now, and all those are now filled. We will keep picking names, but everyone else will be on the waiting list."

The crowd became more subdued. The applause that greeted each name was halfhearted and the air in the room felt damp and heavy. People who already had their answer began to head for the door. Alma wanted to follow them.

"Number one sixty-seven," Smith finally said. "Alma Febles."

Leyda jumped from her seat, the way she was poised to do all night. She flung her arms around her mother's neck and sobbed.

"They picked our name, they picked our name," she stammered through choking tears. Her mother simply stroked the little girl's back. She didn't have the heart to explain about the waiting list just then.

The Other Side of the Fence

Mary Dorman was sitting at the pock-marked wooden table in the conference room of the Grinton I. Will Library, taking notes on the legal pad in front of her and pretending that what she was hearing made sense. She would have killed for a cup of coffee, but although there was an automatic coffee-maker on the shelf near the door, it was always empty. There was a television and a VCR, too, but they were both unplugged. Mary suspected that Bob turned all these things off each evening so that there would be no distractions, nothing to do but listen to him talk. That would have been easier, she thought, if she'd had a clue as to what he was talking *about*. All she knew for certain was that it had little to do with the housing.

Bob was Robert Mayhawk, who had entered her life with a phone call several weeks earlier. It was a brief call, less than ten minutes, but sometimes that's all it takes to change everything.

"You don't know me," Bob Mayhawk had said, "but you were recommended by someone who thought you would be perfect for a project I am working on. About the housing." He'd seemed worried that she would hang up.

"I would appreciate it," he continued, "if you would just listen to what I have to say."

Mayhawk explained that he ran the Housing Education

Relocation Enterprise program, known as HERE, which had been hired by Municipal Housing to help move the new tenants into the townhouses. There would be an orientation, he said, classes that everyone would be required to take before they would be permitted to move. Volunteers (much later she would learn that there would be a modest stipend) were needed to help with that orientation. That was why he was calling. Would Mary be interested?

She was very interested. In the months since she watched the first townhouses arrive, Mary had often found herself thinking about the people who would occupy them. Talk at the Save Yonkers meetings had always been about the effect of the newcomers on the neighborhood, not about the effect of the neighborhood on the newcomers. What would it be like, she now wondered, to live where you are not wanted? There were rumors on the east side that armed guards would supervise the move, particularly after the pipe bomb, and that homeowners on all sides of the townhouses were buying weapons, just in case. How could anyone be expected to feel settled in their new home knowing that? The judge's plan was more than just an assault on her community, she decided, it was twice the evil. Cruel not only to the homeowners who already lived near the site, but also to the tenants chosen to move in.

She had shared those thoughts with a number of people and one of them had obviously shared them, in turn, with Bob Mayhawk. He did not ask her anything about herself for most of the phone call, and Mary assumed it was not because he didn't want to know, but because he already knew. In fact, he asked only one question, near the end of the conversation, and it was less about the past than about the future.

"How do you feel about the housing right now?" he said.

"I think it's wrong," Mary answered. "I don't believe in it. But it's here. And the people who are moving in to it had nothing to do with what went on and I feel bad for them. I don't think they should be blamed for any of this."

"So you would like to be involved in our project."

"Yes," she said. "I would."

He seemed relieved. Mary wondered how many other people he had called before someone took the job.

The first meeting, like all the others that followed in recent weeks, was held at the Grinton I. Will Library. Bob Mayhawk, slim and dapper, with close-cropped salt-and-pepper hair and the bearing of a former Marine, had turned out to be one of the strangest men that Mary had ever met. During his initial telephone call he had hinted at his concern for secrecy. On closer look, that concern was an obsession. Do not tell anyone about the work you're doing here, he instructed his team, and do not ask me any questions about that work. Mary had assumed that her first HERE meeting would be an information session, that she would find out what she would be doing in this new job and when she would be doing it. But she came home that first night knowing little more than when she left. Mayhawk said he would tell them what they needed to know only when they needed to know it.

At every meeting since then he had asked them to solve a series of mind games and puzzles, all taken from the book he had written and published himself. Called *Mayhawk's Law,* it had a muddy brown cover with its title in gold letters, and it was filled with odd stories. One was about a family whose patriarch was deciding which of his three children should inherit the family business. Each child submitted a brief memo outlining his qualifications. Which one, Mayhawk asked, was chosen? Another puzzle was about a cheetah, an ostrich, a gazelle, and a gnu. Giving them nonsensical information about each (the gazelle has sore ankles, the gnu did not use the eastern passageway), Mayhawk instructed the group to "determine which animal used which passageway and the order in which each animal finished the race."

Mary knew she could have walked away from Mayhawk, and from HERE, and from the cheetahs and the gnus, but something, maybe the mystery of it all, brought her back every night. She never did figure out his quirky guessing games, though she did come to see that the moral of most of them was "assume nothing." She took that lesson to heart, but not as Mayhawk had intended. Instead of wondering how the gazelle might have injured his ankles, she wondered what she did not know, and should not assume, about Bob Mayhawk.

The brief biography in the back of his book said he had been a "corporate investment specialist" on Wall Street and that he was the founder of "The Center for Personal Strategic Planning," which held seminars on "motivation, goal setting and goal achievement." He had also been a business professor at the State University of New York.

That he had a background in business made sense to Mary. He had the air of authority of a businessman, someone used to being in charge. His clothes were casual, but in a studied sort of way, as if he had tried hard to look as if he wasn't trying. His entire manner was formal and distant. Mary couldn't imagine that he had many close friends. Even his face was a mystery. Although his hair was graying, his skin was youthful. How old was he? Mary wondered. "Black people," she thought, "never look their age."

That, of course, was the biggest surprise. When Mayhawk called she had assumed he was white, and she had also assumed that the others in this program would be white—people from the neighborhood or people who worked for Municipal Housing. Who else to teach the new residents how to live on the white side of town? Instead, Mayhawk was black, as was his assistant, Verna Earl, and the rest of the team, which consisted of Verna's daughter, Dee, Dee's friend, Jeff Clark, and Bea Clark, who was not related to Jeff and who was a resident of Schlobohm.

There was one other white face in the room, and although it was familiar, Mary was not certain that it was entirely friendly. Lucille Lantz had been the founder of an anti-housing group called the People's Union. Like Mary, she described her fight against the housing as one of principle, not race. "It's about unfairness," she would say, in her deep, smoke-filled voice. "While I must struggle to pay my rent to live in east Yonkers, others are allowed to live in the same neighborhood with better apartments paying lower rent." To Lucille, the key word here was *rent*. The People's Union was a splinter group, formed out of the bickering between the home-owners of Save Yonkers and those, like Lucille, who were east side tenants. But it was not Lucille's long-ago allegiance to a rival team that made Mary uncomfortable. It was Lucille herself.

A small, coiled woman, wound tight as her auburn perm and burning hotter than her ever-present cigarette, Lucille was the

Show Me a Hero

type who was always protesting something. Before the housing, there was the school desegregation plan (she had been PTA president). Before that, a campaign for change in the rules about foster care (she and her husband, Paul, had been foster parents a dozen times over the years, and also had four children of their own).

Each fight made her more brassy, more savvy, more political. In time, she even reworked her name to help her cause. Lantz, she decided, was a pleasant enough Austrian name, but it carried no weight in Yonkers. "Lantz, how unusual," shop clerks would politely note whenever she paid by check. Her maiden name, Rizzetta, brought no such comment and required no explanation. "If I'm trying to get the attention of someone who's Italian, it's stupid to use Lantz," she decided, as she started signing her numerous letters to the editor "Lucille Rizzetta Lantz." "The people who run this city are named Vellela, Spano, Martinelli, Spallone," she said, "and I should use Lantz?"

About the only thing Mary and Lucille had in common was that they had both fought the housing and they had both come to realize that their fight had been lost. Yet even as they traveled to that same conclusion, the two starkly different women took strikingly different routes. While Mary's disillusionment had been gradual and quiet, Lucille's had been very sudden and very public.

The night before the City Council voted to comply with Judge Sand, the executive committee of the People's Union met at Lucille's apartment. The council would cave, they all agreed, and Lucille made what she thought was a practical suggestion. "It's time we woke up and smelled the coffee," she said. "We have to figure out a way to make the housing work."

In the convoluted world of a protest movement, those are fighting words, and everyone in the room began to shout. Until that night Lucille had believed that people say things in anger that they do not really mean. By the time the fracas in her dining room had ended, however, she had come to believe that what people say in anger is what they really do mean, but usually have the self-control to keep to themselves.

"People are about to lose their jobs," Lucille argued. "Yonkers is about to cross a line that should not be crossed."

"That's a sacrifice that has to be made," they answered.

"Sure," Lucille said, "it's not your sacrifice. You can say that sitting in that chair because it's not your paycheck. In some families, both the mom and dad work for the city and they'll be losing everything. I can't ask someone to lose their salary for me."

"Sacrifices have to be made," they insisted.

"It will destroy the city," Lucille said.

"Having them live over here will destroy the city."

"Not as surely as being fined a million dollars a day."

"Maybe you want them living in your backyard, but I don't want them living in mine."

Lucille worried that her glass-topped dining table would shatter with all the pounding. By the end of the night she had submitted her resignation, and she never heard from most of the executive board again. The local paper ran a short article announcing her departure, and Lucille had spent the day waiting for her phone to ring off the hook with calls begging "Come back, we need you," but no one called.

Until Bob Mayhawk. She had been suspicious during their first telephone conversation, especially when Mayhawk refused to tell her who had recommended her for this job. "Friends," he had said, but Lucille did not think she still had any friends. She had been chosen, she concluded, as a declaration of change, evidence that not only had the opposition been defeated, it had been converted. Those videotapes of POWs denouncing their countries at gunpoint came to mind.

If that was Mayhawk's game, Lucille decided she would play it. If she could not beat the housing from the outside, she might as well keep her eye on things from the inside. She had not been to any kind of public meeting in Yonkers since the night she resigned from the People's Union. It felt good to have a new cause. But, she reminded herself, this wasn't her fight anymore. She would never allow herself to get as involved in anything as she had in 1988. This time she was a visitor, an onlooker.

That distance gave her a freedom that Mary sensed, but did not understand. Long after Mary had stopped asking questions of

Mayhawk, Lucille was still at it. He didn't answer Lucille either, but, unlike Mary, she didn't seem to mind. Lucille was equally unfazed by the mysteries of *Mayhawk's Law*. The ostrich won the race, she announced. The gazelle came in second, the cheetah was third, and the gnu was fourth. The gazelle's sore ankles were irrelevant to the outcome, a stray fact, a red herring. "Don't be distracted by things that aren't important," Lucille said, easily summarizing the mysterious point of the exercise. Mayhawk nodded.

Mary's first conversations with Lucille Lantz were awkward. Although an outsider to the conference room would assume that the two women had much in common, Mary, at first, could see only their differences. One was a leader, the other a follower. One still thrived on confrontation, the other had lost her taste for it. One was certain of her view of the world, the other doubted her own judgment. Lucille was the confident, certain, confrontational one, Mary thought. And herself? The compliant, unsure, searching one.

And yet, as Mayhawk might say, things are not always as they seem. True, the fight to stop the housing had pushed Mary from observer to joiner. It had also rechristened Lucille—first Lantz, then Rizzetta, then back again. But change is a process, not a destination, and the next part of the fight, the struggle to implement the housing, would bring a whole new set of transformations.

"Assume nothing," Bob Mayhawk would say.

Only after leaving his classroom would Mary grow to learn what that meant.

A Field Trip

A line was forming at the corner of Ashburton and Broadway, a short walk from Schlobohm, when Mary Dorman arrived. Seeing the crowd, she pulled a folded piece of paper from her pocket, shook it open, and quickly scanned the rows of names. There were obviously more people on the line than on the list. The letter from Municipal Housing had clearly assigned each tenant a time — one group in the morning, one in the afternoon, two groups today and two tomorrow. But since this was the first group, and everyone was so eager to see their futures, they had apparently decided to ignore the instructions.

The letter also said "No Children," but there were children everywhere. And it specifically said only one member of each household could take the trip to see the townhouses, but no one seemed to have come alone. Billie Rowan brought along her brother. She wanted his male point of view, because this would be John's home, too. Norma O'Neal was with her friend Phyllis, who had been her eyes on so many other important occasions. Alma's sister Dulce brought her daughter Rita to translate the tour into Spanish.

The bus pulled up a few minutes later — a sleek luxury charter rather than the creaky yellow school bus Mary had been expecting. The seats were blue and velvety, the windows were tinted a dark gray, and there was even a microphone in the front. It was as if someone with some power had worried that putting several dozen people, mostly black and Hispanic, into a full-regalia school bus and *busing* them across town would carry too loaded a message.

Mary understood that every step was a possibility to stumble. In the weeks since she had started this job, she'd been feeling increasingly awkward and clumsy — puzzled around Bob, self-conscious around the tenants. That second affliction had made itself known only days ago, when Bob gave the HERE team their first official assignment and sent them door-to-door in the projects to survey those who would move into the new townhouses.

Mary expected to feel fear, but instead she just felt white. For nearly sixty years, she had thought of herself simply as a person — not a white person, just a person. Even during the worst days of the housing fight, when racial slurs punctuated so many protest meetings, she did not think of herself in terms of her race. Her religion, yes. Her family ancestry, yes. But not the color of her skin.

Walking the hallways of Schlobohm, however, she started see-

Show Me a Hero

ing herself as the tenants might see her. White. Middle class. Irish Catholic. Proper. What more did they need to know? She could almost feel the blue of her eyes behind her chunky prescription lenses, and her hair practically ached with silver gray.

Had all this not been so new, she might have stepped back and seen the obvious—that this was how it felt to be black in a white world. This constant awareness of living inside your own skin is what the tenants of the townhouses would feel every morning, walking out their door and into a neighborhood where their face advertised their address. But Mary's bent had never been philosophical, and as she made her way from one apartment to the next in Schlobohm her thoughts went in another direction entirely. If these tenants looked at her and saw only a set-in-her-ways white lady, she worried, how could she do this job? And if she could not, why did it suddenly bother her so much?

As the meetings with the tenants wore on, her self-consciousness spread and she became exquisitely aware of her words, her assumptions, the sound of her voice. Too often what she said turned out to be slightly wrong.

"Everything is so clean," she gushed in the first few apartments, amazed that the homes were not grimy and rancid like the hallways. "You go from that dirty, dirty hallway, and then you're in this nice house, this home," she said. "You keep it so clean."

She thought it was a nice thing to say, until she said it one time too many. "Yep," one woman answered, "we try to clean the bathrooms once a week, whether they need it or not." The comment hit its target, and Mary felt stupid and small.

Afraid she would stumble again, Mary kept her seat belt on and her mouth shut during the first part of the bus ride, waiting until the driver crossed the Saw Mill. Not until she saw her familiar neighborhood of Lincoln Park did she feel comfortable enough to take the microphone.

"Right now we're passing St. John's Church," she said of the building that gave her street its name. "I go to church there."

Rita Manzueta leaned over and translated for Dulce. "*Esta iglesia se llama St. John's,*" she said. "*Pienso que es Catolica.*"

Would her mother make the trip to the west side every Sunday, Rita wondered, to go to church with Aunt Alma? Or would a new home mean a new church, someplace like St. John's?

"That's Morely's supermarket," Mary continued from her seat up front. "It's a good supermarket. The people there are very nice."

"There's the Yonkers Raceway," she went on. "I'm glad the housing was built near here, because, before, when this was just an empty lot, people coming out of the racetrack would throw their garbage here. Now that the housing is here, maybe they won't." No one else laughed at the misguided attempt at a joke.

The bus turned the corner, from Central Avenue onto Clark Street, the site of the first groundbreaking and the place where Mary first realized that the fight was over. The driver slowed, but did not stop. The tenants pressed against the right-side window, like airplane passengers over the Grand Canyon. It was the first time that most of them had seen the townhouses.

"They're gorgeous," Phyllis raved to Norma, who saw only the green of the trees and the pale yellow of the buildings, but who liked what she saw.

The buzz inside the bus grew louder. Mary stopped talking because no one was listening.

"That's public housing? Not like any public housing I've ever seen."

"I'm gonna plant me some flowers."

"Maybe my kids can have a swing."

"You could put a grill back there. You could have your own barbecues."

"I would like to know why they won't let us get off the bus. If we are allowed to move into the neighborhood, why aren't we allowed to walk around there?"

They would walk around soon, but not yet, Mary explained, then directed the driver past the four other sites. First, to Trenchard Street, built on the remains of School 4. Mary had been to a birthday party for the building, complete with pointy hats, candles, and a cake, and she had mourned its passing as deeply as if it had been a person. Now School 4 was gone and twenty-eight townhouses stood in its place. Mary could barely recall what the school building had looked like.

"See how convenient the public transportation is?" she said, shaking off the memories and pointing to a bus stop near the site. "The number 20 bus goes right past here."

Next, to Wrexham Road, another twenty-eight units, surrounded by stately apartment houses, down the block from the leafy Sarah Lawrence College. During the months of construction the site had been a favorite of graffiti vandals who were fond of several huge boulders, too large to be economically removed, that stood sentry between the clusters of townhouses. "Death to Sand" was a favorite message. Or "Yonkers Forever." But as the bus drove past, Mary saw no trace of the spray-painted anger. It had been made to disappear as completely as School 4.

"So close to the Cross County Shopping Center," Mary said. "Just a short bus ride away."

Onto Helena Avenue, fourteen units on a street of single-family homes. A street almost exactly like Mary's. "Very quiet here" was all she said.

Finally, to Whitman, with forty-eight townhouses, the biggest of the sites and the one Mary liked the least. To her it seemed isolated, with no real neighbors, too much like the projects it was meant to replace.

"This is where we can get out and look inside."

Mary climbed down first, then waited at the bottom of the steps, helping the occasional toddler. "Is this the place they bombed?" one young mother asked, hesitating a moment before stepping onto the sidewalk. "Which apartment was it?"

Not the ones they were visiting. Municipal Housing had unlocked two model apartments, both far away from the now repaired bombing site. For nearly half an hour, the tenants peeked in every Formica cabinet in those apartments, nodding approvingly at the shiny linoleum, the two-door refrigerator, the gas range, the stainless-steel sink, the oak staircase. They even used the bathrooms.

Upstairs, Norma and Phyllis paced the hallway, pretending it was dark, worrying that Norma, unused to stairs, would take a wrong turn one night and tumble down the dozen steps. "You could put up one of those gates," Phyllis suggested. "The ones that keep babies safe."

Downstairs, Billie Rowan paced the living room, gauging its size. All around her, others were complaining that the 12'9" by 12'6" space was too small, but Billie cheerfully announced that she didn't care. The only furniture she owned was a bed frame, a mattress, and the portable playpen that Johnny and Shanda shared as a crib. "I don't have nothing to fill up these rooms anyway," she said, walking back and forth nonetheless, mostly because everyone else was. "When you have nothing, then everything fits."

In the kitchen, Doreen James was opening and closing the back door. It felt flimsy in her large hand, just as Sheila and others at READY warned it would be. Doreen had noticed a gap under the front door, too. And the window frames seemed cheap, like they would bend with use. She thought of pointing out the flaws to "the bouncy white lady" in charge of the trip, but quickly squashed the impulse. She jiggled the back door again, wondering whether Jaron would catch cold this winter because the townhouses were drafty.

Outside, Rita and Dulce were pacing the fenced-in yards—four strides wide, ten strides long. Not nearly as big as they looked from the bus, but far more land than they had in Schlobohm. They could put a small grille in the yard. Alma could bring Virgilio, Frankie, and Leyda for Sunday dinner.

As Rita and Dulce walked back and forth, up and down, a white couple, who Rita assumed lived in one of the private homes nearby, came and watched them from the other side of the fence. "This is going to be a nightmare," the woman said to her companion. Rita did not translate for her mother.

Mary was smiling as the bus returned to Schlobohm. It had been fun taking these women across town and, like some fairy godmother, presenting them with their homes. She still thought the housing was wrong, and that Judge Sand had been wrong, but she

Show Me a Hero

found that she was happy for the people whose lives would change because of that wrong. Their excitement was contagious, and on the ride back to the projects she gave her home telephone number to anyone who asked, so they might call her with questions.

Stepping out of the bus, her smile faded a bit. Lucille was waiting on the sidewalk, bouncing on the balls of her feet as she took a few last drags from her cigarette, and looking annoyed. Mayhawk had assigned the morning tour to Mary and the afternoon one to Lucille. Pointing to the long line and all the children, Lucille asked, "Who are all these people? What do I do, kick them off if they're not on the list?"

Mary shrugged. "I didn't. They all fit. Just don't tell Bob."

"Why bother with instructions?" Lucille wondered, as Mary walked away.

The question was not just an idle complaint. Lucille saw the tenants' inability to follow rules as a more cosmic inability to control the whole of their lives. Like Mary, she had gone door-to-door in the projects, and had been impressed by the cleanliness and order in most of the apartments. She was struck by the fact that these tenants, whom she had long thought of as the enemy, were really prisoners in their own homes. But these insights, this new sympathy, did not cause her to forgive all.

"The apartments are clean, but what about the outside? The hallways? The stairwells?" she wondered. "I live in an apartment. My hallways are not filled with crap."

She knew it was chic to believe what Oscar Newman believed, that the very buildings are to blame. Her own life made her think otherwise. Decades ago, after World War II, Lucille had grown up in a place that was just like Schlobohm—but very different. The Martin Ray projects, which had stood across the street from where the Grinton I. Will Library is now, were built during the same spurt of exuberant construction that had led to the first projects in Yonkers. Her playmates at Martin Ray were all children of returning veterans, and the projects were clean, neighborly places, filled with promise. There was a stigma back then—"They called us war brats"—but hard work and good behavior were sufficient to move a family up and out. Lucille felt no hint of such promise here.

No, it was not the buildings, nor the stigma of living in the buildings, she believed. It was the way people chose to respond to their environment, not the environment itself.

"I am not racist, but I am prejudiced," she'd often said back in 1988, and the passing years had not changed her views. "I see that there are different characteristics that come with different groups of people. You aren't gonna change that by moving them to the other side of town. I've been to the projects. I've seen the awful buildings. The gunshots. The window bars. The stench. Who destroyed those buildings? I'm sorry. It's not the landlord. The landlord doesn't urinate in the hallways."

Lucille knew that the only tenants allowed to enter the lottery in the first place were those whose apartments were neat and whose rents were paid on time. She had hoped, had assumed, that the result would be people most likely to take charge of their own lives. But the size of this crowd and the presence of these children hinted otherwise. Mary excused the rule-breakers as enthusiastic. Lucille saw the same enthusiasm, and was pleased by that, but she also saw confirmation that there were things about these tenants that could not be changed by something as superficial as a move across town.

Everyone did fit on the oversized bus, and Lucille began her tour. She too spent an hour at the two sample townhouses, hearing the same questions, reacting differently.

"The living rooms are so small," the tenants said.

"Everything looks smaller without furniture," Lucille answered. Silently she thought, "If you had brought a tape measure you would know exactly what would fit."

"Will we get screen doors?" they asked.

"I can ask," she said.

She thought: "My apartment's on the second floor. I don't have a yard right off my kitchen."

Inspecting the empty air-conditioning sleeves, they wondered if Municipal Housing would be providing air conditioners. Peering in the space upstairs set aside for a laundry closet, they asked about washers and dryers.

"You need to supply your own," she said.

"I'm a tenant," she thought. "When I find an apartment, I don't think, 'Gimme this, gimme that.' I'm happy if I can find a place that takes kids."

Getting Oriented

As the elevator lurched toward the third floor of the Walsh Road Senior Center, Oscar Newman tried to keep his outlook positive. Optimism did not come easily, however, crammed as he was at the back of the tiny car, one towering white male surrounded by six black women, a strain on the capacity of the slow and inefficient machinery. Tonight's orientation session was scheduled to begin at 7:00 P.M., but it was already well past that time, and the lobby was still filled with women waiting for their turn to ride upstairs. Newman had come to the meeting to keep his housing plan on track. This was not a promising start.

Technically the orientation program was not Newman's department. Smith had given complete control of tenant training to Bob Mayhawk, whom Newman had not even met. It was Newman's sense that Smith was keeping the two men apart, and, until recently, Newman did not care enough about the particulars of the orientation to make a fuss. He was content to focus on the details of the townhouses themselves, leaving the selection of the tenants to Smith and the mysterious Mayhawk. Newman was deliberately uninvolved, and would have stayed that way if not for the recent word from Washington.

Several days earlier HUD officials had informed Peter Smith that, despite earlier promises, federal funds would not be available to actually move the tenants into the new townhouses. Municipal Housing had solicited bids from local moving companies, and the numbers they had received were staggeringly high, probably because the moving companies were frightened of going into the west side projects. HUD refused to reimburse Municipal Housing at those rates — which were about a thousand dollars per household—and in the absence of federal money there would be *no* money, because the Municipal Housing Authority's budget did not allow for an extra $200,000.

The back-and-forth between Housing and HUD was threatening to stall the entire moving process, which was already behind schedule. Newman wanted the tenants into the townhouses as soon as possible, to avoid still more vandalism, and the cheapest solution to this nascent and annoying crisis, he thought, was to ask the tenants to pay for all or part of their move. "They've moved before in their lives," he argued to Smith, "and it's a good bet they didn't hire a mover. Odds are they have a relative who will do it for a few beers and fifty bucks."

So Newman was here to break the bad news to the tenants. Smith had promised to call Bob Mayhawk and warn him of Newman's plans, and when the elevator finally reached the third floor, Newman made his way to the drafty community room. Mayhawk was standing near the front of the hall, looking agitated and staring fiercely at the clock, body language that kept Newman from walking over to say hello. He knew who Mayhawk was without an introduction, and he assumed Mayhawk knew all about him, too.

The session did not start until nearly half past seven. Holding a microphone in one hand and assorted papers in the other, Mayhawk announced that the topic of the day was "The Lease." He then proceeded to read from a sample document, explaining, word by word and line by line, what it meant. It was, he said, the same lease already used by the Municipal Housing Authority for the projects on the west side. In other words, most of them had already signed the paper he was dissecting so slowly. But the refresher reading was necessary, he added, because "we can't assume that because you signed a lease you knew what was in it."

Newman, sitting near the back of the roon, was appalled. This wasn't *training*. This wasn't preparing anyone for anything. He was surprised that Mayhawk, an African-American man, was willing to send these new tenants into their new homes with no real understanding of what they might face. If Newman were in charge, he would teach things straight, without sugar coating, tiptoeing, or talking around the subject.

Show Me a Hero

"You are now living in a new community that has certain un-written rules," he would say. "Even though this is your front walk, you don't walk around in the front in a bathing suit or you don't take a chair and sunbathe in front. You can do it in the back, but you can't do it in the front. Why? That's a rule.

"You have to know that you are under constant observation by your white, middle-class neighbors," he would continue, going directly to what, after all, was the entire point. "The kinds of behaviors that the white, middle-class people would tolerate from each other, they will not tolerate from you. So you have to perhaps work a little harder at it until they calm down and accept you. That has been the case for every group that has ever moved from working-class neighborhoods to middle-class neighborhoods of any ethnicity in this country. It's not going to be any different for you. In other societies they don't worry about it because people don't move between classes. It's part of the American way."

Mayhawk wasn't saying anything like that.

"Management agrees to furnish the following utilities in accordance with the current Schedule of Utilities posted in the Project Office," he said, instead. "Water, heat, electricity and/or gas."

By the time Mayhawk reached section 17 of the second rider to the contract, Newman was begining to wonder whether Smith had indeed called Mayhawk, and if Mayhawk ever planned to let him speak. Maybe Mayhawk hadn't seen him after all? On the slim chance that that was the case, Newman stood up and began to inch his way toward Mayhawk. Mayhawk did not stop talking. Soon Newman was standing just a few feet away, a silent presence demanding an introduction. So Mayhawk made that introduction, then stepped aside.

Newman wasted no time on pleasantries and immediately explained that the housing authority had hoped to pay the tenants' moving expenses, but that the cost was far too high and HUD was unwilling to approve it.

"How many of you could afford to pay three hundred fifty dollars, or half?" he asked, aware he sounded too much like an auctioneer giving the opening bid.

Seven hands went up.

"How many could afford three hundred fifty dollars, if not being able to pay meant not getting in?"

Nineteen hands, and Norma O'Neal's was among them. She would find a way.

"And if you had six months to pay it?"

Thirty-two hands, including Billie Rowan's. Six months was a long time. John would be home by then. She would work out something.

"More than six months?"

A few more hands.

"If it cost only one hundred dollars, how many could afford it?" Newman asked.

"*Cien dolares para mover,*" Rita said to her mother, urging her to raise her hand. One hundred dollars. She couldn't risk this for one hundred dollars.

Mary Dorman, who was at the session per Mayhawk's orders, was angry. Who did this man think he was, playing with these people's lives, acting like a carnival barker, hawking a chance at hope and escape?

Lucille Lantz was also angered by the sideshow. Why are these people just sitting there, taking it? she wondered. Why don't they stand up for themselves, take some control? Standing behind Newman, but in full view of the audience, she began fanning at the air with both hands, gesturing frantically for people to put their own hands down.

Mary joined in. She nearly laughed out loud, picturing how they must look. Two usually respectable women, waving their arms madly, sweating with the effort of it in the hot, airless room. How did she get here? she wondered. Was this simply a reflex, a conditioned response to years of being against whatever Oscar Newman was for? Or was it something far deeper than that? Was she begining to see this from the other side?

Finally, with a flourish, Newman brought the bidding to a close. "How many could arrange their own move?"

Hands were raised throughout the room, a total of sixty-four. Doreen refused to raise hers at all. How dare they disregard the rules like this?

Then Newman changed the subject. Better to cover everything in one visit, he reasoned. The builder had made a mistake, he said, and the space allocated for a washer and dryer in the townhouses would fit only one model, a "piggy-back combined unit, with the washer at the bottom and the dryer on top."

"If we could arrange it that you'd pay one hundred dollars" for that kind of unit "and we'd pay the rest, who could afford it?"

Only a hand or two.

"If you paid fifteen dollars a month with your rent, and the Housing Authority put them in, how many of you could afford it?"

That's when the shouting began.

"How much will the rent be?" someone yelled.

"It depends on your income, as it does in public housing now."

"How long will we have to pay the fifteen dollars?"

"For as long as you have the house," Newman said.

There were boos at that answer, and catcalls, but as the noise level rose, so did fifty-three hands.

"If you used commercial washers and dryers, you'd spend five or ten or even fifteen dollars a week, not counting the inconvenience," Newman screamed over the din. Mayhawk had given him the floor, but not the microphone.

"Why can't we put the machines we already own into the kitchen," one woman asked. Newman raised his palms, pantomiming helplessness. They had seen the size of the kitchens, so they should understand.

Soon after that, Newman left, satisfied that he had explained everything, and the townhouses could remain on schedule. His departure did little to calm the room, however, and Mayhawk spent most of the session trying to quiet the crowd. When that proved futile, he did something Mary had never known him to do before. He ended a meeting fifteen minutes ahead of schedule.

Orientation session number three was held at the same place, meaning the same crowded elevator ensured the same late start. The subject was "Home Maintenance." Oscar Newman was not there. In his place were far more friendly representatives of Con

Edison, the Sanitation Department, and the housing authority's maintenance office, explaining how to regulate the thermostat, mow the lawn, clean the windows, and take out the trash.

After a very long hour, Bob Mayhawk opened the floor to questions. There were a lot of those, but not many answers.

"Where do we keep the lawn mower?" There certainly were no garages at the new sites.

The man from housing maintenance had no idea, but said he would check.

"Can we paint?"

"Only with off-white, flat paint, the kind that's there now."

"How about glossy?"

"The rules call for flat."

"The rules have never had children who scribble where they shouldn't. Glossy is easier to wipe down."

"I'll check on that."

"Can we plant flowers?"

"You can put flower pots outside, but you can't put anything in the ground."

"No flowers?"

"The rules prohibit anything that requires digging a hole in the ground."

"No bushes?"

"There are bushes there now."

"How about the plastic kind of flowers?"

"I guess so, since that's not permanent, but you should try to keep it tasteful."

"So the rules say that even though this is our home, it really isn't?"

"I'll check on this and get back to you with an answer."

Session four covered security, police patrols, and Neighborhood Watch groups.

"There are two-man patrols of the west side, but only one officer to a car on the east side," the police representative was saying.

"Why do we have to sit through this?" someone whispered.

Show Me a Hero

". . . if there's trouble, contact the Police Department, do not try to handle it yourself. . . ."

"They're treating us like dumb asses," someone else whispered back.

Again Mayhawk asked if anyone had questions.

"Do the white folks have to learn how to be good neighbors?" There was some applause.

"If we have to learn how to accept *them*, are they going to have to take a course to learn how to accept *us*?" Stronger applause.

"What's a Neighborhood Watch? Who they watching, me?" Laughter and cheers.

"Are we supposed to cross the street when we see the white people coming?"

"I saw those white people on television, at those City Council meetings, it looked like they were the ones who needed to learn some manners."

At the front of the room, Mayhawk listened to the wave of frustration, then gave the only answer he could give—one that could not really satisfy anyone.

"Those are very good points. Right now there are no plans for classes for those who now live near these sites. Perhaps such an opportunity will be made available to them. We will see what we can do."

Orientation week finally ended. The tenants had heard more than they'd wanted about utility bills, recreational options, which east side markets take food stamps, which buses would get them back to the west side. In the final minutes of the final meeting, Dee Earl, one of Mayhawk's assistants, took the microphone for some parting words of advice.

The moment had been nearly a decade in the making, and Mary expected that Dee would close with something dramatic, reminding everyone of the struggle to get these new homes built and the monumental significance of being the first to live in them. But Dee's message had absolutely nothing to do with that. She spoke instead about the how the move could change their individual lives, and Mary realized, with the shock of any sudden shift of focus, that the tenants didn't think of the townhouses as history. They just thought of them as home.

"Everybody here is here for one reason," Dee said. "You were interested in doing something for yourself and for your family. And interested in making a change in where you were living.

"Over the next few weeks," she continued, "you will have some important decisions to make. You started out by thinking you wanted to make a move. That's why you're here. Is that still what you want? You need to weigh everything that's been laid out before you in order to decide—are you ready for that final move?"

Now it was Lucille who was surprised. This woman was talking as if there was a choice to be made, as if the tenants might actually decline the chance to move away from this place to the safety of the east side. Didn't they all feel lucky to have been picked out of the bingo drum? Why would anyone turn this prize down?

"A lot of you started the program saying 'I'm ready. No if, ands, or buts. I'm ready,'" Dee said. "That's the way you have to feel. That's the kind of determination this step is going to take. It doesn't allow for a lot of doubts or indecision. If you have doubts starting off, you're going to have difficulty. If you're not certain that you have what you need to survive in a new area, you're going to have difficulty.

"People, things are going to be different," she said, her voice rising. "Different does not only mean better. You're going to have to make some serious decisions that will affect the rest of your life. Are you prepared to make those changes?"

Slowly, Mary and Lucille were starting to understand. They had both spent so many years frightened by the townhouses that they had not seen that the tenants had reason to be frightened by them too. The protests, the pipe bombs. What other dangers were there on the east side? This was a chance to leave a neighborhood where coming home meant grime and fear. But they would be trading that for a neighborhood where coming home would mean prejudice and hate.

"There's been lots of talk back and forth about what's available, what's not available," Dee concluded. "Washing machines, moving

Show Me a Hero

expenses. Valid questions. But what it comes down to is weighing your priorities. What is it that you want? The answers are going to be different for every single person in this room."

Moving In

It was close to 2:00 A.M., and Norma O'Neal was exhausted, but her son Dwayne and his wife, Libby, would not leave. They sat on what little surface was available in Norma's brand-new living room, surrounded by unpacked cartons, making small talk and trying to swallow their yawns. Dwayne had arrived at Trenchard Street at dinnertime, before the sun had begun to set, and now it was inching toward dawn and they were still there. Norma had hinted that she wanted them to go away—"You must be very tired"; "My, isn't it getting late"—but it was not her nature to be blunt, so she sat there and made small talk, wondering when on earth they would finally go.

"You sure have a lot of stuff," Dwayne was saying, for the third time that evening. "Those moving men sure earned their money."

Norma was too sleepy even to nod. It had only been two days since those moving men gathered every carefully packed item from her old apartment and carted it all across town. But, in the way that time seems to thicken and thin with circumstance, the Norma O'Neal who had lived in Schlobohm already seemed a lifetime away from the one living here, in this brand-new townhouse.

Despite Oscar Newman's warnings, she did not have to pay for her own move. Peter Smith helped to broker a deal with the Department of Social Services, and, as Norma said, "the welfare people paid." (Smith found money for the washer and dryers, too, from within the Municipal Housing budget.) Social Service rules required three estimates on any job, so Tasha walked to the three closest moving companies and recited her mother's relevant statistics: five rooms of furniture, two dozen boxes, everything will be packed in advance. An elevator at the old apartment. A flight of stairs at the new apartment. At each stop, Tasha was given a sealed envelope with a bid inside. The three envelopes were given to the county's Social Services bureaucracy, where, somehow, someone had picked a company and arranged for Norma to move.

She would have liked to arrive in her new life with more. At orientation, so many of the people sitting around her had talked—at far too much length, if you asked Norma—about what they were leaving behind. Everything, they said, would be new, and they went on to describe the red leather in store for their living room, and the dark woods they would pick for their bedroom. Norma did not for a moment believe she could afford that. She had barely finished paying off the furniture she already had. Most of it was bought just before she lost her eyesight and, eventually, her job. The bedroom set, with the matching headboard, dresser, and nightstand, was purchased five years ago for $1,600—half down, the rest at $50 a month. The three-piece wall unit, painted to look like mahogany, with big glass doors and shiny brass accents, was purchased six years ago, for $800, nothing down, $50 a month. Two television sets, the kitchen table with four matching chairs, Tasha's bed and dresser—all of it was old, and all of it came along with her. The only thing she had purchased since her eyes went bad was the freezer chest in the kitchen, which she had bought at Trader Horn for $250, the week she received her first disability check. It was big enough to fit a month's worth of groceries, saving her trips to the market every week. And the only thing she had left behind was part of the beige velvet living room set—also $1,600, at Almo's furniture on Main Street—which she was afraid would not fit in her new townhouse. So she gave the loveseat and the chair to her younger son and his girlfriend, keeping the couch for herself.

As it turned out, the extra pieces would have fit just fine. She shouldn't have listened to all the complaining on the bus about how small the rooms were. If she had minded her own counsel, and not a lot of young girls who didn't know any better, she would have a completely decorated living room right from day one. The set was a little worn, of course, because all her things wore out more quickly than they should. None of her furniture was made

Show Me a Hero

quite as well as she would want, and she knew she was paying too much for too little, but that was yet another of the indignities of living in a neighborhood where the merchants know you have no other choice. She had learned to patch and disguise, and she certainly wasn't ready to buy anything new—except, perhaps, the lawn set Pat Williams had seen at Bradlee's, a glass-topped table, four chairs, and a rose-and-white umbrella. It was $600 when Pat first noticed it, but Norma's nephew, who worked there, told her that after the Fourth of July weekend the prices on outdoor furniture were cut in half. And there was a small grill at Bradlee's too. Wouldn't it be nice to invite people to her yard for a barbecue?

"Mama? What do you think, Mama?" Dwayne was still talking. "Are the neighbors nice?"

"I've been keeping to myself, mostly," Norma answered. Why wouldn't he go home?

"A few people poked their heads in when the movers were here and asked if they could come look at the apartment," she continued, since he seemed to expect a longer answer. "People from the neighborhood, I think. White people."

"You let them in?" Dwayne asked, and Norma heard the note of alarm in his voice.

"They were curious, I guess."

"Ma, don't go letting people in. You never know."

"The movers were here. And Caroline. I was safe."

"How is Caroline working out?" he asked, of her new home health aide.

"Fine. Fine," she said, wondering why he was so nervous tonight and when he was going home.

"And the people who put Braille on the stove and things?"

"They're coming next week. They were Johnny on the Spot when I told them I had moved." Of course, he knew that already. It was the part of her new life that pleased her the most. Someone would come and teach her how to listen for traffic when crossing the street, and read the stove knobs with her fingers. No more waiting for darkness in order to check whether a burner was still on by turning off the kitchen lights and looking for a glow of red.

"So, everything's okay here, Ma?"

The Rebuilding

"Oh yes. Everything's okay," Norma said.

Then Libby spoke, for what seemed like the first time in hours.

"I don't think they're coming back," she said, looking at her husband.

"Who's not coming back?" Norma asked.

"I think they're gone," Libby said.

"Who's gone?" Norma asked again.

Dwayne paused a long time before he answered.

"When we came, we parked the car out front," he said finally, "and a carload of people passed and said something nasty to us."

"What did they say?"

"I'm sure they're gone."

"What did they say?"

"Libby's right, they won't be coming back."

"What did they *say?*"

"Nigger, go home."

"Oh. I see."

"We thought we'd set here awhile to make sure you were okay."

"I'm okay. Now go."

But, once they did, she did not sleep well at all. Her body ached with exhaustion, but her mind was wide awake with the possibilities.

To Doreen's relief, Jaron quickly fell asleep in his new room at Gaffney Place. The stalling and clinging she had expected never happened. He just put his head on the pillow and that was that, a simple, trusting gesture that to Doreen seemed to say, "The bed is the same, Mommy is the same, the goodnight kiss is the same."

Doreen wished she could find the same kind of comfort. Jaron's bed was one of the few familiar things in the apartment, because, in her determination to make a new start, she had left everything but that, the dressers, and the kitchen table behind. "That's staying here," she told the moving men at least a dozen times that morning, as they started to carry the living room sofa toward the elevator. "Leave that here," she said, over and over again, when they tried to take the matching chair. Furniture, knickknacks, even some clothes stayed in the apartment when she left Schlobohm for the last time. Let Municipal Housing figure out what to do with them.

As a result, the living room of her new townhouse was completely empty. Jaron had spent the day careening around it with joy—jumping, spinning, running in circles. Then, for a change of scene, he had dashed to the backyard and done the same thing there. His mother had felt safe and smug watching him. But now that he was asleep, the living room echoed with emptiness, the backyard was dark and threatening, and Doreen was having second thoughts. Someone had thrown a rock through the window of the maintenance man's car the day before yesterday. Sheila and the others at READY had wagged their tongues over that one. Was she right to have ignored them?

Doreen had moved here to protect Jaron, but in this uncharted world, so close on the map, but so far in all the ways that mattered from where she had lived before, she was surprisingly uncertain about where to start. Protection in Schlobohm was physical— don't touch the scummy banisters in the stairwells, don't stare at that screaming man, don't pick up that crack vial, don't go outside without holding Mommy's hand. In this new home, with lawns and trees and recycling bins, she felt she needed to protect him from words and thoughts, to somehow protect his feelings, his inner world.

Because old habits die hard, she started to map out a communal approach to the problem. Should she circulate a petition demanding increased security? Form a committee to explore a Neighborhood Watch patrol? Quickly, she stopped. "Worry about Doreen and Jaron," she thought. "Protect yourself."

To that end, she had already wedged two new twin beds into the tiny upstairs bedroom, and made a home for her sister Barbara. If Municipal Housing ever found out, they would all be ordered to leave, but Doreen did not think twice about inviting Barbara to stay. "How can they make you turn away your family?" Sadie Young Jefferson would say. It was hard to be humbled by a rule that everyone was breaking, and, more important, by a rule that kept her from feeling safe.

So her sister was here to make things safe. Why then was Doreen standing in the empty living room, afraid? She walked the few feet into the kitchen, and spent a few minutes rummaging through the unfamiliar drawers until she found what she had only just realized she needed.

The steak knife felt right in the palm of her weighty hands, secure and reassuring as her fingers closed around it. She had never once thought of sleeping with a knife under her mattress when she lived at Schlobohm.

Grasping the knife, she started up the stairs, but stopped and turned back through the kitchen and out the door to the yard, which was already scattered with Jaron's toys. There were empty boxes from the move, and he was using them as a house, or a fort, or something. A pot he had wheedled from the kitchen lay on top of a cracked wooden spoon that Doreen had meant to throw away. There were a few balls, and it was next to one of them that Doreen spotted what she wanted—the aluminum baseball bat her father had given her son for Christmas the year before.

With the knife in one hand and the bat in the other, she stepped back into her tiny house. She locked the door behind her, turned the knob, and tugged to make sure the lock was secure. Once upstairs, she placed the knife under her mattress, the bat under her bed, and went to sleep.

"Happy birthday to me, happy birthday to me." Billie Rowan was humming to herself as she walked up and down the stairs of 115 Gaffney. This was the first place she had ever lived that had stairs, and she was fascinated with them. She was unpacking slowly, one item at a time, shaking each plate, pot, and hairbrush loose from its wrapping of newspaper.

How cheerful to move on your birthday, she thought, with boxes of surprises to unwrap. It didn't matter as much that her only gift for her twenty-second birthday was five dollars from her mother, tucked into a Hallmark card. There was nothing from John, yet, and the children could hardly be expected to shop. So her own belongings would have to do, and she felt a childlike thrill when the newspaper fell away and revealed something that belonged in a bedroom or bathroom, because it meant another sprint up and down the stairs. Seven steps up. Pause. Turn. Six more steps, and you were upstairs. Those thirteen steps made this a real house, not just another apartment. And, just maybe, a real house would lead to a real life, with a man who was home, not in prison, and two children who did something besides try her patience.

"You'll curse those stairs one day," her mother had warned her. But it had been a long time since she had listened to her mother.

By dinnertime, her few boxes were more or less unpacked and she had run out of reasons to run up and down. She and the kids ate some farina (she would have to do some shopping, soon) and sat on the bed in her bedroom, watching television.

A few minutes had passed when a noise that did not seem to come from the TV caught Billie's attention. She went down the stairs, slowly this time, with tension rather than joy, but found nothing wrong in the living room or kitchen. She opened the downstairs closet. Nothing. The back door. Nothing. The front door. Nothing. Everything was quiet—so quiet that opening and closing all those doors seemed a rude intrusion.

She went back upstairs and settled herself on the bed when there was a second noise, different from the last but equally unfamiliar. She went downstairs again, and again she found nothing. The problem, she thought, wasn't the noise, it was the quiet. She could not remember ever being anyplace this quiet. Then came another noise, another search, a fourth noise, a fourth search. Finally she turned off the television and began to put a few of her newly unpacked belongings—toothbrushes, diapers for the kids, clean underwear—into a bag.

She would go to her mother's apartment in Schlobohm, she decided. After all, it was her birthday. Her mother would want to spend her birthday with her. And Shanda and little Johnny would be more comfortable there tonight. It would just be for one night. Except, of course, she had all those errands to run tomorrow — groceries and things, maybe a new outfit for John's first night home — and the only stores she really knew were on the west side.

Maybe she would stay at her mother's tomorrow night, too.

Councilman Nick

It had been early in the morning when Nick first mixed the powder and water in a plastic bucket that had previously held drywall Spackle, and carried it to the end of the long driveway. He and Michael (who had actually mixed cement once or twice before and should have warned him) pushed a long steel rod into the sloppy mixture. Then Nick, Michael, and Nay took turns holding on to the heavy pole, doing their best to keep it upright while the liquid languidly became solid.

As hours passed, Nay went back into the house, first for sandwiches, then magazines, then sunscreen. By midafternoon, Nick tried to rig up a support truss for the pole, using some nearby branches, but it only held for a few minutes.

All this effort was for a street sign that said "Wasicsko Lane." It was green and white, like all the official signs in Yonkers, and even on close inspection it looked like the real thing. But it wasn't. Michael had found a company that specialized in replicas, and he had given one to his brother and sister-in-law as a gift, a way to help confused deliverymen find the hidden house.

"Shouldn't have to wait until you're dead to have a street named after you," Michael had joked as he watched Nick unwrap the box.

Nick had been touched and amused at the time, but now he was feeling hot, tired, and embarrassed. The end of his driveway was in full view of Yonkers Avenue, right next to a traffic light, and each time the cars stopped drivers would stare and honk and wave. Both of his hands were cramped around the sign, so he couldn't wave back. They must have thought he was an idiot, standing there hugging a pole.

Or maybe they thought the sign was real. Then he would not look like an idiot, but like an egotist who names a street after himself. Hadn't he gotten flak when he put WASICSKO on his license plates? Even worse, what if they thought that he *wanted* them to think that the imitation sign was real? Then he would look like an egotist and a fraud.

The fact was, he sincerely had no interest in the kind of recognition found in a municipal sign. When the townhouses were first going up, it was Nay who raised the possibility and Nick who rejected it.

"Wouldn't it be great," she said, "if they named them after you?"

No, Nick had answered, it would not be great. "They start to name things after you when you're washed up or you're dead," he said. If asked, he would graciously decline the honor.

No one ever asked.

He was painfully aware that no one had asked about a lot of things lately. Despite his expectations, he had not become part of Terry Zaleski's inner team. Neither had he been invited to the lottery, although other members of the council were there and a few had even been given the honor of pulling some of the names out of the bingo drum. He *had* been invited to a small ceremony where a few tenants were given symbolic keys, but he was left to find a seat in the audience while people like Terry Zaleski gave speeches from the podium.

A few days after that ceremony, Nick and Nay had gone on a cigar run to the townhouses to greet the new residents. He knocked on doors, shook some hands, and was invited to tour a few half-finished apartments. All the tenants were polite, but they did not seem to know him and they had no idea what he had done to get them there. He worried that the only people in town who did remember him were the angry, unforgiving voters he would have to face for the rest of his career.

Dinnertime neared on the sidewalk near Yonkers Avenue. The

pole no longer tilted when left unattended, and Nick brought out a shovel. He dug into the rocky earth until he had blisters, then he rolled the bucket into the hole and covered it with dirt.

In the waning sunlight, he stood with Nay and stared at the sign. "Wasicsko Lane." The pole was slightly crooked and an overhanging branch obscured some of his name.

Sitting on the Lawn

For every cause there is a meeting. Mary's weeks of mind games in the Will Library and her further weeks of orientation at the Walsh Senior Center were just the beginning. Now Bob Mayhawk had assigned each HERE team member her own housing site, at which she would hold weekly meetings with her tenants. Meetings, as her husband Buddy would gently remind her, were not real life. Yet they had come to define her life, and, for the next few months, they would be part of life in the townhouses as well.

Mary's site was Clark Street, within walking distance of her home, and she was holding her first meeting out on the lawn, in the narrow space between two clusters of townhouses. It was not the get-together Mary had planned, nor was it the kind that she was used to. During the Save Yonkers and then the Concerned Citizens days, someone volunteered their living room and, usually, their coffeepot. Camaraderie was not the point of the gatherings, but it wasn't purely a sidelight, either. The sense of belonging mixed with the sense of purpose until it wasn't completely clear which one brought her back to those meetings time after time.

At Clark Street, however, there was no feeling of camaraderie and no sense of purpose. She had rung all twenty-eight doorbells, but she could not find one person who would agree to host this meeting at their home. At first she assumed that was because they didn't have any furniture, or because they thought they would have to buy the snacks, but now she believed it was something

Show Me a Hero

deeper. In the projects, apartments were places to escape to, not places where you threw open the doors and invited strangers inside. Neighbors were as likely to be a source of violence as a source of friendship. Meetings were events where others lectured at you, not ones where thoughts and ideas were shared.

So Mary gave up on finding a living room and settled for this newly planted patch of sod for her first meeting, grateful that it provided some shade against the June sun. Mary was the first to take a seat, glad she was not wearing a skirt, hoping that she would not go home with permanent stains on her khaki pants. When everyone was settled (only five people came, despite the notes she left under every door), she tried to explain why the second meeting should be held inside.

She began with the practical approach.

"We can't keep coming out here," she said. "Winter's going to come. You're going to have to get together in each others' homes."

No one volunteered.

Then she tried a more philosophical argument. "You have to get to know each other," she said, "and not only because we can't keep standing out in the street and having meetings. You have a different life now from people on the west side, but you also have different problems from the people on the east side. You're your own little community, and aren't going to be able to do anything if you don't know each other. You don't have to like each other, but you should be acquainted with each other because you need each other."

That seemed to work. Carolyn Dunclay, a single mother with a handicapped daughter, shyly raised her hand and said everyone was welcome to come to her apartment the following week.

Mary spent a moment enjoying that tiny victory, then asked if anyone was having any problems. The list, at first, was full of minor maintenance chores. Someone's stove didn't work. There was a hole near the lock on some one else's back door. The water in one upstairs bathroom didn't turn on. "New house problems," Mary called them, and promised to send them along to Peter Smith. This was easy, she thought. Maybe Bob Mayhawk was wrong and they wouldn't need to hold a meeting every week.

She was about to wrap things up, when the women started talking about "teaching the neighbors some manners." The anger in the words made it clear that some "new house problems" would take more than a wrench, or a phone call, or even a policy change to fix. The neighbors, Mary learned, had made it a habit to sit on their front stoops and glare at the new residents, giving the tenants the feeling they were always being watched, sending them burrowing into their homes, with the doors shut and the curtains drawn.

In the projects they had kept their children inside for fear of guns and drugs. Did they move here only to lock the doors again, against less tangible threats?

Mary didn't know what to tell them. The cheetah and the gnu hadn't prepared her for this. Like a parent trying to advise a child on dealing with the playground bully, she told them everything she could think of, and hoped that some of it sounded useful.

"Don't worry," she said, "I live there, and I will not let you have any problems."

"You know what I think," she said, "I think you're probably a little nicer than they are across the street. You wouldn't sit in your house and stare at them."

"If I were you," she said, "I would just go about my business. If you see them or pass them, smile and say hello. If they don't say hello back, fine. But nobody can accuse you of not being polite."

That's what they were doing, they said. It wasn't really working. Not only that, there was the problem of the dogs. Every morning and every evening, two neighbors marched their dogs across the newly planted lawns and let them do their business, as if the land was still a vacant lot and the townhouses had never been built. The woman had three huge white poodles. The man had a nasty-looking Rottweiler. Mary, herself the owner of a German shepherd–Labrador crossbreed, was certain this was some kind of protest, otherwise the dogs would simply be walked in the street. Again she gave advice she knew would probably not help anyone.

"If you see them do it," she said, "you could ask them to please put their dogs on the street. If you don't see them, just pick it up

Show Me a Hero

with an old newspaper or something, that's what I do, because you don't want it there."

Lucille's site was Trenchard Street and Gaffney Place, where School 4 once stood, and which was now home to Norma O'Neal, Billie Rowan, and Doreen James. Like Mary, Lucille could not find anyone willing to host the first meeting; she sat outside with the tenants on the hot asphalt of the parking lot. The spot had the advantage of allowing everyone to keep an eye on their children, who had taken to using the newly paved area as their playground. But it was much less comfortable, and much more public, than Lucille would have liked.

She did not spend very long introducing herself. Everyone, she reasoned, already knew her from orientation, and the less said the less likely she would stumble into a sentence she wasn't sure she believed. She opened with a nervous joke. "I guess I should apologize for being white and Italian," she quipped, running her hands briskly though her frizzy auburn curls. She was relieved when there was laughter.

"Is anyone having any problems?" she asked, turning her notebook to a clean page. As she waited for the inevitable list of complaints, she jiggled her pen between her thumb and forefinger, anticipating her own annoyance and trying not to let it show.

There were complaints—several pages of them. But they were not the "gimme gimme whining" kind that Lucille had expected, and her reaction was therefore more complex than she had planned. The problems these women spoke of really *were* problems, Lucille agreed, and she found herself seeing them from their point of view.

"Kitchen," her notes said, "grease splattered from stove leaves stains. Could Municipal Housing install backsplash tile?"

Fair question, Lucille thought.

"Staircases," her notes continued, "raw wood, no varnish, hard to clean. Could steps be refinished?"

Lucille found that a reasonable comment, too.

"Anything else?" Lucille asked, curious about what other glitches were built into the $26 million construction project.

"The lawn mowers—" someone said, but before they could explain further there came a scream from across the parking lot. Two Big Wheels tricycles had collided, and from where the mothers sat it was impossible to figure out which children were involved and whether they were hurt. The women walked to the scene of the pileup with a lack of urgency that suggested they had already done this many times before. Lucille stayed where she was, watching as Doreen James picked Jaron off the ground, then applied a kiss to each knee.

The gesture transfixed Lucille, not because it was extraordinary, but because it was not. As the tenants turned and walked back toward her, she stared at them: all women, all mothers, all representing what she had once feared the most. While others joined the housing fight to protect their property values, or to keep out the drug dealers, Lucille had joined in the name of morality. Public housing, she thought, was filled with families that were not what families should be—single women with too many children, usually by different fathers, with no interest in marriage, and without even the decency to be embarrassed about their situation. People who flout the basic social rules of home and family, she believed, would flout all other rules as well. She could not let such people live near her children. And now those mothers were walking toward her, and Lucille felt seared by the knowledge that right and wrong were not as simple as they used to be.

Be careful what you hate, you might become it, the saying goes, and in 1990, two years after the protests ended and two years before this new housing was opened, Lucille's youngest daughter had become pregnant. She was nineteen years old then, and still in college. The baby's father was someone who quickly disappeared from her life and whom Lucille would be happy to never see again.

Abortion was never really an option. The Lantz family did not believe in it. Lucille and her husband, Paul, assumed from the beginning that they would raise this grandchild, and shortly after the baby was born, Lucille and Paul became her legal guardians, turning their ordered lives upside down. Now there were Disney videotapes in Lucille's living room, and magnetic letters on her refrigerator, and stuffed animals just about everywhere. The two-year-old girl knew that Lucille's daughter was "Mommy" and that Lucille and Paul were "Grandma and Grandpa." She also knew that she had a daddy, but he didn't live nearby.

On a census list, Lucille knew, these women sitting down once again in the parking lot would fall into the same column as her own daughter: single mother, never been married. But staring at them, studying them, she could not accept that the women of the projects and her own daughter shared any common ground. These women had nothing to do with her daughter, she believed, and their children had nothing to do with her granddaughter. She believed that because she had to. If she could not separate their worlds in her mind, then what had the entire fight been for?

Doreen settled Jaron in her lap. As she did, she caught Lucille's stare and tried to decide what to make of this woman, who was alternately helpful and harsh. Doreen had not wanted to come to this meeting. Despite her loyalty to READY, she had sworn off this kind of meeting, because they never seemed to solve anything. She was only here because Lucille had rung the bell and asked her to give this a chance, but what she had seen so far did not renew her faith. The lists Lucille was making would get passed along to Municipal Housing, where Doreen had been sending her own lists for years.

"Where were we?" Lucille asked.

"Lawn mowers," said Doreen.

"I think I can help with that," Lucille said, and explained that she had persuaded the owner of Marden Hardware, more or less down the block from the townhouses, to give the new tenants discounts on hoses, sprinklers, mowers, and other lawn items.

"Ask for Howard," she said. "He's very helpful."

Doreen clenched her teeth, trying to keep her mouth shut. The problem isn't *buying* the mowers, she thought. I work. Her current job, as a bus monitor, might not earn her a lot, but she certainly knew her way around a store.

"We know where to find one," she blurted, aloud. "The problem is, Municipal Housing, they don't give us anyplace to store them."

Not only that, she said, there are no gates to the yards, "so after you mow the front lawn, you have to wheel the thing through the house to mow the back. I don't want to keep dragging a dirty mower through my house."

"Housing will lend you a mower," someone offered.

"Yes, they will," Doreen said. "But you have to go all the way to Walt Whitman to get it, that's two buses, and you sure can't bring it back here by bus, so you can only get one if you have a car. And that still doesn't keep the thing out of my house."

"When the maintenance man came to mow the front last week, I gave him extra and he mowed the back, too," someone else said.

"My boy will take your money instead, he'll start a business and do all the lawns," said one of the few mothers of a teenager.

"Your boy never does the work you say he'll do," snapped that mother's purported friend. "You're always offering him, but he's never interested."

Lucille tried to steer the conversation to more productive ground. She almost asked, "Does anyone here have a car?" but she stopped herself at the last moment, deciding that it contained the assumption that they probably did not. Bob Mayhawk had warned her about assumptions. They too easily lead to offense. Editing herself midthought, she asked, instead, "Who here has a car?" That sounded more upbeat and affirmative. Two women raised their hands.

"How about this," Lucille suggested. "If one person borrows the mower, they give as many people as possible a chance to mow their lawns, too. You help each other out." Not a perfect solution, she realized, but at least it was a start—an active suggestion to counteract the passive complaints. Although there were nods of agreement from the women in the circle, Lucille saw little chance that any sharing would actually take place. Doreen James saw no chance at all.

Show Me a Hero

John Comes Home

Billie had hoped everything would be perfect the day John came home from prison, and, for a little while, it almost was. She woke earlier than usual that morning, and wrapped her hair in a new African print scarf, bought just for the occasion. Then she straightened the few pieces of furniture in the apartment, wishing there was more of it and that the rooms looked more like a home. She had managed to buy a dining set for the kitchen, a secondhand bed for Johnny junior, and a new crib for Shanda. But there was only a bed and a television in her own bedroom—soon to be John's bedroom, too—and the living room held nothing but promises and dreams.

When John finally arrived, she walked with him from room to room, pointing out what was there and what she hoped would be. She feared she had done a poor job of describing the townhouse in her letters, because everything he saw left him wide-eyed with surprise.

"This is nice. This can't be true. They're playing with your mind," he said. "Tell me they're not messing with my mind."

"No, baby," Billie answered, thrilled that he was thrilled, because maybe now he would stay. "Really, baby. This is ours. This is home." That John wasn't on the lease and therefore had no official right to live there was, to Billie's mind, just bureaucratic blather that had nothing to do with real life.

For the first few days everything was just as Billie had hoped it would be. John was at home "twenty-four/seven," and helped take care of the house and the kids. It was nothing like their life in Schlobohm—no gang to tempt John away, no summoning whistles from the street. As the days passed, however, Billie began to find John's evenings at home to be as trying as she had found his nights away. After all her months alone, here he was, and he had opinions.

"Why don't the children have a bedtime?" he asked near midnight one night, wanting to share passion, not parenting, with Billie and finding that Johnny and Shanda were wide awake.

"They go to sleep when they want to," Billie answered. "The

latest they go to sleep is one o'clock in the morning." It was an arrangement that made sense, she said, because "if I put them to bed earlier they won't go to sleep, and then I'll have to keep going back and forth to hit them, so I let them tire themselves out."

"Why do they just hang around here all day?" he asked late one afternoon, when the children were still in their nightclothes and still in front of the television.

"They have a schedule," she answered. They usually woke up by noon, she said, then ate some breakfast and watched cartoons until *All My Children* came on at one, followed by *One Life to Live* at two, and *General Hospital* at three. Then Billie would feed them again and let them run around the completely empty living room for a while. Eventually it would be dinnertime, after which everyone would watch TV until they fell asleep.

"Why don't they play with the other kids?" he wondered. "Or outside?"

She had tried that, she said. Johnny would bring his remote-control car and Shanda would take her plastic truck, but the arrangement never seemed to work. The hitting would start, and the other mothers would always blame Billie's children, so, she said, "Now they play amongst themselves."

Billie did not blame John for thinking the children were undisciplined and out of control, because she thought the same thing. "My kids are bad," she'd think. "My kids have something special. They have something like no other kids. They are crazy bad sometimes." They were born that way, she'd decided, and it didn't help that their father was never around to show them who was boss.

She said exactly that during their first few fights, but then John would sit close to her on the steps, look sweetly into her eyes, and explain, as he always did, that it was not his fault. He'd wanted to be with her, he would say, sounding wounded that she could think otherwise. The law had kept him away. "I want to make one thing clear," he would say. "Always remember, I never done none of this on purpose."

Billie found herself apologizing.

"I'm sorry," she said. "It's not your fault."

They never had that fight again. Instead, they held their battles

Show Me a Hero

on less dangerous ground: Why does he always leave his dirty clothes on the bathroom floor? Why does she always wear her pants so tight that she's "showing off the goods"? Why don't those children have a bedtime?

John was not really bothered by her nagging. He saw it as a sign that Billie loved him, which she believed she did.

Billie, in turn, did not dwell for long on the dissolution of her dream that everything about their new start would be perfect. The skirmishing was familiar, and she was used to it. It was simply the way things were with the two of them. If she had thought, fleetingly, that things could be different, she was not at all surprised that they weren't.

Only the place where they lived had changed. They had not.

The Pretty House

Alma's daughter Leyda was beautiful the morning she graduated from the sixth grade at School 29 in Yonkers, and the day was beautiful, too. Both Leyda and the sky wore the same shade of blue. Her dress, made as a gift by her aunt, was a floaty, satiny material, and years later she would cringe with embarrassment at the thought of how grown-up it made her feel. Pinned carefully to the precious fabric was a single white carnation, her very first corsage. Each girl in her class wore one—a gift from their teacher.

The ceremony was lovely in the appropriately corny way, and Alma wished it would never end. Afterward, Alma, Leyda, Frankie, Virgilio, and the assembled crowd of aunts and cousins went to the Sizzler for lunch. Apparently every other sixth-grade family had the same idea, and the restaurant was so crowded and the service so slow that Alma began to believe that the fates might rescue her and make the meal last long enough to preempt her afternoon plans.

But eventually the steaks were finished, the check was paid, and the inevitable could not be put off any longer. It was time for Alma to take her children to the east side, to see her sister's new town-house for the first time.

The afternoon they spent there was a surprisingly pleasant one. Alma felt a few pangs of envy when she first walked in and saw the staircase, the kitchen, and the bedroom that was Dulce's alone. All these were smaller than she had imagined, but somehow more beautiful. She must have used that word a dozen times during her first few minutes in the apartment.

"It's so beautiful. Everything is so beautiful. So different."

The adults sat inside, some in the living room, where the plants were thriving in the sunny window, some in the kitchen, around the new wooden table. They spoke in Spanish, talking about nothing in particular, and keeping one eye on the children, who ran from room to room playing games to which only they knew the rules.

Every so often, Dulce or Rita or Indy would get up to refill a coffee cup, or brush up some cookie crumbs, or take a plate to the sink, and Alma would be jolted by the simple act of prideful ownership. Filling *their* coffee cups, cleaning off *their* table, placing *their* plate in *their* sink. Welcoming *their* guests to *their* home. As they did these things, they seemed to stand a little straighter or smile a little quicker, or so it appeared to Alma. When a room is clean and orderly, those who enter it feel cleaner, and more orderly. A scrub brush had been taken to Dulce's life. Alma ached for her own purifying new start.

She thought of her closets back at Schlobohm, filled with countless kitchen items she had bought on hope and an installment plan. What had started with one box of pots had become a compulsion, a mania, and when she failed to win the lottery, she bought an Oster Cool Touch Toaster, then a set of Oneida Stainless Flatware, service for four. A Presto Under-Counter Can Opener followed, as did a Farberware Electric Frying Pan.

As Dulce's move had come closer, Alma's closets gradually filled with measuring cups and salt and pepper shakers. She bought a device to hold plastic wrap, aluminum foil, and paper towels. She owned a thirty-piece microwave cooking set, although she did not own a microwave. She found a silver-plated tray at a garage sale, and she bought it because it matched the crystal salad bowl with silver-plated trim that she had found at a flea market. She was particularly proud of her Mister Coffee ten-cup, despite the fact that she never drank coffee.

"It's just for guests," she explained. "I'm going to have people over."

By the time Dulce left Schlobohm, Alma could fit nothing more in her closets, and she began to stack her unopened purchases all around the apartment. There was a box of percale bedsheets, pink flowers on a beige background, on the floor of her bedroom, and a set of egg cups under the bed.

She was not jealous. She told herself this until she believed it. She was truly happy for her sister, and did not wish that anything be taken away from Dulce. Alma merely wanted the same thing for herself. She wanted to shut herself inside Dulce's quiet, private bedroom and go to sleep.

After a few hours at the townhouse, Alma went to tell her children that it was time to go home. She found them in the backyard, trying to climb the chain-link fence, even Leyda, in her satin dress. Leyda and Virgilio walked dutifully into the house when Alma told them to, and started to say their good-byes. But Frankie refused to make it easy.

"I don't want to go back to our house," he said, accusingly. "I want to stay here, at the pretty house." Alma, fighting her own overpowering urge to stay there forever, had to drag her angry son out the door.

A Visit to Remember

The doorbells were among the many things that chronically did not work in the townhouses. When pressed, they rang, but it was a muffled, apologetic sound, one that rarely managed to summon anyone to the door. Thomas Downer tried a few times, with no result, then knocked loudly and waited. Less than a minute later, a woman's face appeared at the upstairs window, her nose pressed into the screen.

"Who's there?" said the woman, who Downer assumed was Billie Rowan.

"Thomas Downer," he answered. "I'm here on a parole visit for John Mateo Santos."

The face disappeared, and Downer heard a lot of shuffling and shouting, the type of noise that often provided the soundtrack to his arrival at a parolee's door. He stood outside patiently while things were tended to within, knowing he would be admitted soon, not because he was welcome, but because they had no choice. While he waited, he sized up the townhouses.

Gruff, burly, and graying, Downer had been a parole officer for more than a decade, and he had rarely made a home visit to a place as nice as this. A few white-collar criminals, maybe—embezzlers, in particular—were likely to have nice homes, but not ordinary thieves like John Santos.

Technically, Downer knew, he had the right to haul John out of these townhouses and back to jail. Out less than three weeks, the man had already broken the rules. When John was first released, he listed his address as 132 Bruce Avenue, home of his mother, Carolina Santos. Downer had made a standard surprise visit to that address, planning ahead in case John "messed up" and had to be taken into custody by police. Downer noted the layout of the apartment, where all the bedrooms, closets, and windows were, where any backdoors were, where John's room would be, if there were any dogs. The apartment checked out and was approved. During his first meeting with John, Downer made it clear that "if you plan to move out of there, you ask me, first."

But now Downer doubted that John had ever intended to live on Bruce Avenue. All evidence was that he was living here, with Billie Rowan, on Gaffney Place. This did not come as a surprise to the officer. He had learned to form quick impressions of his parolees, and his opinion of John Santos was that he was "unnaturally agreeable." During their first meeting, twenty-four hours after John was released, the young man smiled and nodded while Downer ex-

Show Me a Hero

plained the rules of parole: "find a job or go to school, submit to random drug and alcohol tests, stay away from 'known criminals' " and ask permission before any trip out of the country or any change of address.

"What a little weasel," Downer thought at the time, watching John smile. "He's so 'yes, yes, yes. Yes sir. No sir.' " Experience had made Downer suspicious of people who are "docile and agree to everything you tell them." Usually, he'd learned, "it's just a front."

Standing outside the door of John's new home, however, Downer knew he was not going to bust the man for breaking the rules. He had long since resigned himself to fighting only the fights that mean something, and even from the front stoop it was clear to him that this was a better neighborhood than the one he had already approved on the west side. What would be the point of muscling John for making a move that gave him a better chance?

It was John himself who finally opened the door. He asked Downer to come in, then introduced him to Billie, who was standing near the kitchen, with one hand on each child's head, trying to hold them still. Downer said hello, keeping an eye out for any signs of physical violence against her or the children. That *would* be enough to send John back to jail.

Then he asked if he could have a look around, and Billie gave the tour, starting with the small kitchen (Downer made a mental note of the back door to the yard) and the living room (no furniture, Downer noted, but the floor was clean).

Upstairs, Downer was careful to remember which of the two bedrooms belonged to Johnny Jr. and Shanda. ("If I have to come in there in the morning to take him, I don't want to terrify the children by kicking in the wrong door," he thought, but did not say.) He specifically asked where John slept, too, because that was most of the reason he was there. He looked through the bedroom closet, finding male clothes that appeared as if they would fit John. He opened drawers, counted the number of pillows on the bed, and made sure that the room seemed to be shared. He let himself into the bathroom where he paid close attention to the toiletries (two toothbrushes, shaving supplies). It was, he decided, "very apparent" that John Santos was in residence.

Back downstairs, Downer explained the rules to Billie: "I come by the house. I might come by early. I might come by late. I need to check that he lives here. That there are no drugs or alcohol. No illegal activity of any sort. Do you agree to allow me into your house?"

Billie nodded, hoping the man wouldn't come too often. He was a reminder of John's past, a past she was trying to forget.

"Do you agree to have Mr. Santos staying with you?"

She nodded again, a simple gesture. She could not imagine at the time how Downer's memory of that nod would one day shatter her new life.

Not long after that, Downer left. As he walked past the townhouses, toward his car, he found himself unusually optimistic. There is a saying among parole officers: "One-third of your people will make it because of what you do, one-third will make it in spite of what you do, and one-third will not make it, no matter what you do."

He was beginning to think John Santos might make it. He still thought he was a weasel, lying to Downer and to himself about his plans. But luck can help even a weasel. By moving here, Tom Downer thought, the weasel might have lucked into a future.

Dogs, Drains, and Decisions

Mary's second tenant meeting was held indoors, at Carolyn Dunclay's house, and it was a success. Carolyn provided soda and coffee, and put out a plate full of little sandwiches and another stacked with pickles cut into tiny slices. There was a bowl of ice in the middle of the coffee table, surrounded by paper plates and napkins. Mary stopped at the bakery on the way to the meeting and brought a box of yeasty, chocolate bakery cookies. This meeting felt like a party.

Nine people filled the living room, and Mary, after a week of study of her lists, knew most of their names. The first item of business was to pick a place for the next meeting. When Cynthia Napper, one of a handful of married women in the townhouses, volunteered right away, Mary resisted the urge to cheer.

Next, they elected officers for what would ideally become the Clark Street tenant association. Per Bob Mayhawk's instructions, they were to elect a president, vice-president, and secretary for each site. Flush with success at the cozy feel of her second meeting, Mary added her own touch to Mayhawk's plan and decided that Clark Street should have a treasurer, too.

"If you're going to have your meetings in someone's house, every week, then maybe that week they're not going to have the money for all the food you want to put out," she said. "This way everybody can put in fifty cents and let the treasurer hold on to it."

The problems raised at the second meeting were essentially the same as those raised at the first, although the details varied slightly. The dogs were still using their lawns as toilets. The neighbors were still staring, stonefaced, from across the street. Cynthia Napper told of her first night in the housing, when she looked out her window and saw a young girl from one of the nearby apartment buildings lifting the metal sleeve of Cynthia's in-ground trash can — Newman's treasured trash can — and sprinting back home. Cynthia's husband opened the door and shouted at the girl, who kept running. The staring neighbors just sat on their porches. No one did anything to stop the child. Cynthia was convinced that the adults sent the girl over in the first place.

The new secretary wrote all the comments down, and Mary promised to take them to Peter Smith the next morning. She was certain Cynthia would get new trash cans, she said. And maybe Smith could have the police captain come over to talk to them about the dog problem. As for the staring, if Mary could figure out a way to stop people from talking and staring, she would use it in her own life.

Lucille's second meeting was not as successful. Once again she found herself sitting in the parking lot, although, this time, there were a few more tenants in attendance, and they had brought their own chairs.

She tried to follow Mayhawk's plan, and hold an election, but when she asked for volunteers, no one wanted any of the positions.

"You can't govern yourselves without officers," Lucille said, looking around the circle. Her gaze stopped at the person she thought to be the most likely candidate, the one Lucille had come to think of as "the talky one."

"Don't look at me," Doreen said. "I don't want to govern anyone."

"You wouldn't be doing it alone," Lucille said. "There will be other officers, too."

Doreen looked around the circle. "I don't see other officers," she said.

"I think you'd be good at this," Lucille said.

"I don't think I'm interested."

"Well then," Lucille said, in a voice so achingly peppy that it did not sound like her own. "Why don't we all think about this and hold the election some other time?"

She noticed with relief that a green Oldsmobile had chugged into one of the spaces on the other side of the parking lot. Tony DiPopolo had arrived. Bob had urged the inclusion of local civic groups in these meetings, and DiPopolo was certainly part of a local civic group. She had invited him here because she thought a guest speaker would keep this from becoming yet another gripe session. As he walked from his car, she wondered how to introduce him.

"Tony represents the Cross County Homeowners Association," she said. Then, quietly, while he was still out of earshot, she added that he often said things that were racist, but it might not matter because they might have a hard time understanding anything he had to say. DiPopolo's heavy Italian accent coupled with his staccato style of speech meant that few people could follow him on first acquaintance.

"You have to get used to it," Lucille whispered. "You concentrate completely, and he's clear and understandable for a while, but then you lose him again."

What she chose not to tell the group was of the one memorable

Show Me a Hero

moment, soon after the contempt crisis had ended, when Tony DiPopolo was clearly understood by everyone. He stood up during a City Council meeting and introduced himself, despite the fact that everyone in the room knew who he was. "Mr. Mayor," he said, "my name is Anthony DiPopolo. I represent the Cross County Homeowners Association. Mr. Sheingold," he continued, turning his attentions toward a local newspaper reporter who had covered the standoff, and who happened to be Jewish. "Why you come to City Hall?" DiPopolo ranted. "Why don't you get lost, you liar? How come there's all this Jewish talk around town—Michael Sussman, Mr. Oxman, whatchacall Oscar Newman. . . .

"We give $9 billion to the state of Israel. Every year from 1948 until now, we give $348 million. . . . This is white liberal. . . . You run the newspapers. You run the banks. How come you don't tell people the truth?

"For forty years, we discriminate, Mr. Sheingold? Why don't you get lost, go back to Israel where you come from? . . . You white liberals, you use your relatives for political reasons. I don't give a damn what the hell you are, thank you very much. We were born in this city. . . . Who knows who runs this city? The white liberal, white Israel.

"How about the newspaper, Mr. Sheingold? Who runs the newspaper? You have all your paisans? I never see no Italian Americans, no Irish Americans. All you want is Judge Sand, the god. You got to face the truth, OK? The black American, he is in the minority. . . . He became the majority and the white Americans in Yonkers, U.S.A., he became the minority. And that's the truth."

Lucille was, understandably, surprised when this same Tony DiPopolo announced that his civic group would like to play a part in helping the townhouse tenants adjust to their new homes. She wondered if his feelings had changed, or just his tactics. He didn't keep her wondering for long. After thanking Lucille for inviting him to the meeting, he turned to the women and told them they should be grateful to protesters like himself for forcing the court to build townhouses instead of high-rises. Then he accused them of having a hand in the anti-establishment lyrics of the songs by the rap singer Iced Tea. The riots in Los Angeles were somehow their fault, too. His monologue segued to the subject of day care, and he said he didn't understand why anyone at Gaffney would need day care, since none of them worked.

"I work, thank you very much," snapped Doreen. "I work at jobs it would break your back to do."

Go girl, thought Lucille. Maybe I could talk her into office after all.

Having said his piece, DiPopolo went home, and Lucille braced for what she assumed would be outrage. It never came. The tenants spent no more than a few minutes dismissing him with raunchy names, and then they dropped the subject, as if they expected nothing better from him and were not surprised at what they got.

Only Lucille remained upset. She would never speak to anyone that way. Or would she? Hadn't she? Her own exact words had never been as harsh as Tony's, but she had certainly sat in meetings and cheered as he and others had spoken. She had listened to his speeches for years, and they had never angered her. At worst, she had recognized his excess and excused it as part of the fight, a well-intentioned crusader going a little overboard, or becoming a little too emotional, in the name of the cause.

When she had first read the transcript of DiPopolo's diatribe back in 1988, she had felt a form of sympathy. "Poor Tony," she had thought back then, "he means well. He just doesn't realize how racist he is." Now, sitting at Trenchard, the man's remembered words sounded very different, and she knew it was she, and not the words, that had changed. Is it possible to "mean well," she wondered for the first time, when the underlying motivation is racist?

With the visitor gone, the meeting continued, and once again, the tenants recited their lists of complaints: lawn mowers, screen doors, Con Ed bills, washers and dryers. Lucille had heard it all before. She knew the problems so well she could have raised all of them herself. But rather than being annoyed by the repetition, she was, for the first time, saddened.

Yes, these women had complained before. But apparently no one had listened, because nothing had changed. Just as she had heard what Tony had said before, but it didn't shock or bother her, because she didn't really hear.

A woman named Rose Campbell began to speak. Rose was one of the tenants Lucille liked the most. Tiny, shy, and certain that a single rule infraction would get her tossed out of her new home, she spent hours every day cleaning up around her townhouse, sweeping the sidewalks and picking up other people's trash. So when she received a letter from Municipal Housing, announcing that her mandatory house inspection would be held on Wednesday between 9:00 A.M. and noon, she took the morning off from work, without pay, and waited.

When the inspectors had not arrived by 2:00 P.M., she called the Municipal Housing office and was told that inspections stop for the day at 2:00 P.M., and that she would be put on the schedule for the next day, if possible.

"But I have a letter that says today," she said.

Bring it down and show it to me, she was told.

"That means two buses and I have two small children," she said.

Lucille went home that night troubled by everything—by Tony DiPopolo and Rose Campbell and the apathy and the complaints and by the fact that no one seemed to be listening to anyone else. Later that week, she dialed Municipal Housing. Disguising her voice, as she had learned to do during the protest days, she used the name of one of her tenants in place of her own, and asked to be put through to someone who could help her. She spent a long time on hold before she was disconnected.

She made several other tries that afternoon, and each time she called she used a different name and described a different problem. The people she needed to speak to were either away from their desks or on the phone. She was transferred repeatedly and placed on hold endlessly. She left a few messages, but no one called her back. She did not get an answer to a single question.

There was a torrential rainstorm three days before Mary's third tenant meeting, and the drainage system at Clark Street turned up wanting. The slope of the site sent water rushing from the backyards on one side of the site into the backyards on the other side, where it sat puddled for days.

Uncertain what to tell the distraught tenants, Mary suggested they write a letter to Peter Smith. Bob Mayhawk hadn't approved such activism, but it felt right.

"I'm not sure what he can do, but I'm sure he will send the engineers out to do something," she said. And she believed that. Unlike Lucille, she had not lost her faith in the good intentions of Municipal Housing.

The letter was written, and although it started as a complaint about the flooding, it quickly became a chronicle of other problems as well. To Mary, it read like a Declaration of Independence.

> *To Peter Smith, Executive Director*
> *Municipal Housing Authority*
> *From Clark and Loring Street tenants*
>
> *Clark and Loring Street tenants would like to inform the Municipal Housing Authority of the following problems:*
> 1. *The drains in the backyards in the houses on Clark Street are insufficient to handle the run off from the natural hills in the backyards on Loring Avenue, and the rain collected make the backyards full of mud that does not dry up easily.*
> 2. *Maintenance men are mowing some people's back and front yards, but not others, on an arbitrary basis. Since many of us can not afford mowers, we request that this service remain but be available to all tenants.*
> 3. *We would like a clarification of the cable policy. Many tenants would like to obtain cable, but were told by the cable company that we could not have cable for a year because of housing. We do not understand.*
> 4. *Maintenance men have been walking into our homes without permission of the tenants, which is contrary to MHA policy.*
> 5. *The tenants above the handicapped units do not have access to any backyard. We would like to suggest that*

gates be installed to provide access to the backyards. These gates can be installed easily because they are corner houses.

6. *The tenants that live over the handicapped units have one entrance. Is this not a fire hazard? They have only one way out if there is a fire.*

Thank you for your time in the above matters.

Sincerely,

Tenants, Clark and Loring Streets, Yonkers, N.Y., The Judge Albert Viarillo Townhouses

Mary promised to deliver the letter to Peter Smith the next morning. Flush with the potential power of that first letter, the tenants decided to write a second one, to the man with the Rottweiler who was still walking his dog across the townhouse lawns.

We the residents of the Clark St. townhouses would like to inform you that your dogs have been eliminating on our property. Please be considerate and walk them in the street while passing our houses. Do not permit them to urinate or defecate on our lawns as they pass by. Thank you, the tenants of Clark St. townhouses.

Mary promised she would deliver that letter, too, although she suspected it was a promise she could not keep. No one in her group knew the man's name. They thought he lived on Belmont Avenue, probably on the second floor of an apartment building there, because they had followed him once and seen a light turn on in a second-floor window shortly after he entered. But the only way to be certain that the letter reached its intended recipient, Mary knew, was to stand outside the townhouses until the man and his Rottweiler walked by, and hand it to him herself. There were limits to how far she would go to do this job.

Long before Mary and Lucille expected it, Bob Mayhawk announced that their involvement with the housing was over.

"Just like that?" Mary asked.

"The job is done."

"You mean the funding ran out?" Lucille asked.

"I mean the job is done."

They would never get more of an answer from him than that.

The decision, whatever the reason, made sense to Lucille. "We had a role to play and we played it," she said, a role she was proud of, but one that was finished. "We can't hold their hands forever."

Mary, however, announced that, whatever Mayhawk said, she was not leaving. She would continue to visit the townhouses, to go to tenant meetings, and to help if they asked her to. "I can't just drop them, I'm sorry," she said. "I can't just say, 'Well, so, you're on your own.' "

Mary thought Lucille was abandoning the cause. Lucille thought that Mary was too close to it. Each sensed that she stood in a place that the other could not understand. Mary had started the HERE program as a follower and, over the months, she had grown into a leader. She no longer needed Hank Spallone to tell her what to think or Bob Mayhawk to tell her what to do. All on her own she was doing more good for her embattled city than any of the protests had ever done. Lucille, on the other hand, had started full of answers and left with nothing but questions. She had been determined to keep her distance. But now she was so close that her vision was blurred and she felt she was losing sight of the difference between the tenant's lives and her own.

After Mayhawk disbanded his program, Lucille went home. Mary went over to Clark Street. She had work to do there.

In response to the letter from the tenants, Peter Smith had asked a police captain to attend the weekly tenant meeting that night to see if something could be done about the dogs. Determined that there be a proper turnout for the meeting, Mary began knocking on doors, reminding people to come. Where no one was home, she left a note. By 7:00 P.M., the designated living room was full.

Mary began by explaining the problem to the captain. "People are walking their dogs on the lawn. They are letting the dogs go all over the lawns. I guess when it was a lot they used to let the dogs

Show Me a Hero

just run across it. One lady comes out with these three poodles, and lets them go to the bathroom on this nice lady's lawn."

While she was talking, the woman she was talking about—the owner of the poodles—happened to walk by. Mary pointed her out to the captain, who sent his deputy outside to talk with her. Those left in the room kept up the flow of the conversation, but no one was really paying attention. They were all trying to pretend they weren't aching to watch from the window.

After what felt like a long time, the lieutenant came back and said only that he hoped "it wouldn't happen anymore." A short while later, the man with the Rottweiler came out from wherever it was that he lived. Perhaps alert to the presence of the officers, he walked his dog in the street, taking great pains to clean up after the pet.

Billie's News (III)

With a violent wave of nausea and despair, Billie Rowan faced the fact that she was pregnant. It was the third time in four years that she'd had this same sickening realization, and she wondered what it was like to be happy about a pregnancy. This time, like the last two times, the thought made her miserable.

John, she knew, would want her to have this baby, even more fiercely than he had wanted her to have the others. He lorded over the townhouse like it was his personal accomplishment, something that he owned. "The perfect place for a family," he said, boastful that he lived here while everyone else he knew still lived back over there. That was the problem, Billie knew. This might be the perfect place. But they were not the perfect family.

The fights that started when John first came home had gotten worse over the months. They fought about the clothes he left in the bathroom, and whose turn it was to take out the trash.

"One shoe's over here, the other shoe's over there," Billie yelled one afternoon. "Why don't you pick the shoes up?"

"That's what I have a woman for," he yelled back. "So you can pick me up."

They fought about money, and what brand of soap to buy, and about their children.

"You're screwing them up," he said. "You let them do whatever they want and then you scream and hit them. That's not the right way to do it because you're confusing the child and then they become emotionally disturbed."

"They become disturbed," Billie snarled, "because their father keeps going off to jail."

Billie was certain that a new baby would only make the fighting worse, but she was equally certain that John would disagree. "I'll change," he would say. Or "A baby will strengthen the bond between us." Or "Let's get married." Or "When it's born, I'll take care of it; you don't have to do nothing."

When she could not put it off any longer, she told him. He said all the things she thought he would say—and one thing more.

"It worked," he chuckled, with a broad grin, as he explained how he sabotaged a condom so that she would become pregnant.

It was a test.

"I felt that the love you felt for me wasn't there no more," he said. "So I wanted to see if it was still there. You know why? You always say, 'I never wanted these kids.' I resented that. I wanted to see if it was true."

Now Billie and John had something new to fight about.

"I'm not feeling ready for another baby," she said.

"How could you destroy something that we made?" he yelled.

Billie knew he meant something that *he* made.

"I just can't handle another child," she said.

"How can you destroy Life? It's destroying Life," John said. "Forget how I feel, about the baby and getting closer. This is another way of God saying life must go on."

John knew that Billie worried about God. Though she was not a religious woman, she had always planned to become religious one day, when she felt more worthy. She had rare moments when she felt unexpectedly calm or happy, and she thought that maybe that was what it was like to sense the presence of the Lord. And once or

Show Me a Hero

twice, she believed she experienced a miracle, like the day she had no money and no Pampers, and she absentmindedly reached into the pocket of a jacket and found a five-dollar bill. But these were exceptions to her more usual feeling that she was not yet good enough for religion.

Her fear of God, and her love for John, made her foggy with indecision. She scheduled one appointment at a local clinic, but left without having the abortion. Every evening for a week after that she would find herself telling John that she would have the baby. They would lie down together and prod tenderly at her abdomen, talking of "little feet, little clothes, little noses." Then, every morning, Billie would wake up and press her hand to that same swelling abdomen and think, "What am I doing? I can't have this baby. I do not want to have this baby. I cannot handle this baby."

A week after her first appointment, she made a second one. She didn't tell John. She awoke early that morning, left her children with John's mother, and had an abortion.

Doreen Finds Her Voice

Doreen James sat in the parking lot of Gaffney Place, her large frame balanced on the narrow wooden chair she had hauled over from her kitchen, waiting for her meeting to begin. Circumstance had once again put her in charge—this time she was the president of this townhouse tenant association. There had never been a full election for the position, but Lucille had called and said that she would not be coming to meetings anymore, and since Doreen was the person with the most experience at Trenchard and Gaffney, Lucille thought it would make sense if she took over. Doreen was surprised at how excited she was about the title. She was also determined not to let that excitement show.

She had prepared for this meeting as carefully as she knew how, determined not to run meetings as Lucille had run them, or as she herself had run them back in Schlobohm. She would not, for example, start by asking if anyone had any problems. Of course they had problems. If she let them list them, they would be here all afternoon. Instead, she made her own *short* list of problems, all chosen because she had ideas on how to fix them.

When the other women were seated, Doreen started with the easiest item on the list—a party. It was a response to the fact that the few organized activities over on the west side were not available to those on this side of town. The children would come home and announce, "Mommy, we're going to Playland," because their friends back in Schlobohm had told them that Municipal Housing was having a trip. When their mothers called to inquire, however, they learned that the buses were only for those who lived on the west side.

"That's not right, we're municipal housing, too," Doreen's neighbor Anna Sheets had ranted in Doreen's living room a few days earlier. "You're the pres-eee-dent," she said, pronouncing each syllable with great sarcasm. "You're supposed to fix this."

A party in the parking lot would not be a trip to Playland, Doreen knew, but she liked the idea of doing something exclusive to the townhouses. There had to be some way to get these women to join together.

"We could have a barbecue for our kids before they go back to school," she suggested to the group.

"That's a great idea," someone said.

"You can use my grill," Anna said. "I don't use it."

Doreen wanted to stress that this was more than just talk.

"I'm talking about *really* getting together," she said. "Doing things like neighbors are supposed to do."

"At least we can do something together," Anna said. "We can't go on no trips."

"Let's start a fund," Doreen suggested. "If you all want to donate $5, if you want to donate food stamps, if you want to donate green stamps . . ."

"Why don't everyone just bring something," Anna asked, "and save all this talking?"

That idea caught hold for a few moments, until someone asked how they would be sure that "everyone doesn't bring the same thing, like maybe everyone will bring hot dogs." Group organization and planning are skills that get little practice in the projects, and these women were out of shape. After much discussion, Doreen had the idea that a sign-up list might solve the problem. If everyone wrote down what they were bringing, she suggested, they could avoid duplication.

The date was set for the Sunday of Labor Day weekend, and it was agreed that they would all meet in the parking lot with their grilles, chairs, and food.

"We're really not supposed to use the parking lot," Doreen said. "Municipal Housing sent us a letter saying they don't want children to run in the parking lot. But I could care less. Children need someplace to run."

Item one had gone exactly as planned, so Doreen moved on to item two.

"Let's talk about the Con Ed bills," she said.

A month after they had moved in, the tenants had received their first utility bill in the mail, something most of them had never paid because heat and electricity were included in the rent back in the projects. During the late 1980s, however, HUD had changed the rules and required that all new units must be equipped with their own thermostats. It was done as an attempt to save energy, and money, and to give the residents some practice at living with an eye on the cost of keeping warm. But there was no mention of this added expense of the townhouses during orientation, and to the tenants the unexpected arrival of a Con Ed bill merely looked unfair.

As the months passed, and the Con Ed bills kept coming, utilities became a major preoccupation at the townhouses and, not surprisingly, a hot-button topic at Doreen's first meeting.

"It's a double standard," Anna said. "Why should we have to pay something that the people across town don't?"

This was a tougher problem than the Labor Day party, but Doreen had put it on her agenda because she had made some calls directly to Peter Smith, and she had some answers and some ideas.

Municipal Housing could not simply assume responsibility for the tenants' utility bills, Peter told her. The new federal rules, he said, required that the tenants themselves pay the bills. However, he said, those same regulations also permit local housing departments to reduce the tenant's rent in order to offset the bills. The "allowance" for a two-bedroom townhouse, he said, would be $109 and for a three-bedroom townhouse it would be $129.

Doreen's explanation did not make any of her listeners happy. She knew that it wouldn't, because they had not yet turned on their heat and already their bills were between $70 and $80 each month. The amounts Municipal Housing was offering would not cover the cost once winter came.

"Why do we have to pay any bill at all?" Anna repeated.

"They pay most of it," Doreen said. "If you keep the bill down to $109 or something then they pay the whole thing."

"How can we do that when there are gaps under the door? You can look under the door and see the outside. The wind is already blowing in. We'll be frozen when it really gets cold."

Doreen uncapped her pen. "How many other people have gaps under their doors?"

Nearly everyone raised their hands. Doreen suggested the next part of her plan.

"Maybe you should all call Peter Smith and tell him that," she said. "It's good to talk to one another like this, but I think the more of us that call Peter Smith, then maybe something will happen. Remember this number, 793-8400. Call there and ask for Peter Smith. Tell him you're cold and you can't afford to pay for the heat. Tell him that they got double standards. Tell him there'll be a lot of sick babies and people will start using kerosene heaters. . . ."

"Tell him we're freezing our asses off," Anna snapped.

"Be polite," Doreen warned.

Across the parking lot, a familiar car caught Doreen's attention. Few of the tenants here had cars, and she knew most of the vehicles and their owners. This car did not belong to anyone in the townhouses, and yet she had seen it before.

The driver got out and walked toward the group of women. Short, thin, and birdlike, he, too, looked familiar.

Show Me a Hero

"My name is Tony DiPopolo," he said, and his unmistakable accent refreshed Doreen's memory. She wondered how he dared come back again. *She* certainly had not invited him. But she heeded the advice she had just given Anna and tried her best to be polite.

It wasn't easy. Soon into the conversation DiPopolo returned to the theme of his earlier visit by restating his belief that most of the residents of the townhouses did not work.

"I don't think it's any of your business who works and who doesn't," Doreen said. "We're all human beings, however we take care of our kids."

"Yes, yes," DiPopolo agreed. "You're a human being. I'm a human being. That's my point."

Doreen was confused.

"So you're not fighting us anymore?" she asked.

DiPopolo shook his head vigorously, but, to Doreen's mind, not convincingly.

"How am I going to fight you?" he asked. "There's no more fighting to do. The fighting's over."

"Are you with us or against us?" someone said.

"I'm with you," he answered. "What are you talking about? We want to work together."

Doreen wasn't sure she really did want to work together, and she wasn't at all clear about what this man wanted to work *on,* but she believed everyone deserved a chance to prove they had changed, so she gave a shrug and turned the conversation back to the subject of the heat. Within moments, DiPopolo joined in.

"Why should you pay the heat?" he yelled, trying to make himself heard above the half-dozen other voices. "You don't own the apartments. You can't afford it. I'll do this for you. Write down everything you want, put it down on a piece of paper, and I'll bring it to the secretary, I'll even type it. I'll go to all the politicians, and to the councilmen, and to the congressmen and the mayor and to Peter Smith, and together we'll say, 'How can you expect these people to pay this?' We'll be together. If nobody is going to listen to us, we'll go to the television and the newspapers."

The monologue left Doreen off balance. The words sounded right, but there was something about this that felt wrong.

The Rebuilding

"You say you want to represent us, right?" she said, slowly, trying to put her finger on the problem as she spoke.

"You want me to?" DiPopolo asked, with surprise. "I've got a meeting with the mayor in a couple of weeks. We can talk to him then. It's a meeting on a different issue, you know, about the movies, at the Cross County area over there. There's gonna be five movie theaters. We don't know what kind of people are going to be there. A lot of teenagers. We have to stop that."

Suddenly, Doreen knew what had been bothering her.

"Can I ask you one thing?" she said, carefully but firmly. "Not to put you off, but why are you so against everything? Why do you knock everything before you get it up? You don't even get it up before you knock it. These teenagers need things here, something to do, so they won't be tearing around making trouble. It's better than being out on the street."

There were nods of agreement around the circle.

"Sounds like it would make the city some business," someone said. "I'm always hearing that the city needs new business."

"Sounds like a good place for a movie theater to me," said someone else. "It would be closer to us and we wouldn't have to travel all the way down Central Avenue."

This will have to end, Doreen thought. There will be no more outsiders telling us how to live. She looked squarely at Tony DiPopolo. "We want your help, if you really mean it," she said, firmly. "But you don't represent us. We represent us. When you go to talk to the mayor, or whoever, we want you to go with one of our delegates so we can know exactly what's going on."

"We'll go together, tell him everything that you said, and I'll bring it back to you," DiPopolo agreed quickly—a man who had fought the housing being put in his place by a woman who had defied him and moved in.

"No," Doreen said, correcting him. "You're not gonna have to bring it back to us because we're gonna send one of our delegates, and our delegate's gonna bring it back to us. I don't want you to get a misunderstanding when you leave here. You don't have to report about your meeting, because we'll send our delegate and she'll explain everything. You're just there to stand behind us. We will represent ourselves."

The Beginning of the End

Memory is selective and fame is addictive, a combination that allowed Nick Wasicsko to forget the burn of the spotlight and to remember only the adrenaline rush of being at the center of it all. As the one memory faded, the other grew more tantalizing. Nick was determined to feel that rush again.

Had he had his fifteen minutes? If so, they weren't enough. Would he ever give another State of the City address? Would eleven television cameras be rolling when he did? He was only thirty-three years old. He wasn't willing to be finished yet.

He had hoped to regain some of the glory, or at least some of that feeling of connectedness, by rejoining the city council. But daily contact with Terry Zaleski made him feel not like a player, but like more of an outsider. It also made him feel like an idiot, for actually believing that it could have been otherwise. Zaleski, chosen because he was a blank slate, was showing himself to be a secretive and difficult man. "We backed him because he wanted to be a good mayor but he decided at some point that he was going to be Elliott Ness," said Jim Surdoval, who had been one of the first to leave Nick's camp for Terry's. Zaleski seemed to see corruption everywhere, launching countless investigations. Word inevitably reached the newspapers, ruining reputations, which, Nick believed, was the main goal of the inquiries in the first place.

He was certain he was a target of one or another of those investigations. Vincenza Restiano, the City Council president, was certain that she, too, was being watched, and this gnawing, unsettling suspicion soon became the basis of a most unusual friendship. Nick was a man who had few friends. Until Restiano, none of those friends were other politicians. But Vinni Restiano was not the usual type of Yonkers politician, in ways that went beyond the obvious fact that Yonkers had always been a man's town. Scattered and emotional, nervous in this newly created job, she needed Nick's help. The position of "City Council president" was really Nick's old "mayor" post, but with a different title. Soon Nick was spending more time in her office than in his own, strategizing, even role-playing the way she could run an upcoming council meeting. Nick's drink of choice by now was Sambuca, and the council president started to keep a bottle in her office credenza.

They talked about more than just the hows of politics, they talked about the whys, also. Restiano had been a member of the City Council until 1987, the volatile year in which Nick was elected mayor, and she'd lost her seat to Nicholas Longo because she favored compliance and he did not. So she knew what it was like to lose your dreams because of your beliefs. She also understood how incomplete Nick felt without those dreams, and she had felt his fear that he might never feel complete again.

She once confided to him that she had been so despondent after her 1987 loss that she could understand how people could consider taking their own lives. "I thought about it from Election Day to Christmas," she said. The type of soul attracted to politics, she knew, begins to confuse votes with love, and it pained her to go out in public in the days after she was defeated. "They didn't say, 'Vinni I love you, Vinni I love you, Vinni I love you,'" she said.

Over the months, Nick Wasicsko and Vinni Restiano talked about politics, and about life, and, more and more, about Terry Zaleski. Although his most recent twenty-six-vote victory left him no reason to trust his instincts, Nick believed that Zaleski could be beaten in the next mayoral election. The voters, he thought, would soon tire of Zaleski's "politics of investigation," and Nick planned to be in position when they did. He would never step aside for Terry Zaleski again.

Partly out of crankiness and partly according to strategy, Nick began a very public series of skirmishes with the mayor. By September of 1992 he was embroiled in one of the nastiest, a convoluted tug-of-war over the Yonkers Parking Authority. He who holds the money holds the power in any city, and the Parking Au-

Show Me a Hero

thority brought in $2.5 million in revenue each year, from parking fines and fees at the city's thirty garages. Nick's brother, Michael, was a member of the board of the Parking Authority, a job Nick had given him before leaving office. One of the first things Zaleski had done when he himself became mayor was ask Nick to ask Michael to help oust the man who ran the agency—John Zakian, who had been a supporter of Angelo Martinelli, the man Zaleski had just defeated.

At the time that Zaleski made his request, Nay also worked at the Parking Authority, and her boss was John Zakian, putting her in a precarious, uncomfortable position. Nick, still trying to show he was a team player, did as he was told, and ousted Zakian, even though it meant risking his wife's job. Now, nine months later, Nick was trying to show he was *not* a team player. He was his own man, and he could get his way at the Parking Authority if he wanted to. Robert Jean, who had replaced John Zakian, was an affable enough administrator, who had never really done anything to Nick. But this was politics, nothing personal, and Nick and Michael began lobbying other members of the board to remove Bob Jean. Citing a few irregularities in the wording of Jean's contract, they argued that he should be voted out of his position, and replaced with John Zakian.

By this time, Nay, still at the Parking Authority, was happily working for Robert Jean. The first she knew of her husband's plan to oust another of her bosses was an article in the newspaper one morning, which said that Nick believed that the agency was not being well run under Robert Jean's watch. It quoted Nick as saying that the reason he believed this was because Nay had been telling him so.

"You're trying to crucify me, aren't you?" Nay asked, knowing that she had never told him any such thing.

He promised her that her job was secure. "When John comes back," he said, "he'll be happy to have you work for him."

Terry Zaleski, however, did not want John Zakian back. He realized this was part of a bigger plan, and he wanted to stop it, now. Council elections are on a different cycle from mayoral ones, and Zaleski made it clear to Nick that he would have to defend his council seat in one short year, which was two years before he could challenge Zaleski for the prize position. The mayor sent the message that Nick would face a tough primary—Zaleski would make sure that he did—unless Nick stopped this shoving match over the Parking Authority.

Seeing how important this squabble had become to Zaleski made Nick all the more determined not to lose. He was having fun. The scramble for votes on the Parking Authority board might not compare to the heady tension of the summer of 1988, but it was an adrenaline rush, nonetheless.

Sensing that Nick would not back down, Zaleski tried to compromise. He would dismiss Robert Jean, he said, and launch a search for a replacement—anyone but John Zakian.

Certain that he had the votes he needed to get his way, Nick refused to talk about compromise. Hours before the vote on September 19, Zaleski sent Jim Surdoval over to the house on the hill to try to talk to Nick. Nick, thrilled that the Zaleski forces were actually coming to him, upped the stakes by refusing to open the door. Jim Surdoval used his car phone to call the house, and Nick didn't answer the phone, either. Eventually, Surdoval left, and the Wasicskos headed for the meeting. Nick was anticipating victory. Nay was worrying that her husband was losing his mind.

They watched, nervously, as Michael Wasicsko put forth a resolution containing a list of charges against Robert Jean, including insubordination, dereliction of duty, and malfeasance. It called for his dismissal and the reinstatement of John Zakian.

Reading from a prepared speech, Jean answered the charges in detail. Slowly it became clear to Nay that he was blaming most of the alleged wrongdoing on her. She was too angry to speak. Michael tried to, but he did not get to say much.

"You're trying to cut his throat," yelled a board member who sided with Jean. "Let him talk."

In the end, the key vote, a man Nick was sure he'd had on his side, voted to keep the sitting administrator in office. He had been persuaded, he said, by Robert Jean's answers to the accusations.

Two weeks later, Robert Jean fired Nay Wasicsko.

Show Me a Hero

"Basically she was terminated because, in our opinion, she not only was not competent but was doing everything possible to sabotage the operation of the office," he told a newspaper reporter covering the story.

The Wasicskos barely spoke for days. They rattled around silently in their grand house, staring at the renovations that they could not complete because Nay no longer had a salary.

"How could you play politics with our life?" she asked him.

He didn't promise to stop. He only promised that the next time he played, he would win.

There was an opening for a deputy city clerk at City Hall, a job that essentially reported to Nick's close friend, Vinni Restiano. John Spencer, a Republican who was also at odds with Terry Zaleski, nominated Nay for the position. A few days of articles and editorials followed, saying the appointment was a nepotistic conflict of interest, since the city clerk worked for the City Council. Those accusations didn't wound Nay, not because her skin had toughened, but because she thought they were true.

"It is a conflict of interest, absolutely," she told Nick.

But in Yonkers that has never seemed to matter. Nick abstained from the vote. Vinni lobbied the council on his behalf. Nay soon had a new job, by a vote of 4 to 2.

Trick or Treat

When Doreen lived in Schlobohm, Halloween was not a problem. She simply ignored it. The first year she moved in, she naively taped smiling paper pumpkins and grinning cardboard witches to her door, but within days the decorations disappeared.

She saw them later, stuck on someone else's door, laughing at her. It was a lasting lesson in why, when folks at Schlobohm decorate at all, they limit themselves to their windows. After that, she did nothing for Halloween. A few trick-or-treaters rang her bell each year, but she had no candy for them, and she pretended she wasn't home.

With her move across town, Halloween became a tangle of decisions. What would she tell Jaron about trick-or-treating? If she took him door-to-door, should she venture beyond the townhouses? If she did, how would the neighbors react to the arrival of her little black boy? If she didn't, how would she explain to him, and rationalize to herself, the fear that caused her to shut out the bordering world?

For a time, she latched on to the idea of a party—a way to give the children something to do, so they might not notice what else they were *not* doing. Of course, she had thought a Labor Day barbecue would be a good idea, too, and when that date rolled around she had been the only person to show up. (The meeting with Peter Smith to discuss the Con Ed bills managed to evaporate, too.) But she had agreed to be the president of the tenant association, and she didn't feel right simply letting this holiday go by.

Lacking a better idea, she called Municipal Housing and asked for help. The agency's budget, she learned, included a certain amount of money for holiday celebrations at each site. For Halloween, the site at Trenchard Street and Gaffney Place was allowed seventy-five dollars. As president, the money was Doreen's to use, as long as she provided a receipt.

So the day before Halloween found Doreen at the Sam's Club warehouse in Elmsford, loading a cart with industrial-sized packages of M&Ms, Bit o' Honeys, and Twizzlers. The total was $74.95, and Doreen carefully saved the receipt. "I think I'll keep five cents and really cause a little trouble," she thought, folding the paper and slipping it into the pocket of her jacket.

She and Jaron spent the night of October 30 on their living room floor, stuffing the goodies into brown paper lunch bags. The last thing they added were tiny cartons of unidentifiable juice, which Doreen dismissed as "quarter water," that Municipal Housing had supplied as a bonus. The next morning, Doreen knocked on every door at the site and asked for a head count. "You have one child, I give you two bags," she said. "You have two children, I give you

Show Me a Hero

four bags." The result was a reverse kind of trick-or-treating; instead of the children going to the candy, the candy came to them.

While Doreen was going door-to-door on Halloween morning, Mary was over at Clark Street, visiting Pam Johnson, the tenant who was scheduled to hold the next meeting. It had become Mary's habit to stop by a few days before these meetings, by way of gentle reminder. When she arrived this particular morning, she found Pam standing on a chair in the living room, taping cardboard ghosts to the ceiling. The couch was covered with paper napkins, plates, and cups.

"For the meeting?" Mary asked, taken aback by the display of enthusiasm.

"For the party," Pam mumbled, holding a roll of scotch tape between her teeth.

Climbing down, Pam explained that the party was a last-minute idea, a reaction—the only one she could think of—to a "problem" her younger daughter had had earlier in the week. Four-year-old Anita Johnson was "minding her business" with her own toys on her own lawn, Pam said, when a "little white girl" across the street, in one of the houses where the neighbors had taken to sitting and staring, asked if Anita would like to come over.

Pam walked her daughter to the curb, helped her across the sleepy one-way street, then returned to her stoop and watched as the two girls began to play. They seemed to be getting along just fine, Pam said, when, a short while later, Anita ran to the curb in tears and starting shrieking to her mother, demanding that Pam come and take her home.

Pam never did get a detailed explanation of what happened, but the few sketchy facts she managed to pry from her daughter were more than she needed to hear.

"The little white girl started calling her names, and said she couldn't play with her because she was black and dirty," Pam said. "She wasn't allowed to play with black kids. I told her that girl doesn't know what she's talking about."

Until that moment, Pam had been happy to be at Clark Street.

She had moved from a crumbling apartment near the School Street projects. It had no heat and hot water, it cost her $700 a month, and it was condemned two months after she moved out. There was nothing of her old neighborhood she would miss, she thought the day she left. But in the old neighborhood, no one ever refused to play with her daughter because she was black.

"I was going to have them go trick-or-treating," she told Mary, ripping open a plastic bag of black and orange balloons. Anita was going to be a ghost and her eight-year-old sister, Valentina, was going to be a witch. One black, one white. "But I can't let them go out there now," she said. "I won't let them be rejected like that."

In the days after her daughter was verbally slapped, Pam organized a party. One neighbor bought the skeletons that decorated the walls and ceilings, others provided the balloons, the cake, the paper plates, the candy apples. Municipal Housing supplied the money for the hot dogs and the sodas.

"We invited everyone from the townhouses," Pam said. "I feel bad. I would have liked to invite some of the kids from across the street. I probably should. I know I should. Do unto others. Turn the other cheek. I can't."

Finding Home

On the day after Thanksgiving, Norma was sitting in her bedroom, holding a magnifying glass and cheerfully making her Christmas shopping lists. "Ma," Tasha interrupted from the doorway, "I got something to tell you. Will you get mad?"

Norma looked up at the blurry, backlit outline of her daughter. "According to what it is," she answered.

"Ma, how'd you like to have another grandchild?" Tasha finally said.

"I got three," Norma answered. She really hadn't figured out where this was leading.

"But how would you like to have another one?"

252   *Show Me a Hero*

"Another one?" And then she understood. "Tasha, you ain't *pregnant*?"

"Yeah."

"How far?"

"Four months."

"How come you didn't tell me?"

"Because I didn't know."

"You're a liar," Norma said, but she said it gently, because she remembered writing to her father about her own pregnancy, and she was determined to stay calm. "You're a liar. You did know."

At nineteen, Tasha was not much older than Norma had been when she became pregnant with Dwayne. Unlike Norma, Tasha had not yet finished high school, and was still in the twelfth grade. Norma had worried about Tasha's happiness since the move across town. She was at an in-between age at Gaffney—much older than the oldest of the children, a few years younger than the youngest of the mothers—so she had a hard time finding friends. But, until this November morning, Norma had not worried about Tasha's future. In spite of all the temptations of Schlobohm, Bruce and Dwayne had grown into the men Norma wanted them to be, with college educations and jobs that made their mother proud. She had come to assume that Tasha would do the same.

Still trying to remain calm, Norma told Tasha to call her brother Dwayne, who had done his best during Tasha's life to fill the gap left by her father.

"You need to tell him," Norma said, handing her daughter the phone. It was advice she would regret. Dwayne immediately began insisting that Tasha have an abortion, and Norma all but grabbed the phone away again.

"I don't believe in no abortion. Never have," she yelled, so that Dwayne could easily hear. "Tasha ain't gonna have an abortion in my house."

By evening, her temper had cooled enough that she trusted herself to talk, and she tried to reason with Tasha.

"I'm gonna tell you like it is," she said. "I don't believe in abortion, but I can't tell you what to do. You're almost twenty years old. If you have an abortion you have to have it on your own. I will not go with you. If you have this baby, I can help you. I will not tell you to have an abortion and then later you throw it in my face that I made you have an abortion. I will not make you have this baby and then later have you tell me, 'Well, I didn't want the baby.' "

Sometime after that, Norma's younger son, Bruce, called.

"Ma," he said, "I know somebody that's had an abortion and they want to talk to Tasha."

Minutes later, the young woman herself was on the phone and told Norma of a clinic in White Plains, a short bus ride away, which she described as clean and safe. She volunteered to go along with Tasha for a counseling session. "They'll show her pictures of what will happen and she can make up her own mind and decide if she wants to do it."

Tasha said she wanted to go, and the woman made her an appointment, but it was snowing heavily that Saturday morning, a freak early snow, and the woman could not come to get her. There was no talk of babies or abortions all weekend. Tasha stayed in her room most of the time, and Norma decided not to intrude.

On Monday morning, Tasha came to breakfast and told her mother that she wanted to have the baby. Norma could not see the expression on her daughter's face, but her voice sounded very young and scared.

"Sure," Norma said. "I'll do everything in the world to help you."

Norma had suffered morning sickness throughout her pregnancy with Tasha, but Tasha had not inherited that tendency from her mother, and she pounced happily on Norma's suggestion that they go to a restaurant to celebrate the unborn baby. It would not be a celebration in the truest, most joyful, sense of the word. Norma knew what was in store for Tasha, and she knew how hard it would be. But she also knew that cursing your "lot in life" had no point. What happened was what happened, and then you moved on. She wanted Tasha to have what nineteen-year-old Norma had not had. And a celebratory dinner was a place to start.

Where they should go? Although it had been almost six months since she moved across town, Norma knew very little about her new neighborhood. She said it was her eyesight that kept her home, but she realized that wasn't true. Over on the west side, she had maneuvered herself around the stores of Getty Square with the help of complete strangers, and she had found her way to work by sound and touch. Here on the east side, her surroundings were safer, and, thanks to the worker from the Guild, her senses were better trained, yet she had never been to the supermarket three blocks away. Despite all the court orders and all the millions of dollars spent on the townhouses, Norma's reality came down to this: she did not feel at home on the east side. A judge can mandate housing remedies, but he cannot mandate a sense of belonging or an essence of neighborhood, and Norma had found neither.

When she asked Tasha where they might celebrate, therefore, she expected her daughter to choose the Sizzler at the shopping mall, one of the places they had gone in the days before their move. Instead, Tasha suggested the Clam House, a Yonkers landmark a few blocks from the townhouses. Norma knew the place, although she had never been inside. She could hear the music and laughter when she took her daily walks with her home health aide. She loved music, and she loved seafood. So, several evenings later, she and Tasha walked to the Clam House.

As soon as they entered, Norma was certain she had made a mistake. The restaurant was smaller than she had imagined. The tables were close together, and the feeling was intimate. She felt as if she were intruding, although she couldn't say exactly what she was intruding on. It just didn't feel like the kind of place that she wanted to be. When the hostess started to lead Norma and Tasha to their table, Norma didn't follow, and the woman asked if anything was wrong. "I think we won't be staying," Norma said, and Tasha thought she would melt from embarrassment.

"You're welcome to stay," the hostess said, smiling uncertainly.

"No thank you," Norma said. Then, remembering Tasha, she reconsidered. "We'll take it to go," she said.

Norma ordered fish and chips. Tasha ordered a hamburger plate. They waited while the hostess packed up their Styrofoam containers, and Norma could feel her daughter's quizzical stares. This *was* Tasha's home, Norma realized. While Norma was feeling out of place and uncertain, Tasha was gleeful in these shops and on these streets, a defiant self-confidence that said, "This is MY neighborhood now." And Tasha's unborn baby, well, that would be the real test. If things went as Norma hoped, that child would never view the east side as a minefield, like Norma did, or as a candy store, like Tasha. He would not be gleeful, or defiant, or grateful to live here. He would simply *live* here.

Tasha carried the warm dinners home from the Clam House, wondering, but never asking, why her mother needed to leave. Norma did not try to explain. When Tasha had set the food out on the table, Norma raised her glass of water and made a toast. "My baby's having a baby," she said. "This is a nice house for a baby."

Meeting the Poodle Lady

It was not quite 8:00 A.M., and Anita Johnson was standing by the big living room window, as she did nearly every morning, waiting for her mother to get Valentina ready for school. Anita felt more than ready to go to school herself, but she was only four, and, her mother said, in answer to the little girl's regular pleas, she would have to wait until next year.

Lucky Valentina, already in second grade, went off to the school bus each morning and into realms Anita could only imagine. All those children to play with. The way Anita saw the world, the more playmates, the better.

"Anita loves everyone," Pam Johnson liked to say of her sunny, outgoing daughter, who had inherited her mother's disposition. "Everyone loves Anita."

She used to play every day with her cousins and the others that her aunt cared for, but that was when they lived in the apartment, before they moved to the townhouse, and when her mother still worked. From the townhouse, the trip back to her aunt's apartment would mean two buses or a five-dollar cab ride each way. Pam tried to find day care for Anita on the new side of town, but there was nothing she could afford or that would take social service payments. So Pam quit her job and began to spend her days with her daughter.

For Anita, it was nice. She loved her mother. But she was sure it was not as much fun as going to school and meeting all those children. There were a few children her age in the townhouses, but not nearly enough. The one time she had tried to meet one of the white children across the street, the little girl had called her names and made her cry. Her mother would not let her cross the street again. Standing by the window in the morning, listening to Pam hurry Valentina along, Anita could see that little girl's house. She would think, in the part of her head she used for pretend, about crossing the street, knocking on the girl's door, and saying, "Hi, let's play."

On the mornings—like this morning—when Valentina was being extra pokey, Anita could also see the Poodle Lady. Around the corner, the lady walked, then down the block, past Anita's house. Every morning she came, and, whenever she could, Anita would watch her. She had three dogs on leashes, two white and one a sandy color that, to Anita, looked almost pink. Anita was afraid of dogs, but that was mostly the kind of dogs from back where she used to live. She thought she would probably like this kind of dog—all fluffy and bouncy. She wondered if the lady would let her pet them.

Anita knew her mother didn't like the Poodle Lady very much, but she was not sure why. Something about the dogs using the townhouse lawn as a bathroom. On this morning, as the woman and her trio of dogs came into view, Anita decided to ask her not to do that. Then she and the Poodle Lady could be friends. She stepped away from the window, opened the front door, and stepped into the late autumn chill without a jacket. She practically skipped down the path.

"My name is Anita, can I pet your dog?" she asked.

The woman nodded. "Pat their backs. They like that," she said.

Anita looked up. "Why do you talk like that?" she asked.

"I come from a country called Colombia," the woman answered, smiling. "It's far away from here."

Anita bent down toward the three dogs, reached out her hand, and patted the closest one, hesitantly, behind its head, grinning her happiest grin. Then she pulled her hand back quickly and held it behind her back. The dogs were soft and silky, like she had imagined they would be. She wanted to reach down and touch them again, but they had begun to tug at their leashes, and the Poodle Lady had started to walk way. As she walked, she called out her good-byes to Anita.

"Bye," Anita said back, adding hopefully, "see you tomorrow."

Christmas

Two days before Christmas, just as it was getting dark, Alma's niece, Rita, stopped at Schlobohm to visit her aunt. It had been months since she had last been to the project in which she had grown up and from which she had eagerly fled. In the six months since she and her mother had moved to the townhouses, they had been back to Schlobohm no more than two or three times.

Vague feelings of guilt at that absence brought her back now, a detour on her route home from the school where she worked as a teacher's aide. Guilt mixed with holiday spirit. She had just cashed her paycheck, and the three hundred dollars in an envelope in her purse made her feel flush and generous. So did the shopping bag she carried, filled with a half-dozen presents that she had, to her surprise, received from some of her students.

She used the back door to her Aunt Alma's building, because it was closest to the elevator, and she didn't feel like carting the bulky shopping bag up the stairs. As she opened the heavy metal door, she heard footsteps behind her, muffled, and then louder, the sound of several people running. She turned around and saw they were running toward her.

"Four kids," she would tell the police a short while later. "They were *kids*. Thirteen, fourteen, maybe fifteen years old."

She didn't remember having time to scream before they grabbed her from behind, hit her over the head with something unseen but keenly felt, and pushed her, head first, into the concrete wall. As suddenly as they appeared, they were gone. Her purse and her bag of gifts were gone, too.

She would have nightmares for weeks after that. The details differed, but, in all of them, she was being chased. When she was awake, she was constantly angry, not only at the "kids," but at herself. Thinking back, she was almost, but not completely, certain that she had seen them in Getty Square, that they had watched her cash her check, and that they followed her home. She had let them follow her home. Living in the townhouses had dulled her instincts, thinned her armor, led her to do things she should know not to do. During her years at Schlobohm she had learned how to walk like someone who should not be messed with, how to dress so she would not be a target. She had hated having to learn those rules, but she was furious now that she seemed to have forgotten them. She would never go back to Schlobohm by herself again.

The police officers found her purse, on the roof of her aunt's building, but it was empty. The bag of presents was never found. For weeks she wondered what had been inside all those sweet little boxes. She hadn't unwrapped them. She had been waiting for Christmas Eve.

The afternoon before Christmas, Pam Johnson returned home after spending the day at her mother's apartment, across town. She, Anita, and Valentina were still taking their coats off when a neighbor, clearly excited and achingly curious, knocked on the door.

"A lady was here looking for you and your girls," the neighbor said. "That lady with all the poodles."

Pam had often seen, but had never met, the Poodle Lady whom Anita was so fond of. Anita talked of the woman all the time now, and Pam knew almost nothing about her. She did not know, for instance, that the Poodle Lady's name was Lillian Cadavid, that she had moved from Colombia thirty-four years earlier, and that she had raised three children, two daughters and a son, in half of her two-family house around the corner. Pam did not know that the poodles—named Martini, Brandy, and Alexander—were not really poodles at all, but were all bichon frises, which cost between $800 and $1,200 as puppies, or that each one was a gift for a different Christmas or birthday. And she certainly did not know that it was a source of amusement to Lillian that her bichons "are not too friendly with black dogs." With other dogs, she would say, with a half-suppressed giggle, "very friendly. If it's a little white poodle, they play. But a black dog, no."

Lillian did not know Pam's name, either. Fond as she was of Anita, she never asked the little girl her last name, although they met in front of Anita's townhouse nearly every day. Lillian thought it best not to know. "So often the mother has a different last name than the child. So confusing, or awkward," she thought. In anonymity there is distance, she believed. "I'm not going to be her friend," she thought. "I won't invite her in for tea."

Lillian did not know that Pam was one of the tenants who complained to the police about the "poodles" during the first summer in the townhouses. And Pam did not know that Lillian was unrepentant when the officer approached her in the street the night of that meeting.

"I pay taxes, I don't see that anybody owns the street," she said. "The people in these houses they think I'm doing this because they're living there? Well, they don't know that this is my routine. I don't want anybody to intimidate me. For a few days I thought, 'Where can I walk my dogs now, because the houses are there?' And then I said, 'No, I'm gonna keep my route.' And I did."

All Pam knew, all she needed to know, was that Lillian was kind to Anita and Valentina, and that she had got Anita past her fear of dogs. She had got Pam past another fear, too. Knowing that one white neighbor could be friendly somehow made the other white neighbors seem less threatening.

All Lillian needed to know was that Anita was special. That seeing her stand on the curb, waiting to pet the "poodles," made the morning dog walk fun. Lillian had feared the townhouses, even protested against them, but Anita made her think the new housing might not be too bad.

About an hour after the neighbor left word that the "Poodle Lady" had been to visit, Lillian stopped by again. This time, Pam and her daughters were home, and Lillian gave them the small Christmas packages she had brought — bags filled with candies and hair ribbons — which were received with proper thank-yous. Everyone — Pam, Lillian, Anita, and Valentina — stood in the doorway while the gifts were given and received.

Pam did not invite Lillian in. Lillian did not expect her to.

Two days after Christmas, Virgilio, in a rare moment out of Alma's sight, was walking to the store. He had instructions to pick up a few groceries for his mother, and he planned a detour for a slice of pizza for himself. He practically bounced as he walked, not only because he was momentarily his own man, but because of the virginal white Nikes on his feet, two days old, first time out on the streets.

A few weeks before Christmas he had asked his mother for new sneakers, and instead of saying no, his were fine, a little dirty and worn, maybe, but fine, she had said okay, she would buy them as his Christmas present. He thanked her then, and again when he took the shoes out of their box Christmas day, but he didn't think something you need should count as a present. A present should be something you want.

As he walked up the hill out of Schlobohm, thinking of sneakers and pizza, he noticed some kids a few feet in front of him, older and unfamiliar. They were looking at each other, then looking at him. His steps slowed and lost their bounce.

"What size are your sneakers?" one of the boys asked.

"Why do you want to know?" Virgilio asked, meeting their gaze and trying to act nonchalant and tough. He had never been jumped in Schlobohm. He knew that was about to change.

"Let's take the shoes," another of the boys said. "Take the motherfuckin' shoes."

"Ten and a half," Virgilio said, and he started to run, the sneakers thudding hard against the pavement.

The boys didn't follow. His Nikes were probably the wrong size.

"His feet are too big, his feet are too big," Alma said, with laughter bordering on hysteria, when Virgilio arrived home, out of breath and without any groceries. "They left him alone because of his big feet."

Later, she scolded him. "If you weren't going anyplace special you shouldn't have worn your new sneakers," she said. She needed to believe that the incident was caused by something he did, something she could forbid him from doing again.

"They're just sneakers," Virgilio said, not too convincingly, as he kicked the shoes off into the corner of his cramped, cluttered room.

1993

The Murder

The screams began just before 8:30 A.M. at 28 Lamartine Terrace, on the southwest side of Yonkers, in a neighborhood tottering between fairly safe and somewhat frightening. "Help me, he's killing me. Help me, I'm dying," shrieked Helen Sarno, a seventy-year-old woman who lived on the seventh floor. She had thick white hair and a proud bearing. Her neighbors, and she knew many of them, called her "Miss Helen."

"Help me, he's killing me."

The couple downstairs were only half awake when they heard her. They pulled on their clothes, grabbed their baby, and ran up one flight to find the reason for the cries.

"Help me, I'm dying."

The man across the hall from Miss Helen was about to walk his dog when he heard her. He shooed the pet back into his apartment, yelled to his stepdaughter to call the police, and headed toward Miss Helen's door.

"Help me, he's killing me, help me, I'm dying."

Another neighbor on the hallway was shaving when the screams began, and he raced out wearing only his undershorts, with the Magic Shave lather still on his face and a baseball bat in his hand.

Together they banged on the locked door, and yelled, "Leave her alone," and "Open up." In time, a male voice from inside said, "It's okay. It's her son, we're having an argument."

"Help me," Miss Helen screamed again. Those were the last words from the apartment. Soon, the cries turned to moans. Minutes later, even the moaning stopped. The only sound the neighbors heard was the pounding of their own fists against the door.

More time passed. Five minutes, maybe ten, and then, suddenly, the door burst open and a man bolted into the hall. He was young and Hispanic, about twenty years old, with a slight build, about 5'4" and 120 pounds. He was wearing a jacket, green denim jeans, a red sweater, and Timberland boots, all of which were covered with blood. There was a white fuzzy winter hat pulled over his head—an attempt at disguise, perhaps? With a quick motion he yanked the door shut behind him, so it locked, keeping the neighbors from racing into the apartment.

He started to run around the men in the hallway, but there was not enough room, and his only option was to barrel through them. They tackled him, but he tried to escape, so they pounded him with their fists and with the baseball bat. He crawled a few inches, losing the hat in the process, and they tackled him again. Then he slithered out of his coat and out of their grasp, and ran down the emergency stairwell.

As he left through the front door of the building, a police cruiser, responding to a neighbor's call, pulled up and the officers saw an Hispanic man, in green jeans, a red sweater, Timberland boots, and no coat, walking onto the sidewalk. It was too cold to be without a coat on a January morning, three days into the new year. A young woman leaned out a window on an upper floor, pointed to that man, and yelled, "That's the guy, that is him. Stop him." The man dashed around the back of the building, and the officers followed. He was cornered, and, after a struggle, he was handcuffed.

"I was just trying to help the lady," he said. "They say I tried to hurt her." As the officers placed him in the cruiser, the woman at the window gave them a thumbs-up sign.

By this time, a third officer had gone upstairs, learned what had happened from the neighbors, and tried to open the locked front door. Then he climbed onto the fire escape of an adjacent apartment, in order to try the kitchen window. That, too, was locked from the inside, but he could see through the curtains into the kitchen, and what he saw was a room awash in blood. The floor was all but covered by a spreading circle of deep burgundy, looking sticky and sickening. In the center of the circle was an ice pick.

The officer asked for a blanket, which he held over the window

Show Me a Hero

with one hand while he smashed the glass pane inward with the other. Then he climbed onto the kitchen table and jumped down over the pool of blood, following two sets of bloody footprints through a small entryway and into the bedroom. It was there that he saw the elderly woman, Helen Sarno, slumped on the floor, against the side of the bed. She was dressed in a blood-saturated housecoat. There was a pocketbook open on her bed, containing a cafeteria club card from St. Joseph's Medical Center, a bus schedule, a senior citizen discount card, some grocery coupons, and thirteen dollars and sixteen cents. In her lifeless hand, she clutched a small black change purse. Later, detectives would find a single string of rosary beads inside.

The officer went to the door, unlocked it, and let the paramedics in. There was nothing they could do. Helen Sarno had died from one of five separate puncture wounds—to her face, her neck, her upper chest, her lower chest, and her back. The wound to her neck penetrated her jugular and her trachea. The wound to her back went through her lung and into her heart. That wound was four and a half inches deep, meaning the ice pick had been plunged practically to the hilt of the blade.

Detectives brought some of the neighbors out to look at the handcuffed suspect in the backseat of the police car. One at a time, they stared through the window and said, "That's him." A short while later, the prisoner was brought to the police station, where his bloody clothes were taken away as evidence, and he was given a prison-issue jumpsuit. The cuts on his head and hands were photographed, then bandaged. His fingerprints were taken, and he was questioned.

When he was asked his name, he answered, "John Mateo Santos."

When asked his address, he said, "115 Gaffney Place."

The heroics of Helen Sarno's neighbors were reported in the newspaper the next day, and John's address was soon the talk of the east side. John Santos. Now the abstract fears of the homeowners had a name. He stood for all the murderers and drug dealers that were, quite certainly, being imported from across town. That the slaying of Helen Sarno took place on the west side, near the high-rises, not on the east side, near the townhouses, was nothing but a stray, pesky fact, lost in the outrage.

The anger was aimed everywhere, at places that made sense and ones that did not. There were calls for a death sentence against John Santos, even though, at the time, New York State had no death penalty. There were calls for Peter Smith's resignation. More than one politician suggested that monitors be assigned to each of the sites, to keep tabs on who came to visit, and how long they stayed. There were demands that the townhouses be shut down and the entire exercise be declared a failure.

Mary Dorman felt the full force of the outrage. Days after John's arrest, there was a meeting of the Lincoln Park Taxpayers Association, Mary's association, but she was pointedly not invited. "Mary Dorman lied to us," a former friend of hers shouted. And, in fact, Mary had. Not knowingly, but significantly. For six months, she had been assuring her neighbors that Municipal Housing was scrupulously policing the new sites, and that anyone who caused trouble was swiftly removed. Municipal Housing leases, she had been telling critics, were only for thirty days at a time, meaning that troublemakers could be taken care of quickly and easily. But the news stories about John Santos included the fact that, to date, not a single person had been told to leave the townhouses.

Billie Rowan, of course, felt the heat, too. Two weeks after John was arrested, she was faced with eviction from Gaffney Place. Her future in the townhouses was threatened not because of what John had done—not even the dense regulations of the Housing Department hold one adult responsible for the actions of another—but because what he did brought to light the fact that he lived there in the first place. John was not on Billie's lease, but he told the arresting officers that he lived in her townhouse. If he did live there, it was grounds for her eviction.

Billie Rowan was accused of doing what people everywhere in public housing were doing and what a high percentage of her neighbors in the townhouses were doing—living with the men in their lives without benefit of marriage license or lease. Officially,

Show Me a Hero

there were three men listed on three separate leases at Trenchard Street and Gaffney Place, but, unofficially and unabashedly, there were men everywhere, at every hour. They kept their clothes in the undersized townhouse closets, slept in the bedrooms, which could barely contain their double beds, ate their meals in the beige-on-beige kitchens, received their phone calls on the phones that were not in their names, and, depending how careful they were being, often received their mail in the communal turn-key mailbox at the curb, to which they were not entitled to have a key.

They were there because the women they were with did not care about the rule. Just as Doreen James had asked her sister to stay in the early months of the housing, and then never asked her to leave, her neighbors more often than not decided that who they shared their lives with was their business, not the tenant supervisor's. It was an attitude that troubled Peter Smith, not because he couldn't change it, but because he completely understood it, making the rules far more painful to enforce.

Housing regulations require all *permanent* members of a household to be listed on a lease, meaning people who truly live there and can be expected to live there in the foreseeable future. But for too many women in the projects, permanence is a matter of definition. Was John a permanent part of Billie's life? Stopping in between stays in the penitentiary? Leaving for several nights at a time without telling her where he went? She knew she could wake up any morning to find him gone, and she would not be the only woman she knew to be suddenly and sporadically alone. Why tell Municipal Housing that something is permanent, when you aren't at all sure yourself?

But rules are rules, and despite Peter Smith's feelings of empathy, his department hired an investigator to track suspected cheaters. There was no shortage of tips for the investigator to follow, since people on the wait list for public housing in Yonkers —a list that is fifteen hundred names and five years long—often snitch on people who are already occupants of the housing. The completion of the townhouses had only increased that tendency.

Despite a healthy supply of leads, however, the allegations were usually impossible to prove. The department would call the alleged offender in for an "informal conference" on the charges, and that offender would almost always come with proof that her "paramour"—the term favored by the department's lawyers—really, truly lived someplace else. Every year, the housing authority would hold about 180 informal hearings on charges other than nonpayment of rent. Of those, only twelve to fifteen would ever be evicted.

One of those, Smith suspected, would be Billie Rowan. He had no choice but to begin proceedings against her. Too many people were watching this case, demanding that an example be made of someone.

On January 15, Smith signed a letter to Billie Rowan informing her that she was entitled to a hearing on the charges before a council of tenant representatives. She stood accused, the letter said, of violating "Paragraph No. 6 Clause B of the Resident Monthly Lease Agreement which in part states the following: The tenant agrees not to assign this lease, nor to sublet or transfer possession of the premises; nor to give accommodations to boarders or lodgers without the written consent of the management. Upon information and belief that on January 3, 1993, John M. Santos was arrested and charged with 2nd degree murder and gave his address as 115 Gaffney Place. Mr. Santos is not listed on your lease as a member of your household."

Smith knew when he signed the letter that he would not attend the hearing. Billie had two young children, and he expected that this case would break his heart. He would leave this to the agency's lawyers.

Doreen Raises Her Voice

"What's the matter with Municipal Housing?" Doreen James asked in outrage as she struggled to settle her wide self into Mary Dorman's compact car. She didn't wait for an answer. "What's the city doing this for? Punishing her for something that her guy did? She said he didn't live there. They should leave her alone. She's a fine person, she has two kids. She didn't cause the trouble. Why are they wasting their time bothering her?"

The meeting Mary and Doreen were driving toward was not, officially, about the housing. It was the first in a series of by-invitation-only meetings that Mayor Zaleski was holding, one in each quadrant of the city, to hear what neighborhood leaders had on their minds. A few days earlier, an assistant to the mayor asked Mary to contact the tenant representatives of the southeast town-house sites, and Mary had called Doreen and offered her a ride.

"He's an asshole in my book for using her address," Doreen was saying, abruptly switching the focus of her anger from the housing authority to the alleged murderer. "Our men know better than that, than to risk their women and families. So many people get busted, and they use the men's shelter as an address."

In other words, the way a man in this world protects his loved ones is to deny they are his.

"They make rules like we're children," Doreen said. "They say she broke a rule, 'cause it says in the lease, no boarders, nothing like that. But I read the lease today. The lease states that heat and hot water is included, and, for us, it isn't. Why give me a lease stating heat and hot water is included, and as soon as I fuck up something in my lease, I'm out, but they can break their part?"

The community room at the Scotti Community Center was filled with a dozen round tables, with six to eight chairs at each. Mary and Doreen sat at an empty one, near the back, and watched as the room filled. Confronting authority is harder in the flesh than in the abstract, and Doreen was far quieter than she had been in the car. Mary did almost all the talking.

"That's the mayor, at that table up there, and the people sitting with him are his commissioners—police, fire, public works, things like that," she said, giving a verbal tour of the room, not at all surprised that she recognized almost everyone and was not speaking to many of them. At Mary's own table, there was no one but Mary, Doreen, and Carolyn Dunclay, the tenant from Clark Street who had been brave enough to host Mary's first indoor meeting. "Just me and these two very black women," she thought, growing increasingly self-conscious at the glaringly empty seats around them. She talked and pointed and recited lists of names, as if she could somehow fill the chairs by filling the silence.

Finally, Sister Mary Alice from the St. John the Baptist Church walked over and joined the small, uncomfortable group. Mary gratefully jumped up, introduced the sister to Carolyn and Doreen, then headed off to the refreshment table at the back of the room to find a plate of cookies for her now respectably sized group.

She had walked only a few feet from her table when she met Tony DiPopolo, there representing the Cross County Homeowners Association. "Peter Smith has to get that lady out of Trenchard Street," he said, without pausing for small talk. "We can't have that going on."

"We have to wait and find out what happened," Mary said. "It's not fair, Tony, to just throw her out because of some bad publicity. The poor lady, she's got two kids. You don't just do that."

The meeting began forty minutes late because the representatives of the Lincoln Park Taxpayers Association, the group that had so recently spurned Mary, were not yet there. They still had not arrived by the time Zaleski finally stood up at his table near the front, described the purpose of the gathering as "finding ways to make this city even better," and asked each of his commissioners to describe who they were and what they did. When they were through, the mayor stood up again and asked everyone in the room to introduce themselves and say what organization they were from. It was like Career Day in Yonkers.

Mary coached Doreen. "When it comes to you, just get up and say what your name is and that you're the tenant representative for Trenchard," she whispered. And Doreen did get up, but introduced herself, instead, as the representative of the Andrew Smith Townhouses, which, Mary had forgotten, was the site's formal name.

Then it was Mary's turn. As she stood, she felt a shimmer of panic. Who should she say *she* was with? Her official role with the HERE program had ended six months earlier. Could she still say she was a representative of HERE? Her relationship with the Lincoln Park Taxpayers Association was strained, at best, but since no one from the group was there to contradict her, should she say she was with them?

"I'm Mary Dorman," she found herself saying. "I'm from Lincoln Park, but I'm not here representing Lincoln Park. I'm part of the HERE team, the housing relocation team, and I'm here representing the tenants in the low-income housing on the east side."

The mayor next opened the floor to a general discussion of ideas and concerns. First there was a lot of talk about graffiti. Then there was an even longer conversation about school crossing guards. Zaleski patiently explained the funding and manpower shortages that kept the city from solving both those problems. As he was speaking, several members of Save Yonkers walked in and took seats near the door. Although the mayor did not pause, Mary thought he looked momentarily alarmed.

She was alarmed, too. She knew these people, and worried that they were there to "bring up the incident with the murder."

She was feeling tough and protective on the heels of her public declaration that she stood with the tenants. "Don't you cause trouble," she thought, glaring at the group from Save Yonkers. "Because I'll get up and punch you if you do."

The murder did come up, but not because of anyone from Save Yonkers.

Tired of hearing about graffiti and such, Doreen James raised her hand, remained seated in her chair, and said what she had come to say. As soon as she started speaking, the room became silent, and it stayed that way until she was done.

"I would like to talk about the comments of the two gentlemen on the City Council," she said, referring to a report she had seen on the news the night before about the calls for action in response to the murder.

"The tenants who live in the new sites are very upset about

what they are saying. We do not like their comments about screening people, and checking on who we have as company and things like that. How would they like it if that type of thing were said about them? I'm sure they would be upset. The tenants are decent people, and the tenant who may be evicted because of this is, too. That man, Santos, did not live at Gaffney Place, and it shouldn't be assumed that he did just because he said so."

Mary listened, proud and relieved. "She was magnificent" was how Mary would describe the speech to Buddy later. "Eloquent. And her English was great. I don't think she made any mistakes as far as that goes, and I was glad because I didn't want her to mess up her English at all, the way they can do sometimes."

When Doreen had finished speaking, the police commissioner stood up to say, yes, Doreen was correct, the man in question had just been released from prison, and it was likely he was not really living anywhere. The Second Precinct officers spoke, too, and said there were no unusual problems at any of the sites.

Then Doreen raised her hand again, and asked if there were regular police patrols at the new housing sites, and the commissioner said, yes, there were patrols all the time. Why, he said, did she want to know?

"Because I never see you unless there's a problem," Doreen answered. "No one just comes around just to check how we're doing."

Speaking of graffiti, she said, as the commissioner looked uncomfortable, did the officers know that "at the park across from Trenchard, the kids hang out and do graffiti, and probably do drugs, and it's not the kids from the housing, because our kids aren't that old, it's the kids from the neighborhood"?

The commissioner and the officers consulted among themselves, then said, no, they had not known about that, but "someone would look into it." Doreen shrugged, a gesture more eloquent than her speech, her usual silent flip of the shoulders that said, "I'll believe it when you show me."

The conversation moved on to other people and other topics, but Mary heard none of it. She was too busy watching the buzz of movement around her table. First the chief officer from the Second

Show Me a Hero

Precinct came to Doreen, handed her his card, and said, "If you have a problem, please call us. We're really interested in what goes on. It doesn't have to be trouble before you call us."

Then a man Mary knew from her protest days, and who snubbed her in public in the months since she had joined the housing program, came over to talk to Doreen. He complimented her on her words, and then suggested she take pictures of the graffiti in her playground as evidence of the problem. Mary was dumbstruck. "This was one of the bigots," she said during her kitchen postmortem with Buddy. "I have no idea how she won him over."

Finally, Tony DiPopolo appeared at Doreen's elbow. He was standing just two or three feet from Mary, and he had to realize that she could hear every word. Without looking at Mary, he, too, complimented Doreen. "What you said about that poor lady was very good," he said. "Well, if he didn't live there, I hope they don't throw her out."

The Fear That Never Goes Away

The day after the mayor's meeting, someone shattered Nick's fourth-floor office window from the outside.

"Probably a prank," the officers told him, and he tried hard to believe them.

The next morning, the telephone woke Nick and Nay at 7:30. It was not the private line, but the one listed in the telephone book and paid for by the City of Yonkers, a perk granted to all elected officials so they might seem more accessible. From their bed, the Wasicskos could hear the muffled tape of the answering machine, and any thoughts of more sleep ended as soon as the frantic caller left her message.

Something about a dead cat—their cat?—and a car. They pulled on sweats, laced up winter boots, added hats, gloves, and scarves, and went outside.

Their car was parked at the bottom of their long driveway, as it had been all winter, a precaution against possible snowstorms. They had to trudge nearly all the way to the sidewalk, therefore, before they saw what someone clearly wanted them to see: lying on the windshield was an orange tabby, one of a group of strays Nick had adopted during this particularly cold winter.

The cats never came into the house, because the dog tortured them and they made Nay sneeze. But every night after dinner, Nick brought out a piece of aluminum foil piled with leftovers and placed it by the front door. He also covered the floor of the outside shed with blankets, so the animals would have some place relatively warm to sleep.

Now one of those cats—the one who looked like Morris in the Nine Lives television commercials—was dead, staring at them blankly with still opened eyes. They did not want to touch the animal, but from where they stood they could see a wound in its throat and another in its left leg—two round, bloody circles. Neither Nick nor Nay had ever seen a bullet wound before. They had no doubt that they were seeing two now.

Lying next to the frozen creature was a well-used leather glove— a work glove of Nick's that he kept in the garage next to the house. The glove scared them more than the grisly cat. Had it not been there, they could have dismissed the incident as an odd happening not directed specifically at them. But the glove snatched away any such hope. The glove made it clear that someone had been up their hill, next to their house. More important, it made it clear that someone wanted them to know he had been there.

"You go in the house, I'll take care of this," Nick said, and Nay practically ran back indoors.

The police came a few minutes later. They took some pictures, asked some questions, then carried off the cat.

"They think it's a prank," Nick reported, after they had left.

"They took that glove from our *garage*," Nay said, frightened in spite of the window alarms and motion detectors they had installed years ago, during the first round of renovations. "If they can get into the garage, they can get into the house."

"They killed what they thought was my cat," Nick said. "I've gotten bullets in the mail, but . . ."

The sentence hung unfinished in the air for a while, because neither of them wanted to complete that thought out loud.

Billie's Hearing

Billie Rowan took the number 20 bus up Central Avenue on the morning of her eviction hearing. She had persuaded her mother to take care of Shanda for a few hours, but two children were more than the woman was willing to handle, so Johnny came along with Billie.

He fell asleep on the bus, and did not wake up as Billie carried him into the squat, mustard brick headquarters of Municipal Housing. He slept through the ride on the elevator, too, and the walk down the shabby corridor to the conference room, and he stayed asleep as she moved him from one arm to the other, while she shrugged out of her winter coat. She didn't dare try to remove his coat, for fear that he would not sleep through that. So she took her seat, settling her bundled, dreaming son on her lap.

As those who would judge her arrived, they cooed their concerns for the little boy. "Why don't you lay him on the floor? Wouldn't he be more comfortable?" they asked, but Billie said no. She wanted to point out that this same child was the one whose house they were trying to snatch away, but she sensed that the less she said, the better. During the questioning that followed, she held Johnny against her, a shield wrapped in a parka and mittens.

The two of them were seated at one end of the table, near the door. "It's like it's dinnertime at Central Avenue," she thought, "and they're all here to eat *me*." At the head of this feast were two white men who looked like lawyers. They introduced themselves, but Billie saw no reason to try to remember their names. Along the sides of the table were five women, most of whom looked like her. Same skin color, about the same age, probably all mothers, too. They were the members of the Tenants Committee, the ones who would decide her future.

Billie was relieved that she already had some acquaintance with two of them. She fully expected she could talk her way out of this mess, if she could just speak to people who would understand. Sadie Young Jefferson, who seemed to be acting like the boss of the group, had been Billie's actual boss when she worked, years ago, as a trainee during a county employment program, answering telephones in a government office. Next to Sadie was Caliope James, also a member of READY, and Doreen's great-aunt. When John was first arrested, Doreen had told Billie, "Call if you need anything." Maybe Doreen could help after all.

The man who seemed to be the head lawyer opened the meeting by explaining that Billie was being "evicted for violating Paragraph 1, Paragraph 6B, Paragraph 11, and Paragraph 21 of her lease. The essence is that she has living with her a person that she did not report to her tenant supervisor and under federal regulations that should be reported in order to determine the accuracy of her rent."

Under the housing authority's rules governing eviction hearings, he explained, Billie was to speak first and "present her evidence to refute the finding of the Housing Authority that she be evicted." Then he asked that Billie be sworn in, like in the movies, and she was told it was her turn to speak.

"They told me I would be getting evicted because John Santos was residing with me, which was not true," she said, holding Johnny tight with one hand, and taking a folded sheet of paper from her pocket with the other. "He was released and his place of residence was 132 Bruce Avenue. I have a paper here stating that. And I feel I shouldn't get evicted because he was not residing with me. With whatever proof you have, he was not residing with me."

She handed the letter to the lawyer, who unfolded it, read it, and did not look very impressed. For the first time Billie wondered if she should have brought her own lawyer or, at least, a friend.

"This only indicates that as of August 12 he indicated to the State of New York Executive Department Division of Parole in his Certificate of Release to parole supervision that he would reside with his mother, Carolina Santos, at 132 Bruce Street," the lawyer said. "Do you intend to produce Carolina Santos as a witness?"

"Yes," Billie said. "She'll make it here." She said it with as much confidence as she could fake, since she had not even thought of asking Carolina to come. Then she paused for a moment, and decided she should lie as little as possible. "Maybe if I can get her to come in or maybe write a statement and get it notarized or whatever and bring it in, then I would do that," she said.

Sadie started to speak. She sounded warmer toward Billie than the lawyer, but not nearly as sympathetic as Billie had hoped. "Do you know this gentleman, by the way?" Sadie asked. "Do you know that man that they're talking about in that letter there?"

It was a tone that seemed to say, Tell us you never met the man, Billie, and this will all be over. But Billie knew she could never get away with that.

"Yes," she said.

"How do you know him?"

"He's my boyfriend. He's the father of my two children." This was promising, Billie thought. Maybe if she could explain how she was trying to make a life with John, trying to make them into a family, maybe that would seem more important than the details of the lease. But another tenant interrupted Sadie, and brought the questioning back to the letter Billie had introduced as her only piece of evidence.

"Just because it states on that piece of paper that he said he was going to reside there doesn't mean anything," she said. "I could say I live in Washington, D.C."

"I understand," Billie said. "But I'm here now because he said he accidentally put my address and they want to evict me for that."

Caliope James asked, "If he was living at 132 Bruce Avenue, why would he give your address?"

"Probably under shock or whatever," Billie said. "I spoke with him and he just answered right away, he said."

"Why," the lawyer asked, "would he give that address when he indicated in writing to the parole board he was going to live at 132 Bruce Ave?"

"Like I said, he was being arrested for murder."

Sadie broke in, trying, it seemed to Billie, to provide a way out. "Has he ever stayed on your premises?" she asked.

Billie certainly couldn't tell them the truth.

"Well, no. He came to visit frequently. He was there constantly because of the kids and because of me."

"But he never lived there?"

"No, he never lived there."

The lawyer looked as if he knew better. "Did you tell anybody that Mr. Santos lived with you?" he asked.

"No."

"Did you tell your caseworker?"

Billie thought of the glass-walled cubicle at the Social Services office, of sitting there with John and signing form after form, declaring him an "essential person" in her household. Signature after signature, hers and then his, saying that they live together, and pool their money together, and prepare meals together. She had gone with him to make the changes soon after her abortion. It wasn't a baby, but she thought it might prove that she still loved him. And the extra eighty-four dollars a month his presence would bring wouldn't hurt. It would pay the bills, and make John feel like he was the man around the house.

Of course, she should have realized that this lawyer would find out about that.

"Yes or no," the lawyer said, while she hesitated. "Did you tell your caseworker?"

"No. I did not."

"Did you tell Mr. Santos' parole officer?"

All those visits to the townhouse to check on John. Naturally he would know about that, too.

"No."

"You didn't tell any of these people that he lived with you?"

"No."

"When you went for your grant, did you indicate to the Department of Social Services that Mr. Santos was living with you?"

"Well, no."

"Are you, in fact, receiving an additional grant because Mr. Santos is allegedly living with you?"

"When he was home I was receiving, yes, a grant for him."

"So you did report to the Department of Social Services that he was living with you, did you not? You're under oath."

"Yes," Billie said, softly. "Yes."

She tried to make the argument that John wasn't really living at 115 Gaffney, but that the money was coming to her house instead of his house, for personal reasons that she couldn't explain. Why then, the lawyer asked, was the monthly check made out to Billie? Why didn't John receive a separate check, instead of Billie's receiving her regular monthly check, with an increase of eighty-four dollars after John's name was added?

She had no answer to that because there was only one possible answer, but she could not say it. John's money was a part of her grant because John was a part of her household. Instead, she said weakly, "If I knew it was something under false pretenses or whatever, I wouldn't have done it that way."

The lawyer would not let that rest, either. "How long have you been under a grant?" he asked.

"Maybe two or three years."

"In that period of time you've visited the Department of Social Services several times to give information regarding how much you're going to receive in the form of a grant, right?"

"Yes."

"And they've advised you as to how you're entitled to a grant, did they not?"

"Yes."

"Did they not tell you the only way you can get a grant is for the people residing with you?"

"Well, not that I remember. It's been a while."

"Are you trying to tell me I can get a grant for someone who doesn't live with me? How can your grant go up if you're just telling them that 'he doesn't live with me'? You know better. You've been on social services for two years. You know you can't get an increase in a grant unless you tell them, 'I have another child who resides with me' or 'Someone else has moved in with me and I need additional moneys to support them.' You know that."

Billie said nothing.

Sadie spoke next, and any trace of sympathy was gone. Her look was the one a stern teacher gives a troublemaker. READY's latest project was the formation of a screening committee to make sure only the most responsible applicants would be allowed the privilege of living in public housing, and Sadie's tone made it clear that Billie was to be an example to others.

"Let me say this to you," she said. "These people that you see here are residents of public housing. So we know what we put on an application. It is not like we come out of the sky and don't know Housing. We are familiar with Housing, their rules and regulations." In other words: We know he would not have been put on your grant unless he lived with you, and we know that you know that that is against the rules.

From there the conversation became ever more hostile. Little Johnny felt hot against Billie's chest. She couldn't believe the sound of her pounding heart did not wake him.

"Since, I take it, he is incarcerated," Sadie asked, "has D.S.S. been in touch with you and pulled that money out of your grant, or are you still getting it?"

"No," Billie answered, she had not stopped the money yet. "I've been going through emotional changes. I haven't even gotten to them yet."

"In other words," said Sadie, "you're still receiving money for him?"

"Yes."

"Is that legal?" asked the lawyer, clearly quite interested.

"No," Sadie said.

"No," Billie agreed. "I have to get in touch with them."

Sadie nodded curtly. "I have no more questions," she said.

"Do you have any more evidence to give?" Billie was asked, and she said she did not.

The lawyer then called a number of witnesses, all of whom worked for the Housing Authority and all of whom testified that the rules were explained to every tenant. Next, the lawyer brought out the sheets from the Department of Social Services, showing four people listed as members of Billie's household: Billie herself,

John Santos, Shanda Santos, and John Billlie Santos Jr. He brought in John's parole officer, Thomas Downer, who described how, at John's first meeting, "he informed me that he was moving in with Ms. Rowan at 115 Gaffney."

"Were you satisfied that he was living at 115 Gaffney?" the lawyer asked, after the parole officer described his visits to the townhouse to check on John.

"Completely," the officer said.

"Did you tell Mr. Downer that he was living there and that you agreed for him to live there?" the lawyer asked Billie.

"Yes," Billie said, having given up completely. "I told him that. Yes. The answer is yes."

As each witness testified, someone reminded Billie that she could ask questions, and, each time, she answered that she had no questions. When all the witnesses had finished, Sadie turned to her and said, with a mixture of curiosity and concern, "Ms. Rowan, because of the seriousness of this, and you have two children, and it is a possibility you might be evicted, did you ever consider bringing someone to represent you? I'm talking about Legal Services or something?"

"Well, no," Billie said, certain now that that would have been a good idea. "I didn't know of no one to contact."

The lawyer started to gather his papers together. "I have no further evidence to introduce," he said, "and I have no further witnesses. Ms. Rowan is free to make whatever statements she wants to the hearing panel."

Billie shrugged. "I have nothing to say."

The lawyer did. "Briefly," he said, addressing the committee, "I can state that she's offered no concrete evidence to substantiate the fact that Mr. Santos was living with his mother and not living with her. You have the uncontroverted evidence of these witnesses and the documentary evidence that substantially proves that he was, in fact, living with her. I, therefore, would hope this panel would move for her eviction.

"Okay," the lawyer said. "That's it. You have thirty days to make your decision."

Out in the Street

One of the municipal tasks that appears to strain the abilities of the City of Yonkers is plowing snow. Despite the fact that Westchester County usually sees at least one major snowfall a year, the plows and salt spreaders of Yonkers still struggle with the task. Days after streets in neighboring villages have been cleared down to blacktop, cars in Yonkers are still driving on gray-brown carpets, packed to ice by time and traffic.

It's not that the plows don't come by. They just don't have much effect. Instead of clearing the snow, they seem to push it around or flatten it down, and the streets are often as slick when they leave as when they arrive. The inconvenience and mess result in a blizzard of letters to the local editorial page, followed by explanations from Parks Department officials (cars parked illegally on narrow side-streets are mentioned frequently) and promises from city leaders that the situation will be studied.

So when more than a foot of snow fell on Yonkers in March 1993, it was entirely predictable that the road through the center of the Andrew Smith townhouses was not properly plowed. What was striking was how completely it was not plowed. Two days after the storm, when the surrounding side streets had at least had a snowy path of sorts carved down their centers, the drifts were still thigh-high on Gaffney Place. The plows zigged and zagged throughout the neighborhood, but never turned into the townhouses. Those in charge of such things had not added the new extension of the street to the plowing schedule. It was as if the townhouses simply weren't there.

Billie Rowan trudged through the snow to reach her mailbox that March morning. She hadn't bothered with a coat, and by the time she slogged to the sidewalk and back, she was shivering and the few envelopes were wet.

The first one she opened was her welfare check from Social Services, reduced to $479 a month now because the lawyer at Municipal Housing had sent a letter saying John was no longer entitled to his $84 allotment.

Next in the pile was a long, handwritten letter from John, addressed to Billie Santos. Like the others he had sent from the county jail over the months, this letter was upbeat. "He's okay, because his fingerprints is not on the ice pick" was how she described them. "They still want to hold him, though, being that he was there when it happened, so I don't know, maybe he'll be released soon." She was almost certain that she believed him when he said he didn't kill the woman, but she was also angry with him. If she had chosen to have a third baby, rather than an abortion, he would have been in prison for the birth of that child, too.

The last letter in the stack was from Municipal Housing, and Billie thought about throwing that one directly into the trash, pretending it never existed. Instead, she ripped it open at the side, then waded through two pages of dense legalese, titled "Recommendations of Hearing Committee." The information she was looking for was in the last paragraph: "After hearing all the testimony and reviewing the exhibits introduced into evidence, the Resident Hearing Committee . . . recommended for the eviction of Billie Rowan, 115 Gaffney Place." She was told to be out by the end of the month.

She knew she could fight back if she wanted to. Public largesse in all forms comes with an elaborate, cumbersome appeals process, and Billie knew the odds were she would lose in the end—every one she knew of seemed to—but the fight could last a long time, and she would be allowed to stay in the townhouse until it was over. She just didn't have the stomach for that route. John would be home soon, she figured, and she would probably forgive him. Her plan was not to fight, but to flee. Away from Yonkers. Maybe South Carolina, where she had distant, rarely seen family.

Several days after the snowstorm, Billie searched through the classifieds for a new apartment, a temporary stopping place on the way to her new life. She was not at all surprised to find that there were very few places she could afford. She was paying—or, more accurately, Social Services was paying—$271 a month for her townhouse. John's sister, Yolanda, had agreed to share the new place with her, so they would need something large enough for the two women and their four children. A two-bedroom would do, if some of the children slept in the living room. They could afford about $600 a month. In Yonkers, which has the lowest average rents in southern Westchester, the average rent for a two-bedroom at the time was $889, and even a one-bedroom, at an average rent of $682, was more than she could afford.

Most of the ads in the real estate listings hinted at a world that had nothing to do with Billie's life. Duplexes with gardens; six rooms with a balcony; two bedrooms with an on-site gym and a pool. All for more than $1,200 a month. Those that were the right price — "1 BR apt, freshly painted $659/mo"; "1 BR good area. Elev. $520 mo" — were too small. Those that were the right size — "Charming 4 rooms (2 bedrms), eat-in kitchen, elevator building, $750" — were too expensive. And some, even if she could some-how afford them, did not want her: "3 rms. Nice apt in private house. Nr RR Sta. Working couple pref. Ref. req."

A few ads, on the other hand, were clearly seeking her business and that of others receiving DSS checks from the Department of Social Services:

"YONKERS, DSS OK, Studio, 1,2,3 & 4 BR apts, $500 & up. IMMEDIATE. Natuzzi."

"YONKERS 1,2,3 & 4 Bdrm apts, DSS OK, Gd area. Lv msg."

"YONKERS 1,2 & 3 BR, A1 Condition, $500 & up. Immediate occup. Ridgeview Realty."

She called the last of these numbers, the one that sounded the most like a *real* ad, and the only one that listed the number of an agency, rather than someone's last name or some anonymous in-structions to leave a message. A broker named Elias Rabady an-swered her call and told her he specialized in apartments on the southwest side of town. Not that he lived there — he lived several miles away, in the far more affluent village of Ardsley (average two-bedroom rent: $1,083). But he represented several landlords in southwest Yonkers, on the "tree streets" — Elm, Maple, Chestnut, Poplar, Ash. Billie knew the area well. It was where people lived until they were lucky enough to qualify for a shabby, noisy, de-pressing apartment in Schlobohm.

As a rule, Mr. Rabady sternly explained, Ridgeview Realty did not like renting to single-women-with-children-who-want-to-share, because "you have a fight, someone moves out, and then you call and say you can't pay the rent anymore." But this was a rule that was regularly broken, because single sharers with children were often the only apartment seekers willing to live on many of the tree streets. So Billie and Yolanda were shown a four-room apartment at 63 Oak Street, a seedy, redbrick walk-up that even Mr. Rabady described as "a little crummy."

There was trash piled up out front, and a smell that seemed equal parts cooking grease and stagnation, even on a frigid day. The apartment, one of nine in the building, was dark and cramped, but reasonably clean. There was no refrigerator, but the heat seemed to work and was included in the rent, which was $650 a month. A one-month security deposit was required, as well as a broker's fee of 15 percent of the yearly rent, or $1,170.

Billie and Yolanda said they would take it. Mr. Rabady filled out the Shelter Verification forms, sections A, B, and C, as required by Social Services to approve payment. He spelled Billie's name wrong on the application—instead of Rowan, he wrote Rowanne—and indicated that monthly checks be sent to the landlord at a P.O. box, even though he had said the landlord and his family lived "right down the block from this building."

Billie dragged herself home, defeated. She sat in the kitchen, in the dark, for what seemed like an hour. The children had not eaten dinner, but she didn't have the energy to fix a meal. She didn't even have the energy to move. When she had lived in Schlobohm, she had always guessed that there was a better life. Now she *knew* that there was. It had been easier before, when she could only guess what she was missing. How could she bear to live with the certainty of what she did not have?

The next morning, at the mailbox, Billie crossed paths with Doreen James.

"You're going backward," Doreen lectured when Billie told her about the apartment. "You can't let them push you backward. Your man screwed you. It happens. Don't screw yourself double by not fighting back."

Billie did not move to Oak Street. She simply stayed where she was, past the March 31 deadline, in spite of the notice that arrived in her mailbox to inform her that Municipal Housing had asked the city court of Yonkers to enforce her eviction. A court hearing, the letter said, was scheduled for May 1. Two days before that hearing, on April 29, Billie called Westchester/Putnam Legal Services, whose number she had got from Doreen James. In surprisingly little time, papers were filed on her behalf challenging the city court's jurisdiction over the case, and her future was put on indefinite hold while the Supreme Court of Westchester County considered that challenge.

She never contacted Mr. Rabady to say she would not be moving to Oak Street. She simply did not send him her money, and he soon figured out that she and Yolanda would not be coming. A short while later, he threw her file out.

A Petition

Norma O'Neal had never met Billie Rowan before the afternoon that Billie arrived at Norma's door, carrying a petition and a pen. Norma had certainly heard of Billie a lot in recent weeks, however, ever since her boyfriend's arrest had made her the talk of Gaffney Place.

"I know about your troubles," Norma said after Billie hesitantly introduced herself. Norma has always had a soft spot for people with troubles, and she asked Billie to "come on inside and sit down."

Seated on the couch, Billie explained to Norma that her Legal Services lawyer thought a petition signed by the neighbors, saying that they wanted her to stay, might help her case. Billie had written out the message herself, at the top of the page, in round, artistic letters. Because Norma could not read the words, Billie read them to her:

"We the undersigned," it said, *"see's Billie Rowan as posing no*

threat to our community. She is a very loving and kind neighbor &
should remain a tenant of the Andrew Smith Townhouses. She has
had no complaints & shows compassion towards others. We think she
deserves another shot for her and her children's sake for they to may
suffer for anothers man misfortune."

As she read, Norma rocked the basket of her month-old grand-
son, Shaquille, born to Tasha in May after a difficult labor and an
emergency cesarean section. He was a fussy baby, and sometimes
he cried from midnight to dawn. Norma walked the floor with him
those nights, grateful to being doing so on Gaffney Place instead of
back in Schlobohm. It felt so much more hopeful to have a baby
here, where it did not feel like tempting fate to plan for the future.

"If they make you leave, that's not fair to your children," Norma
told Billie. She reached over to take the petition, and Billie placed
it in her hands. "It's not fair for children to be paying for something that older folks did.

"You can't say, because he left your house and did this someplace else that it's your fault," she continued. "That's just like, say,
Tasha, if she goes across town and kills somebody, you gonna
throw me out of my house because of her?"

"He didn't live with me," Billie said. The lie came more easily
now. "He was around all the time because of the children and
everything, but he lived at his mother's. His address was his
mother's."

"And maybe he sleeps over once in a while," Norma said, with a
friendly, conspiratorial wink. "Is that anyone's nevermind?"

She took the pen that Billie offered. In shaky, oversized hand-
writing, she signed her name.

Nick Runs One Last Time

Nick began the summer as he had begun
so many other summers—deciding whether he wanted to run in
the next election, and, if so, what office he wanted to run for. A

citywide redistricting plan was to take effect during the election of 1993, and the way the lines had been redrawn, Nick's house was in a heavily Hispanic district. A local activist named Fernando Fuentes had made it clear he would run for that seat, and Nick was not eager to challenge him.

The only other options, as he saw them, were to move across town or to run for city judge. The first was out of the question. He had already poured too much money into his house. The second was appealing, but when he approached the executive committee of the Democratic party and told them of his plans, the response was frosty. The committee, comprised almost completely of people loyal to Terry Zaleski, said they were sorry, but there was already a strong Democrat running for that position. Given Nick's combative relationship with Zaleski, the mayor's refusal of support only made Nick more determined.

Hoping to make an end run around the mayor, Nick approached Vinni Restiano for help. He asked her to "carry his petitions," a common practice in local elections, in which the supporters of one candidate gather signatures for their candidate as well as a second candidate. In effect, he was asking for her endorsement, her partnership, and he was stunned when he did not get it. Not knowing of his plans, she had already promised her support to another candidate for city judge and she intended to keep her word.

What happened next would be the subject of much debate after the election. The way Nick described it, he was approached by Jim Surdoval, on behalf of Terry Zaleski, with a suggestion. There was an office perfect for Nick's experience and talents, Nick would remember being told by Surdoval — City Council president. If he challenged Vinni Restiano for that position, the mayor would support him.

Surdoval, in turn, would remember that the suggestion of such a scenario "definitely came from Nick," but that "we embraced it quickly." Zaleski's office had polling data that showed Nick was much better known than Restiano, and would probably win a primary. In the general election, however, Nick was much weaker. A primary between Restiano and Wasicsko could well benefit

Zaleski, by eliminating both hostile council members at the same time, Surdoval said.

The fact that the party had already given its support to Restiano did not seem to bother either Jim Surdoval or Terry Zaleski. That support had been given earlier in the year, before the budget process had gotten under way, and before Restiano had voted to override the mayor's veto of the budget, something Zaleski refused to forgive.

The fact that Restiano was a friend, and that Nay worked closely with her at City Hall, did bother Nick, but he didn't feel he had a choice. He needed to run for office in 1993, and this seemed to be the only office available. He felt he had to hold his nose and do it. The council president's salary of $46,507 was twice what he earned right now. Zaleski's offer of assistance was a calculated one, he knew, but he had turned low expectations to his advantage before, and he liked the idea of shocking the Zaleski camp with a victory. In the meantime, he would try not to dwell on the image of his petitions being carried by Zaleski's supporters.

He took the deal.

Telling Nay turned uglier than he had expected. She was kneeling on the ground outside the house when he came home, pulling weeds in the scruffy square of dirt that she stubbornly insisted would one day be a garden.

"I'm going to primary Vinni," he said.

She jumped to her feet. "Stay the hell away from me," she said, pitching her spade and her gloves to the ground, then running toward the house. "I don't think I know you anymore."

When she reached the doorway, she turned and glared. "You know what?" she shouted. "I'm going to work for Vinni. What the hell are you doing this for?"

Nick could not rally the strength to tell Restiano himself. He knew the news would reach her, and he was not surprised when the phone rang several hours later. She was calling from her car and Nick couldn't tell if they had a bad connection or if she had been crying.

"So, you made your decision," she said. "What a coward. You

couldn't pick up the phone and tell me yourself? After all we were to each other, the friendship we had."

Nick noticed that she spoke of their friendship in the past tense.

"Don't think this is going to be easy," she warned. "I know you've gotta do what you've gotta do. But I'm gonna do what I'm gonna do."

Nick did not make his plans public for several weeks, and when he did, he did not hold a formal news conference. He announced his candidacy by calling the newspaper and saying "I plan to run for council president."

In the interview that followed that announcement, he sounded lukewarm about his own candidacy. He was running, he said, because he was "disillusioned about how this new form of government is working." Restiano, he said, had made "what I consider to be some bad judgments," and Yonkers government is "at a standstill." He concluded by saying that "one of the improvements that could be made" would be to have "an experienced person in the council president's office, who would be able to work with all the parties and use some leadership to make the government work in spite of personalities."

He hoped it sounded more rousing than it felt.

Alma Searches for Home, Pam Finds It

Alma Febles followed the news about Billie Rowan closely, watching Yonkers Cable nightly for updates, listening to gossip on the bus or at the market, then trying to place what she learned on the matrix of what was good and bad for her own life. In the days after John Santos was arrested, when politicians and homeowners were screaming with a rage that had not been seen in Yonkers since 1988, Alma was distraught. She knew 121 more townhouses were scheduled to be built—eventually. But the furor over the murder, she feared, might mean that "eventually" would never come.

Show Me a Hero

She lost her appetite worrying about the townhouses. She tossed for hours at bedtime, then awoke with a start in the middle of the night and could not get back to sleep. She cried whenever she thought the children weren't listening. She paced and fretted and all but fell apart.

Over time, her anguish deepened. If Billie Rowan was found guilty by Municipal Housing, the news reports said, she would be the first east side tenant to be forced to leave. One vacated apartment in one year, and it took a murder to bring that one about. So there would be no new townhouses, she was certain, and there would be no vacancies in the existing townhouses. She had no way out.

Tentatively, fearfully, she began to search for an apartment outside the projects. Unlike Billie, who looked at places she could afford and was unsettled by what her money could buy, Alma looked at places where she would actually want to live—three-bedroom apartments in safe neighborhoods—and was chastened by what they cost.

A friend at work told her about an apartment for rent across the street from Fitzgerald & Fitzgerald. It had two bedrooms, but they were very big, so she and Leyda could share. The building was clean and safe, with an intercom system and new carpeting in the lobby. For days, Alma stood outside her office and stared at that building, imagining what it would be like to take a key from her pocket and open its lock, to ride in its elevator, to invite people over for parties, to call it home. One morning, with a burst of resolve, she dialed the number given to her by the friend, and learned that the rent was $825.

With a recent raise, Alma earned $360 a week at Fitzgerald & Fitzgerald, or $18,720 a year, plus some Social Security payments for the children. Hers was a real job, like the ones that politicians are always suggesting welfare mothers get, and she was no longer on the public dole. Her rent was 30 percent of her gross income, or $532 a month. After deductions for health insurance and taxes, however, she took home $256 a week, or $1,109 a month, meaning her rent was nearly half of her disposable income. She had no savings, because the philosophy behind a sliding rent scale—charge as much as the tenant can pay—does not allow for savings. So she certainly was not able to spend $300 extra dollars each month for a new apartment.

Briefly, she thought of renting one of these palaces anyway, because her children were asking her almost nightly when they were going to move. Frankie, barred from the Schlobohm playground by Alma's rules, was becoming increasingly pale, pudgy, and withdrawn. But at least he still listened when she told him to stay inside. Virgilio, a freshman in high school, had begun to come home long after school ended, saying only that he had been out with "friends." Alma had never met any of his "friends." He would not invite them over, because he would not tell them where he lived. She could find a second job, she thought, or beg the children's fathers for some help. Maybe that would allow her to live where she thought she should live, at least for a while. She knew that things would probably come crashing down around her eventually, and she would likely end up back in public housing, but she would have had a shot, somewhat like a prisoner who knows he will be caught, but attempts to escape nonetheless, for the brief pleasure of freedom.

Alma eventually gave up on that plan, however, not because of the money, but because of the rules. If she moved out of Schlobohm, she would lose her place on the waiting list for the townhouses. She had been entered in the lottery as a public-housing tenant, and if she was no longer receiving public-housing assistance, she learned, she would lose any chance, however slim, of moving to the one place she both wanted to live in and could afford.

When school ended, she sent Frankie and Virgilio to Santo Domingo for most of the summer, where each one stayed with his own father, each of whom paid for one ticket. She worried constantly, particularly about Frankie, but she didn't see that she had any choice but to let him go.

In early August, feeling baked by the concrete and brick of Schlobohm, she spent $300 she did not have to fly herself and Leyda to Florida, the cheapest summer destination she could find. They stayed with friends—Alma slept on the couch and Leyda on

Show Me a Hero

the floor—and they swam in the ocean, but the change of scene did not lift the depression that had enveloped her since John Santos was arrested. When her sons arrived back home, they were tanned and rested. Frankie had lost a lot of weight and looked more like a lean teen and less like a chubby boy. He had spent all his days outside, he said, riding bikes, playing ball, and "doing stuff kids do."

It was during the brutal heat waves of summer that Pam Johnson loved her townhouse the most. The thermometer would swear it was as hot on the west side as it was here on the east side, but it felt worlds cooler. The difference certainly had nothing to do with air conditioning, because that was as unaffordable a luxury to her here as it had been on the other side of town. Each townhouse was built with pre-cut aluminum sleeves where air conditioners might be placed, but only one or two of those slots were actually used in all the townhouses of Clark Street. In the homes that faced the townhouses, the houses that had been here first, beige metal casings jutted out of countless windows and walls, humming the heat away. So, when the weather was hot, the people on Pam's side of the street went outside to cool off, while the people on the other side of the street went inside.

One August day, when it was 100 degrees before lunch, Pam dragged her daughters' plastic pool onto the front lawn and filled it with water. She didn't put the pool in the backyard, where she knew it probably belonged, because the engineers who built the townhouses had not thought that drains were necessary in every backyard, and an afternoon of water play there would leave the grass so flooded it would take weeks to dry. But the front yard sloped down, toward the drains in the street, and there were ample spigots out front, so out front was where Anita and Valentina played.

As always happened when Pam filled the pool, children materialized from the other townhouses, wearing bathing suits if they had them, shorts if they did not. And, as also always happened when Pam filled the pool, the neighbors across the street peered from their windows, and sometimes from their front stoops, not saying anything, just staring.

There was still hostility from those neighbors. The Man in the Brown House, for instance, who often yelled at the children, "Go home, go home, I don't want you on this side of the street." But there were also signs—perhaps it was the weather—of a possible thaw. There was the Poodle Lady, who had followed her Christmas presents with Easter baskets, and then started to bring treats for no reason—headbands, coloring books, hair barrettes. And there was the Man with the Rottweiler, who had stopped letting his dog stand and growl behind the Plexiglas storm door, where it had petrified the children. One day, Pam passed him while he was walking the dog, and he nodded hello. More recently, when a few children from the townhouses were playing a radio while standing on a corner, leading some anonymous homeowner to call the police, the Man with the Rottweiler came out to tell the officers that the music wasn't really too loud.

Watching the townhouse children play, Pam saw pure happiness. She wondered what the neighbors across the street saw when they watched the same scene. She suspected they thought it was too noisy, or too public, or too something, and she half expected the Man in the Brown House to step out and tell her so. The splashing had been under way for about a half hour, when Valentina went running into the house, then came racing back, her arms filled with plastic buckets. She and Anita filled them from the spigot and hurled arcs of water at their friends. Soon everyone was armed with buckets, and cups, and hastily emptied trash cans, and everyone, children and adults, was soaked and gleeful.

The water fight went on for nearly an hour. Pam paused for a moment during that time and happened to glance across the street. The neighbors were out on their sidewalks and stoops, dozens of them, standing and staring, despite the pounding heat. But the looks on their faces were not what Pam expected. They were smiling. They were even laughing. They looked as if they wished they could join the ruckus.

"This is *my* neighborhood," Pam found herself thinking. "This is where *I* live." Then she doused Anita with a bucket of water.

A Death and a Decision

Doreen James was worried about her sister. Barbara was clearly sick, although she would not admit that to Doreen. She stayed in bed late, went back to bed early, ate little, talked less, and winced with pain even when she was sitting still.

As summer ended, Barbara began having violent seizures, sometimes one every day. In the middle of a conversation, she would start shivering, then shaking, then her eyes would roll back and she would look, Doreen thought, as if she was in an evil trance. Minutes later, when she was conscious again, Doreen would try to persuade her to go to the hospital, but she always refused.

One afternoon, Barbara came along to keep Doreen company at a routine checkup. Doctors' offices always made her anxious; it was in such an office, after all, that she learned her fiancé had died. This time, the sisters were sitting together in a waiting room, when Barbara's seizure began. Doreen ran for a nurse, and Barbara was admitted to the hospital for several days, but was discharged without a solid diagnosis. When Doreen asked her sister what the doctors found, Barbara would not say.

In early September, Doreen invited the whole family over for a barbecue, but Barbara never left her room. She had terrible pains in her leg, and she felt too weak to walk. This time she agreed to go to the hospital, where Doreen learned that Barbara's blood pressure was dangerously low and, more important, the circulation in her leg was nearly completely blocked. The leg would require surgery.

Doreen stayed with Barbara at the hospital for the rest of the day, and did not leave until close to eleven that night, when the nurses all but ordered her to go.

"I'll see you later," Barbara said, as Doreen turned and waved good-bye at the door.

The operation was scheduled for early the next morning, and Doreen could not be there. Her mother had promised to call when it was over, to tell her that Barbara was safely back in her room. At lunchtime, there was a knock on Doreen's front door, and when she opened it she found her mother standing on the threshold, frail and confused. "I have something to tell you," she said. "She didn't make it. She died during the surgery. She was too weak." Barbara James was thirty-four years old.

When Doreen came home from the funeral she found a notice from Con Ed in her mailbox, warning that her power would be cut off because her bill was past due.

Furious, she crumpled the letter into a ball and hurled it across the room. Then she sank to the floor and cried, tears of grief and frustration, tears for her sister but also for so many other things— things she did not understand she'd lost until this moment.

"I don't want to live here anymore," she said aloud. "This isn't home."

Over the next few days the raw emotion ebbed, but the realization remained. She did not want to be here. Doreen had left Schlobohm not because she was tired of fighting to make things better there, but because she was tired of fighting *alone*. She moved to the townhouses hoping things might be different, that her neighbors would stick together and solve all the problems that had followed them from the other side of town.

Contentment is relative to expectation, and Doreen's expectations were the highest at Gaffney Place. Norma O'Neal came looking for someplace a little better than the place she had left. She found it and, despite its flaws, she was content. Pam Johnson wanted someplace safe, where her children could have waterfights and other types of fun. She was content, too. Doreen wanted much more—solidarity, a feeling of community, a chance to put all Sadie Jefferson's lessons into practice, a sense that she was making a difference.

"I thought that people could stick together here," she said, by way of apology, to Sadie. "But people don't stick together. They're doing the same thing they did on the other side of town. Their own thing."

She didn't understand how others could isolate themselves so easily. She had tried to be an island, just Doreen and Jaron, when she first moved to Gaffney Place. Despite her best efforts, she was soon holding meetings and writing letters, fighting as hard as she

Show Me a Hero

knew how. Sometimes the fighting worked, and Peter Smith okayed small improvements like the new screen doors that had arrived during the summer. But most of the time, nothing changed, and the Con Ed bill was mocking evidence of that. During her last months, Barbara had gently scolded Doreen, saying she was looking for something that didn't exist. Most white people ignore their neighbors, too, she said.

Maybe Barbara was right. Doreen alone could not transform this collection of townhouses into a neighborhood. This wasn't home, and she would stop trying to make it home. But she would not stop looking for someplace that was.

Several days later, when enough time had passed that she was certain she was not acting on impulse, Doreen called Municipal Housing. As she dialed, she felt the calm that only a firm decision can bring. Valerie Carroll, the tenant supervisor, came on the line. "I want to move out of here," Doreen said.

Valerie was surprised. She had never processed a request to leave the east side, she said. Hundreds of people were waiting for a chance to move in.

"You don't understand," Doreen said, "I'm not asking to leave the east side."

Valerie was confused.

"I want Dunbar Houses," Doreen said, of the small enclave in Runyon Heights, where Sheila lived, where Sadie lived, where Jaron would see black faces that lived in houses, not housing. Maybe there she would feel like she belonged.

"There's a long list ahead of you," Valerie said.

Doreen said she was willing to wait.

Nick vs. Vinni

Once Nick launched his campaign against Vinni Restiano, council meetings became ordeals for him. They reminded him of the worst days of the housing standoff, except now there was cold silence in place of heated shouting. Then, as now, he was isolated and on his own. This was still Restiano's council, and his last-minute decision to try to change that did not sit well with most of the people who worked for her or with her. Rather than face the chill in the back offices during breaks in council meetings, he would stand out in the hall alone.

Mary Dorman found him there one evening near the end of the primary campaign. He was leaning against a wall, hands in his pockets, staring at the worn tiles on the floor.

"How do you stand it," Mary asked, "when nobody's talking to you?

"I don't mind, I'm used to it," he said, and actually sounded as if he meant it. "But," he said, "I feel sorry for my wife, because these are her friends."

It had become an ugly campaign. The two former friends had nearly identical voting records, and that, coupled with Restiano's feelings of betrayal, left the candidates nothing to attack but each other. Restiano accused Nick of nepotism—putting Nay in a City Council job—even though Restiano herself had lobbied the council to make that happen. Nick accused Restiano of being more of a Republican than a Democrat, even though he had helped her craft many of her political positions. When Vinni received the support of nearly all the unions in Yonkers, Nick charged that she was a puppet of special interests, despite the fact that he had received the same endorsements from the same groups in his previous campaigns.

Restiano did not miss a chance to remind Nick that she had the official support of the party, while he was a pawn in Terry Zaleski's latest chess game. "I'm the candidate of the party by acclamation," she told audiences. "My opponent is the mayor's candidate by desperation."

In their few joint appearances, she seemed hurt and he seemed defensive. During a televised debate a week before the vote, she spoke bitterly of the new, nakedly political Nick, someone she did not recognize and did not like. "You only think of the next election," she said. "It's time to start thinking of the next generation. Get over it, Nick. The people are on to you."

Show Me a Hero

Nay was caught in the crossfire. Each day a few more pieces of her job were taken from her and given to others in the office. First she was asked to stop preparing the council minutes, then the council agenda. Then she was told there was no reason for her to come to council meetings. Next she was "discouraged" from working overtime. Meetings were held that she was not told of, and memos that should have routinely come over her desk no longer bore her name. If she was five minutes late from lunch, someone was sure to notice. Eventually, the only job left her was handing out forms to couples needing a marriage license.

After spending each day launching other people's marriages, she would come home and widen the cracks in her own.

"I'm sick and tired of being a part of this whole ugly disgusting mess," she would vent at Nick. "I paid for your politics when they fired me from the Parking Authority. Now I get to pay again? Maybe I'm being selfish, or a baby, but I am not the politician, you are."

"It sucks," she would yell at him, "this great thing you did, deciding to run against Vinni Restiano. I have to work with these people. They're gonna make me pay big time. And if you lose and she wins, that's it for me, for my job, for everything. Did you think about that?"

Nay did not go to work on the day of the primary. The city clerk's office is responsible for administering elections, and it would not look right if the wife of one of the candidates seemed to be in charge of the vote.

Vinni Restiano called early on primary day morning, after the polls had opened. Nick was in the shower, but he was not the Wasicsko Vinni was looking for.

"Your husband screwed me over," she hissed at Nay. "If he can do it to me, he can do it to you. What exactly does he care about anymore, anyway?"

Restiano hung up. When Nick walked in he found his wife clutching the receiver, looking stricken. She repeated the conversation.

"What do you care about?" she asked him.

He didn't have an answer.

After the polls had closed, Nick and Nay went to wait for the returns at Mannion's restaurant, a political hangout where the walls are lined with glad-handing photos. It was supposed to be a victory party, but it quickly became clear there was very little to celebrate. Three of the four candidates backed by Terry Zaleski lost their races, including Nick, who trailed Restiano by 363 votes out of a total of 7,836.

He won all the districts on the west side. She won all the districts on the east side.

The only race won by a party designee was in Nick's old district, where Fernando Fuentes squeezed to victory with a twenty-two-vote lead, 553 to 531.

Hank Spallone, who was trying to return to the council, won his Republican nomination fairly easily, 647 to 589. "I think it was me, my personality and what I stand for," Spallone said, analyzing his win. "The people want me back because I always did what I told them I'd do."

At ten o'clock, Nick conceded the race. From the pay phone at Mannion's he called Restiano's home, where she was awaiting the returns with supporters, since she had not been invited to join her own party's party. She was polite, but icy, and Nick left the restaurant immediately after the call. Neither Nick nor Nay said one word as they drove back home.

Mothers and Children

Billie didn't think she was throwing Shanda into the crib with unusual force. But the little girl hit the mattress with such a jolt that the supporting hooks ripped from the frame and the mattress collapsed to the dusty wooden floor. Billie sank to the floor, too, shrieking hysterically. Hers were shrill, piercing shrieks that sent Shanda cowering to the corner and brought Johnny running from the other room. He stood in the doorway staring at his wailing mother and cringing sister, until Billie ordered: "Just get away from me. Leave Mommy alone." She was afraid of what she was angry enough to do.

Shanda's whining had triggered the moment. She had spent most of the day whining—a high-pitched, repetitive tone, like a keening bird—and no amount of hollering, punishing, or spanking had made her stop. Billie was trying to exile the child to the crib when it collapsed. As the pieces of manmade wood clattered around her, something else collapsed as well—Billie's carefully constructed fiction that all was okay. She was not okay. She was fuming, frightened, and falling apart. Her hair was coming out in clumps. Her blood pressure was higher than its usual worrisome levels, and she had stopped taking her medicine because the side effects made her miserable.

Until the day she smashed the crib, Billie had been proud of the fact that, in all the months since John was arrested, she had never cried; proud that she had accepted each successive piece of humiliating news with a deep breath and a cigarette. "Crying is a waste," she told her mother, who, it seemed to Billie, would urge her to cry whenever they were together. "Crying don't fix things, it just makes them wet."

Instead, she had found—or thought she'd found—ways of dealing with John's absence. When the children asked for their father, she did not tell them where he was, answering Shanda's demands for "my Daddy" with silence or a quick change of subject. When pushed, she told them that the "Bad Boys" had taken their father away, a concept they knew from a television show they often watched in the late afternoons. She would rather they believed that John had been snatched into the TV screen than try to explain what prison was.

Once, and only once, Johnny angrily challenged her explanation, with information Billie assumed he got from the other children on the street.

"He's locked up," he taunted, eyes narrowing.

"No," Billie said, "he's not locked up, the Bad Boys got him." Johnny looked confused, but dropped the subject.

Johnny, who had always liked pretend gunplay, immersed himself in imaginary violence, running around the house yelling, "I'll kill you. I'll shoot you." Billie thought she had to do something, but she wasn't sure what it should be. First, she took Johnny's toy gun from him, but he fashioned replacements from his sandwich, or his finger, or whatever else was in his hand at the moment. So Billie went to the toy store and found a battery-operated learning center, where children picked an answer, then pressed a button, and were rewarded by bells and beeps. The recommended age on the box was "6 to 10 years." Shanda was two. Johnny was three. Billie bought the toy anyway, spending more money than she had planned in the belief that something expensive would best teach her children.

When she opened the machine, she realized that the cards required reading, and since neither Johnny nor Shanda could read, she had to sit with them while they played. They were excited about it the first day, but Billie put the machine away after fifteen minutes, because *All My Children* was about to begin. Shortly after that, Billie's mother bought Johnny a toy car, which he liked as much as the learning center, and Billie was pleased to have him play away from her.

Billie knew she was not the kind of mother she wanted to be. "Patience, patience. Patience and patience" was how she described what she did not have. "And understanding what a child don't know, and what they do know. And just patience."

She also knew she did not have the life she wanted, a life where her man was around more than once every few years. She couldn't think of any real person who actually had a life like that, but she believed in it nonetheless.

Now, however, with her daughter's crib in a heap in front of her, Billie saw that she wasn't handling the gap between what she wanted and what she had. In the months since John's arrest, several people, all trying to be helpful, had suggested that her problems were more than she could solve on her own. "I don't need no therapist," she said, not defiantly, but sadly. "This is something I will have to solve myself. They could tell me, 'You need to calm down,' but they don't live here. They don't see what I go through, they don't actually feel what I feel inside. Nobody can help me."

For nearly an hour, Norma had held her tongue while five-month-old Shaq fussed, cried, and refused all of Tasha's best efforts to coax him to sleep. Then, over the sound of Shaq's screaming, she heard Tasha screaming back, and Norma stood at the bottom of the stairs and ordered Tasha to come down.

"Give me the baby," Norma said.

"No," answered Tasha, with a rasp in her throat, a hint that she had been crying herself.

"Give me the baby," Norma said, and Tasha did as she was told.

Norma took Shaq, who was still fussing, into her own bedroom, and placed him in the center of her bed. Then she had a talk with him. "What's wrong with *you?*" she demanded. "Grandma don't take that. Who do you think you is?" She said the words over and over, a gruff yet kindly lullaby, and eventually the baby fell asleep.

He slept in Norma's bed all night, and the next morning Norma used much the same tone on the mother that she had used on the son.

"Tasha," she said. "I'm your mother. I'm here for you. I'm here *with* you. Some girls do not have a mother, or do not have nobody to care. That's why you find a lot of young girls killing their young babies. They can't take it. That's why I'm here for you. Anytime Shaq gets too much for you, you give him to me. When I had you all, when I had Dwayne and Bruce, I didn't have a mother. She was dead. I had nobody to help me. But you got me. Anytime it gets too hard for you, bring him in my room."

On the last day of September, Alma saw a photo in the paper, showing a townhouse shell being lifted onto its foundation by a crane. Fourteen new units of court-ordered public housing were under construction at Midland and Teresa avenues, the accompanying article said; they had all been prefabricated in Pennsylvania and were now being bolted to steel beams that had been cemented into the ground in Yonkers.

Alma crossed her fingers.

On the first day of October, Alma saw an article in the paper about a shooting in a lobby at Schlobohm. A sixteen-year-old boy had been shot in the foot at 4:45 in the afternoon by another boy whom he knew from the project's basketball courts. There appeared to be no motive, the article said. The shooter simply pulled out a revolver, inserted one bullet, spun the chamber, and shot into the victim's right foot.

Alma opened her hall closet, now overflowing with kitchen appliances she might never use, and mourned.

If she could do it over again, she thought, she would not have children. Children only brought heartache, she had learned, and constant reminders of the life she could not give them. If it was only her, by herself, she would have enough to live safely and simply. Why have them, she asked, only to apologize silently to them each day for everything they are missing?

A Hero

Nay was not fired the morning after the primary, a fact that provided the Wasicskos a little financial relief, but no peace of mind. The last time Nay had been fired, it had made headlines, and the couple respected Vinni's political savvy enough to assume that she was waiting until her reelection was final before carrying through on her threat. It would not help her to have that sort of publicity at this time. And there was probably some bonus satisfaction in watching Nick and Nay sweat.

The kitchen renovation was well under way, and now the conversations on Wasicsko Lane were not about how to decorate it, but how to pay for it. On the nights when they managed to

Show Me a Hero

fall asleep, they would find themselves awake again at 4:00 A.M., worrying aloud in the dark.

"What are we going to do when you get fired?"

"What *can* we do?"

"We'll lose the house. How are we going to pay for this?"

"Maybe we can ask my parents to help us out again until we get jobs."

"I've made a mess of everything, haven't I?"

Nick had started his job search cautious yet optimistic, as befits a politician. He believed he would get a job. A good job. He had talent, he reminded himself. He was nationally known. Promises had been made. He had connections.

What he wanted was simple—to stay in the Yonkers area in a position with visibility and prestige. His motives were also simple —he hoped, eventually, to run for mayor again, or maybe for city judge, with the Senate or the governor's mansion still beckoning in the distance. And his plan, at first, seemed simple, too. He contacted Terry Zaleski, who directed him to Jim Surdoval.

He knew that politics was about never looking desperate, so he approached Jim with studied nonchalance.

"Well, I guess if I'd worked harder I could have won this thing," he said. Then he added: "So, what's next for me."

"There are no positions in the Zaleski administration for you at this time," Surdoval said.

Nick tried to maintain his team player poker face. "Make me commissioner of whatever," he said, hoping he sounded relaxed and in control. To himself he thought: Invent something. I have a home. I have a mortgage. I have bills to pay.

"It would look like a payoff for running against Vinni," Surdoval said. "It wouldn't look good." He paused, and softened. "I'll work on something," he said, before showing Nick the door.

Nick offered his hand, and as they shook he said, "If there's anything I can do to help with anything, just let me know. If you want me to pick up someone's campaign fliers from the printer . . ."

He stopped midsentence. How had he gotten here, a former mayor offering to run errands?

Anger often fuels action, and Nick, furious mostly because he had thought he was so savvy when he was being so naive, came home and scrawled his résumé in longhand for Nay to type later. He had been a finalist for the Profile in Courage Award, he wrote of himself, in the third person, "for his courageous stand against angry crowds and voters opposed to court ordered desegregation," and he "was elected the youngest mayor of any major US city in an upset election over a six term Republican."

Then he wrote letters to accompany the résumé. They were proud, confident letters, because he still remembered what it was like to feel that way.

"*Dear Mr. Secretary,*" he wrote to Henry Cisneros, President Clinton's secretary of housing and urban development,

> *I applaud your efforts in Vidor, Texas. It is gratifying to see the Federal government shouldering some of the burden of fairness that is all too often politically difficult for elected officials.*
>
> *I was the Mayor of Yonkers in 1988 and 1989 when Federal District Judge Leonard B. Sand ordered construction of 200 units of public housing in predominantly white east Yonkers. With international attention focused on the lengths the Yonkers City Council was willing to go to pander to their political bases, I at the age of 28, led the effort to obey the Court mandates and maintain order in Yonkers. The voters showed their disapproval in 1989 by denying my re-election bid.*
>
> *However, the New York Times and the Daily News editorially supported me and my position. Senator Moynihan nominated me in 1991 for the John F. Kennedy Profile in Courage Award. I was named one of the three finalists that year.*
>
> *Encouraged by this support, I successfully ran for City Council from my west side district. I narrowly lost a bid for the City Council Presidency last week, winning the west side but losing the east. In spite of my successful efforts, along with HUD, to implement much of the court ordered*

Show Me a Hero

construction, east side residents are resentful. My elective
prospects are not good due to my principled stands on
housing, but my commitment to public service is undeterred.

I am enclosing my resume with the hope that a role for me
may exist at HUD that will under your stewardship
reinforce the message that quality desegregated housing is a
national priority. As an attorney with a national reputation
for political courage and a commitment to fair housing, I
believe I can contribute to your mission. Thank you.

It was signed, Nicholas C. Wasicsko, Esq.

Though the specifics were different, he wrote much the same
message in his letter to Judge Sand, who was looking to appoint a
federal master to oversee the final stage of the housing plan.

"My record of support for the more controversial public housing
portion of your order, I believe, contributed to the successful imple-
mentation of that phase," his letter said, in part.

> *My steadfast courage in the face of vehement opposition*
> *earned national recognition as well as the respect of Yonkers*
> *residents most in need of fair housing. I fought hard to insure*
> *that the public housing built pursuant to the court order*
> *would be accepted by the host communities by being low*
> *density, scattered site, and attractive in appearance. While*
> *these efforts were successful, my high profile position cost me*
> *re-election.*
>
> *At the end of this year, I will be leaving public office. I am*
> *looking for a position that will allow me to continue in public*
> *service to further the goals I have spent my entire*
> *professional career fighting for, equal opportunity and*
> *fairness, in housing, and the law. I believe that I could use*
> *my unique assets to insure the success of this consent decree.*
>
> *Affordable housing, albeit court ordered, should not*
> *engender the blind resistance it has in Yonkers. The goal is to*
> *provide housing opportunities for members of the plaintiff*
> *class and others in need in Yonkers. I believe I am uniquely*
> *qualified to successfully continue the Court's work.*

Then, he added: *"I respectfully request that this letter be kept con-fidential if you decide further exploration of this matter is not appro-priate. Thank you. Nicholas C. Wasicsko, Esq."*

These letters and others were sent on September 20, 1993, less than a week after Nick lost the primary. By the second week in Oc-tober, when he had received no response from anyone, he went back to Jim Surdoval, who had, as promised, "done something," though hardly all that Nick had hoped. The mayor had passed Nick's name to Assemblyman Oliver Koppell, who was the nominee to be New York's attorney general, recommending Nick for a job as an assistant attorney general. He had also recommended him to a number of New York City law firms.

Rather than being heartened by the help, Nick was frightened and depressed. He did not want a job as a lawyer. He had never ac-tually practiced law and he was petrified that he would fail. The depth of that fear became clear when his uncle, probably as a favor to a nephew in need of money, asked Nick to draft his will, and the project came to consume Nick. He spent an entire Saturday in the Barnes & Noble bookstore, flipping through trade paperbacks on how to write a will, and he left with one hundred dollars' worth of books. "I don't remember anything about this," he said when Nay asked why he was turning a small project into a life crisis. "I want to do it right."

Each day, the righteous, motivating anger he had felt turned more fully into self-pitying, paralyzing fear. He still attended po-litical events, but he stayed on the sidelines, asking acquaintances "Why is it that people who do the right thing seem to get squashed?" and "Do you think my political career is over?"

He sent out more job letters, but where his earlier ones had been self-assured and eloquent (if a bit starched and earnest), these clanked with a false bravado. He did not even bother to proofread. *"I am writing with interest about the position of lawyer lobbyist,"* said his three-paragraph note to the general counsel of a company whose ad he found in the classified section of the *New York Times*.

> *As a former Mayor with high recognition among state officials, I believe I can be a strong asset to your*

*organization. I know the chairmen of Senate Mental Hygiene
and the Assembly Health Committees. Many state officials
are also acquaintances.*

*Although my background does not include experience in
the health care area, I am astute and a fast learner; I had to
be to be elected Mayor at 28!*

*I am available for an interview at your convenience.
Thank you.*

He never received an answer.

A Tragedy

On the morning of Friday, October 29, 1993,
Nick tried to get Nay to take the day off. He lay in bed at eight and
watched her as she dressed for work: blue skirt, white blouse,
blue-and-white blazer.

"Make it a three-day weekend," he said. "Go for a walk and look
at the leaves."

"The leaves are all dead, and I don't have any vacation
days left," she answered. "Vinni wants me out. Let's not give her
ammunition."

So Nick got out of bed, dressed quickly—green Dockers pants,
white sneakers, and the green sweater Nay had given him, to cheer
him up, the week before—and he drove Nay to work at City Hall.
They talked of the things husbands and wives talk about when
they catch a few minutes together during a hectic day. The kitchen
cabinets had arrived, and were lying, in their cartons, all over the
kitchen floor. They had to shop for a refrigerator on Friday night.
They had to meet the tile man at the house on Saturday morning. It
looked as if Vinni Restiano would easily win reelection.

On the way home, Nick picked up the *New York Times* and the
Herald Statesman, and read the second one first, scanning it frantically for any news of the investigation into embezzlement at the

city's Industrial Development Agency. As mayor, he had chaired the agency, and, more recently, he had been a member of its board, appointed by Terry Zaleski in 1992, before their relationship went sour. The investigation had already uncovered the apparent embezzlement of hundreds of thousands of dollars over several years, and a low-level employee at the agency had admitted to taking some of that. Now the mayor's investigators were looking at the expense accounts of others at the agency. Nick knew he had not done anything wrong while a member of the IDA board and that he was not among those being accused of wrongdoing. But lately he had been overwhelmed by a fear that in the uncontrollable arena of politics, innocence is no defense.

One morning, a few days earlier, he had read an article about the investigation—one that made no mention at all of his name—and called Nay at work, so agitated he could barely speak. "They're making allegations and they're ruining people's lives," he said, blaring into the phone. "This is not funny. I hope when it's their turn, let's see how funny they think it is."

Nick's rage made no sense to Nay, and his raw fear alarmed her. "Nick, stop screaming, what's the matter with you? I know it's upsetting, but you have to calm down."

That night, he told her he was being followed, but he did not say by whom. He spent hours at the library, searching through microfilms of past newspaper stories, constructing a chronology he could use to make his case. In the space on his timeline for August, when news of the alleged embezzlement had begun to make headlines, he wrote *"Post mortem reveals scandal."* In the space for November, all he wrote was *"?"*

On the morning of the October 29, however, there was no news of the investigation, and he spent a few hours making telephone calls, including one to his secretary, during which he asked her to reserve some tickets for him—two for a Human Rights dinner that same night and two for the Democratic City Committee Annual Dinner to be held on Halloween. Shortly before 11:00 A.M., he changed out of his Dockers and into a suit and tie, to do his councilman's duty at a ceremony to open a new county welfare office. He stood near the back of the room with a former aide, Kathy

Show Me a Hero

Spring, and they talked about the IDA. "We all get tainted by it one way or another," he told her. During the ceremony, Mayor Zaleski called Nick's name from the podium and introduced him to the audience. Nick waved to the crowd and smiled.

The ceremony lasted no more than half an hour, and Nick returned home, changed back into his more comfortable clothes, and worked in the kitchen for a while with Michael, unpacking the cabinets and talking about the IDA. He told Michael that he was sure he was being followed. Michael was concerned, not about the investigation, but about Nick. Why was this man, who had endured death threats for supporting the housing order, losing his composure over something so trivial?

At one o'clock, Nick drove to City Hall to pick up Nay for lunch. During their hour at the Broadway Diner, he complained that he was tired of being followed, and, because he was certain a tracking transmitter had been placed under both his cars, he planned to switch vehicles with Michael. Shortly before two, he dropped Nay back at City Hall.

Early that afternoon, Michael walked into the living room to ask for help lifting some cabinets. There he saw his brother, holding a gun and looking terrified. Nick raced out the door, saying only that he had to run an "errand." He would not tell Michael where he was going.

Minutes after he left, Nay paged him on his beeper. He called her back and told her he was at a pay phone a block away from the house. He said he was going directly home to help Michael. Forty-five minutes later, he drove up to the house, left the car engine running, ran up the stairs, then down them again. He took the cash out of his wallet, but left the wallet behind. He took the keys to his Chevy Geo and his Ford Taurus off the key chain, and left the key chain behind, too.

All afternoon, Nay tried to page him, because she was frightened at his stories of transmitters and tails. Unsure whether she should be worried about his safety or his sanity, she dialed his beeper at least ten times, periodically pressing the numbers "9-1-1," their code for an emergency. He did not answer. At 4:30, when her work was done, she stood in her customary spot at the front door to City Hall and waited for Nick to pick her up. Half an hour later, when he had not arrived, she walked to the end of the City Hall driveway, and a half hour after that, when he still wasn't there, she called Michael and asked him to drive her home.

While Nay was waiting for Nick, he was sitting on a hill at the Oakland Cemetery, about two blocks from his house and a mile from City Hall. He was leaning against a tree and looking out over the cemetery, where his father and grandfather were buried. Beyond their graves he could see the Palisades rising up from the Hudson, the twin spires of St. Casimir's Church, the gables of City Hall.

It was closing time at the cemetery, and the caretaker, Fedor Feciasko, walked over and asked him to leave. Nick said he would, and started walking down the hill, toward his red Geo, with the license plate that read WASICSKO. But when the caretaker came by again, a few minutes later, Nick was back by the tree, staring down on Yonkers. The caretaker opted to leave and give the former mayor, whom he recognized from television, a little more time. He waited until 5:15 to approach Nick again, and, as before, Nick stood up immediately and walked toward his car.

At 5:20, Feciasko made one last trip up the hill, where, he would later tell one of the dozens of police officers who soon swarmed the scene, "I saw he was lying over here. I saw the gun in his hand, and the blood."

Nick Wasicsko had shot himself once through the head with the .38 revolver he almost always carried. Nay could not believe he did not leave her a note, but none was ever found.

Within hours, the stream of praise began.

Said Mayor Zaleski: "It's an extraordinary tragedy. All of the people of Yonkers send their heartfelt love and sympathy to the family. It's just a tragedy. A loss beyond words."

Vinni Restiano: "I feel like I've been in a car crash and the other driver died. Even though we've been political adversaries in this last primary, Nick Wasicsko was a friend, and I'm shocked and hurt for his family. Nick was a real intelligent individual and he had a life ahead of him. He must have really been hurting inside for him to have done this to himself. There was nobody smarter."

Hank Spallone: "Terrible. Tragedy. A real tragedy. We were on opposite sides of the political spectrum, but we were always very friendly. I'm just shocked. Such a fine man is gone. The result of somebody trying to do the very, very best he knew how."

Nicholas Longo: "He took the tough times with a lot of character and a lot of strength. He stood tall. I have to wonder what's happened in five years. The fellow who withstood what was taking place in 1988 was not the fellow who walked into the Oakland Cemetery tonight."

Nicholas Wasicsko had been baptized in St. Casimir's Church. He and Nay were married there, too, beneath the kaleidoscope of stained glass. And, on a gray and frigid election day morning, St. Casimir's was where he was mourned. It was the first election day in almost a decade when his name did not appear on the Yonkers ballot.

More than a thousand people packed the church, filling the polished oak pews and spilling out into the entryway, where they stood, coats still on, tears flowing freely, through the hourlong farewell mass. Nearly every candidate for every local office was present, and all the traditional last-minute campaign events were canceled. Henry Spallone, who defeated Nick for mayor in 1989, was there, as was Angelo Martinelli, whom Nick defeated in 1987. Vinni Restiano cried. Nicholas Longo cried. Neil DeLuca cried.

From her pew in the middle of the crowd, Mary Dorman was astonished to see Oscar Newman slip into a nearby row, then bow his head in what looked like true sadness. He sat there, by himself, for the entire service, never making his way to the front, where the dignitaries were clustered, and not saying anything to anyone. "He's here because he wants to be here," Mary said, impressed by a man she thought could not impress her, "not because he wants people to see him here."

Nay sat in the front pew, stunned, numb, and in a haze of grief. From the time the police commissioner himself had arrived at her door and taken her to the cemetery to identify Nick's body, she had coped by refusing to think. It took all her energy merely to walk and talk. She was so overwhelmed, so drained and leaden, there were moments she felt, for fleeting and frightening seconds, that she might die, too, if she didn't remind herself to breathe. Thinking was more than she could handle. She didn't dare to think, she barely functioned.

Nay stayed wrapped in her protective fog through the calls from the reporters, the questions from the police officers, the decisions and minutiae that come with death. Nick's wake was a blur. After a candidate for judge approached her there and offered his condolences, she thanked him and wished him well on election day. "Good luck on Tuesday," she said, standing in front of her husband's gleaming casket, and Michael overheard and was horrified. "What are you doing?" he asked. And she answered, honestly, "I don't know."

Mayor Zaleski also came to the wake. First Nick's mother, and then Nick's brother, refused to shake the mayor's hand. But Nay walked up and thanked him for coming. "Stop being a politician," Michael said. But Nay did not know how. "I guess I'm losing my mind," she said. "Nick hated him, but he is here, and he is the mayor. . . ."

Now, at the funeral, she was still willing herself not to think. It worked for most of the morning—she did not dissolve in tears, or scream, or faint. But then, near the end of the service, The Reverend John Duffell took the pulpit to begin his eulogy, and the weight of the moment all but crushed her.

It was Father Duffell who had found Nay her first job at City Hall, and who insisted on driving her to the interview so she would not turn and run. During her early years with Nick, they would run into Duffell at events around the city, and he would warn Nick to take care of her, because "she's my favorite girl." From this same pulpit, Duffell had married them. And at this latest central moment in her life, he stood in front of her again, and said the things that she would have been thinking had she not been so afraid to allow herself to think.

Show Me a Hero

Nick was "a man full of promise, a man full of suffering," Duffell said, and his death "makes us realize what's important: not the politics, but the human beings. If only all the things that were said about him these past few days could have been again and again and again and again said to him."

But he did not stop with soothing generalities. He went on and assigned blame. He spoke of the "McCarthyism of Yonkers," and described the city as a place filled with politics, hate, rumor, investigation, and fear. The kind of place where a man who had done the right thing, as Nick had done with the housing, could be destroyed because he was right. And where a man who had done nothing wrong, as Nick had done with the IDA, could take no solace from, and find no safety in, his innocence.

"Why did he do what he did? We'll never know," Duffell said. "But perhaps, some of the fear and darkness that seems to be overshadowing the city had a part to play, where reputations are destroyed on the front page of the local newspaper, by investigations, perhaps valid investigations, revealed prematurely before their completion, before charges are filed."

Nay stopped feeling numb and began to feel angry. She was angry at Yonkers, and at the mourning politicians who surrounded her. As she followed her husband's casket out the front door of St. Casimir's, she was angry at herself, for being one of those politicians, playing by the rules that Nick had taught her, wishing all these people well in their elections, thanking them for dropping by.

As the four-block-long funeral procession snaked its way past City Hall, she was also angry at the screaming crowds who hounded her husband in 1988. So many of those people were watching now, she knew, as the motorcade passed by. People who had quieted their voices, but who had never shed their hate, and who made it clear with their votes that they could not forgive him. They would never let him be City Council president, and they certainly would not let him be mayor again, or senator, or governor, or judge, or any of the other things that had seemed so possible when he was the country's youngest mayor.

Then, as Nick Wasicsko was buried on the same hill where he had died, she was angry mostly at her husband, for caring that he would never be any of those things. For leaving her to rebuild her dreams from scratch, because he could not bear to pick up the fractured pieces of his own.

1998 : Epilogue

A decade has passed since the summer of contempt in Yonkers. It has been six years since the first tenants moved into the townhouses, and five years since Nicholas Wasicsko's death. That is time enough to tackle the question: Did it work? The answer is as it has been since the beginning — it depends upon how one defines success. My measure, then and now, is double-layered: Did it transform the lives of the tenants without chipping at the dreams of those who came before?

For Alma Febles, the townhouses have been everything that she had hoped, a gift made all the more precious because it took so long. More than two years after the lottery, Alma was still waiting. Even the second wave of construction would not help her, she feared, because her lottery number was so high. I put her in touch with Mary Dorman, who took her on as a personal cause. There were many more two-bedroom townhouses than there were three-bedroom ones, Mary said, and she suggested that Alma write to Peter Smith, offering to accept one of the smaller units.

On October 28, 1994, Alma and her children moved into their new home. They threw a party. Knowing that the family had all the kitchen implements they could possibly need, my housewarming gift was a snow shovel, tied with a big red bow. The right to shovel her own walk, Alma had told me, had become one of her definitions of home.

She is past forty now, and she still does not have her elusive, solitary bedroom. She says she doesn't mind. Virgilio has already left the townhouse; he joined the Marines. In another blink of the eye, Leyda will be gone, too; she plans to go to college and become a fashion designer. Alma knows her new home will be lonely with both of them away.

The townhouses have been Norma O'Neal's salvation, too. Her health has deteriorated steadily in the years since she moved to the east side—she's had a stroke, lost part of one foot to diabetes, and now requires dialysis twice a week. When she suffered her stroke, it was a neighbor from the townhouses who answered Tasha's frantic call in the middle of the night and kept Norma breathing. A home health aide now comes—on time, every morning—and helps with the otherwise unmanageable tasks of her day. "If I were still living in Schlobohm," she says, laughing with the relief of being alive, "I would be dead."

It took far longer for the townhouses to bring contentment to Doreen James. Although her name remains on the waiting list for Dunbar, she is now less determined to make that move. In the years since Joe's death she has lurched from one escape route to the next—to Schlobohm, to crack, to her parents, to the townhouses. In the years after Barbara's death, she came to recognize the pattern.

She is still involved with READY, and proud of the changes the group has helped bring to the west side (they are not active in the townhouses). On READY's watch, more than $30 million in federal, state, and city funds have been spent improving security in the high-rise complexes. And after years of lobbying, Sadie's plan to allow current tenants to thoroughly screen prospective tenants is officially in effect.

But even as she is seeing the clout of grass-roots activism, Doreen is easing it out of her life. "Sadie says you can't solve other people's problems until you fix your own," she says. Part of her new life plan includes a full-time job at a chain hardware store on the east side, and night school, where she hopes to take the courses that will allow her to become a social worker in Schlobohm.

And Billie Rowan? She sees the townhouses as a cruel municipal tease, a trinket given to her briefly, then roughly snatched away. The five-week-long trial of John Mateo Santos was front-page news in Yonkers. He did not testify, but his Legal Aid lawyer argued that he had struck up a conversation with Helen Sarno at a local deli, and that she had invited him to her home for a cup of coffee. At first he declined, and they each went their own way. Then John changed his mind and returned to the elderly woman's apartment, only to find her covered with blood and near death. Perhaps he himself became bloody trying to lift her from the floor, the lawyer said.

Billie believed him. The jury did not. They believed the prosecution, who charged that "this guy, John Santos, stabbed Helen Sarno to death using an ice pick, and when her neighbors responded to her screams for help, he tried to talk his way out of it, and when that didn't work, he tried to fight his way out of it, and when that didn't work, he tried to run away."

They found him guilty. Judge John R. LaCava gave him the maximum sentence of twenty-five years to life for what he described as a "cowardly, senseless, and inexcusable murder."

It would be several years more before another court decided Billie's own fate. She believes that Municipal Housing would not have worked this hard to evict her from an apartment in Schlobohm but for the spotlight on the townhouses. They had to "make an example of me," she says. In time, Billie lost the last of her appeals, and was evicted in October 1995, nearly three years after the murder. Shortly before she moved, she told me, "I hope my kids remember this place, so they can find a way back here." She fled Yonkers, and left no forwarding address. Wherever she is, I wish her well.

Despite fears that the ills of the west side would travel with the tenants, life is still relatively peaceful on the east side. There have been some problems that have brought the police to the townhouses — complaints of loud music, domestic squabbles, fights among the children. In April 1995 the boyfriend of a Trenchard resident set her townhouse ablaze while police officers waited downstairs to arrest him on another charge.

But in general, the police say, they are not called to the new housing sites more often than they are called to any other cluster of homes. Said Bob Olsen, who was the Yonkers police chief during the years after the townhouses first opened: "The doomsday scenario never materialized."

In short, the townhouses do what Oscar Newman had hoped they would do—they blend into the neighborhood. Their construction is not perfect. The doorbells still don't work, the window frames are warping, and the screens are peeling out of nearly all the screen doors—doors that Doreen worked so hard to get. The upkeep of the sites could be better, too. Without access to lawn mowers, most of the tenants have all but given up on maintaining their yards, and the insufficient closets inside have led many families to store things outdoors. As a result, some yards are unkempt and shabby looking, but no more so than the yards of some of the private houses nearby.

Those gripes aside, however, Newman's general philosophy seems to be working. The tenants think of their homes as their own, and care for them as well as they can. Lately there is talk of how they might eventually be able to buy the units. Even Peter Smith, who found Newman to be difficult and self-aggrandizing at times, gives him credit. In a summary report to Newman, Smith wrote: "For me, the best test of the Defensible Space theory was not the way the residents took over their own grounds and then began to defend the entire project. I kind of expected that. But it is the way they take care of their garbage cans next to their front walks. I, frankly, did not think that would work. Making garbage disposal an individual thing, and making it clear to the whole world that if there was a mess on their front yard, it was the tenant's own doing, that brought something out of the tenants that showed the whole world how badly they had been prejudged."

So, the lives of the tenants have changed for the better, and the worst fears of the east side homeowners have not come to pass. Is that success? Is it enough?

Norma O'Neal will grab a sandwich at the corner diner every once in a while, but she still will not eat at most of the other restaurants in her neighborhood. Doreen James will not fill her prescrip-

Show Me a Hero

tions on the east side because pharmacists there do not know the ins and outs of Medicaid. Instead, she travels across town to a pharmacy on the west side. Pam Johnson's pediatrician has two offices, one west, one east. But only the office on the west side accepts Medicaid, so when her children are sick she takes them back to the old neighborhood.

In short, the tenants in the townhouses live in a bubble within a bubble. They are still visitors in their new neighborhoods, and they have almost no interaction with the white homeowners whose world they were sent east to change. Was this what Judge Sand envisioned when he wrote his 657-page opinion? Was it worth ten years and $260 million so that two hundred families could live in nicer homes and be ignored by their neighbors?

I asked Sand a version of this question when I interviewed him for this book, and it was the only moment, during hours of conversation, that made his tone go sharp. The number of townhouses—two hundred in a city of nearly 200,000 people—was chosen by the NAACP and the Justice Department, he said. He accepted their number, but he did not choose it, and he would not comment on whether it was sufficient to remedy the perceived wrong. What he did say was that the point of all this was never *integration*. It was *desegregation*, and the differences are not merely semantic. Yonkers is, technically, desegregated. A group of people, a category if you will, is now allowed in where before it was deliberately kept out. But Yonkers is *not* integrated. Black and white are not woven into the same fabric, the same community. Time might accomplish that. A judge cannot.

There is still anger on the east side. A walk through the neighborhood, a knock on random doors, finds that the anger is quieter than before, but it has not gone away.

"So far it's not so bad," says one homeowner, washing down his driveway with a hose. He lives two doors down from the townhouses. "But they're still on their best behavior. I feel like we were screwed over. We *were* screwed over. I'm just too tired to fight about it."

A block away, another neighbor points to the FOR SALE BY OWNER sign on her front lawn. It has been there for several months and she expects it will be there for several months more.

"I'm not selling to get away from them," she says of the townhouses. "But it's because of them that I can't sell. Would *you* buy a house around here?"

It is, in fact, still difficult to sell a home in Yonkers—anywhere in Yonkers. But is that only because of the housing? Is it the presence of the townhouses alone that has lowered property values? Some, like Nicholas Longo, Peter Chema, and Hank Spallone, believe unequivocally that it is. Others argue, and I agree, that the real blame lies elsewhere. Yes, Yonkers has a black eye. But who threw the punch? The most lasting bruises were not inflicted by the townhouses. They were caused by the fight itself.

"All that publicity left people with a bad taste," says Neil DeLuca, who has finally left government for the private sector. "Even people who don't remember the details have this gut feeling this is someplace they don't want to be."

Says John Spencer, the current mayor: "The damage that was done, the people of Yonkers did it to themselves."

John Spencer became mayor because of a backlash against Terry Zaleski. After Nick died, Zaleski's "politics of investigation" came into new focus in Yonkers. Nay and Michael told Nick's story passionately and publicly, emphasizing his fears that he was the subject of an inquiry by the Zaleski administration. Jim Surdoval vehemently (and, to my mind, convicingly) denied that Nick had been part of the IDA investigation, but the mere suggestion that the former mayor might have been driven to suicide by political shenanigans was enough to cause talk around town. It was one of a number of reasons that Zaleski lost his 1996 reelection bid.

Spencer is a former bank vice-president who had served two terms on the council and who had been Republican majority leader when Nick was Democratic minority leader. Despite their different political affiliations, the two men had been friends, and it was John Spencer who had secured Nay her job as deputy city clerk.

Show Me a Hero

Spencer, by general agreement, is an outstanding mayor, and his greatest accomplishment is that he has coaxed, rallied, and dragged Yonkers toward maturity. It is time, he has said, to stop blaming Judge Sand for all that went wrong in the city, and to make things go right from now on. Betting all his political capital that his was a city transformed, John Spencer made sure that one of his first acts as mayor was to request a one-on-one meeting with the judge.

"Your Honor, it's a new day," he remembers saying. "It's gotta be a new day. We've been through too much. I just got elected overwhelmingly in Yonkers on a vow of leadership, to lead this city. Leadership is getting people to work together.

"Philosophically," he said, "I do not believe in government way, way up top shoving anything down the throat of the people. It doesn't work."

Answered Sand: "I share your philosophy, but how would you do this?"

Spencer argued that it was ill advised to insist that the city *build* the second stage of Sand's plan, the eight hundred additional units of affordable housing. The new construction approach, he said, would entail yet another search for sites, which would stir up old feelings again. Why not use existing, unoccupied co-ops, condos, and homes? he asked. And why not allow the city to choose the units, with a minimal amount of intervention from the court?

It was not the first time the idea had been suggested, but it was the first time the judge had been this impressed with the messenger.

"Keep an eye on this guy," he told me a few days after the meeting. "This is someone I can work with."

The resulting plan, finalized in 1998, requires the state to designate a total of 740 units of affordable housing. Some of the units will already exist, some will be built from scratch, as decided by the city. The State of New York will pay half of the $32 million cost of the plan, per Judge Sand's orders. In February of 1998, after his conversation with John Spencer, Sand ruled that the state's Urban Development Corporation was partly responsible for the segregated housing pattern in the first place.

The Rebuilding

At the hearing to finalize the plan, Sand was both reflective and optimistic. "There have been many occasions since the outset of this litigation in 1980, when I sat on this bench experiencing frustration, and a failure to appreciate why, when the parties had the same objectives, it was so difficult to reach a consensus," he said.

"I am very pleased," he continued. "The goal of increasing housing opportunities in Yonkers will be materially implemented. There will, at long last, be an end to this phase of the ongoing saga."

Judge Sand is not the only one impressed by the changes in Yonkers. In the spring of 1998, the Emergency Financial Control Board voted unanimously to disband itself, giving Yonkers full control of its own finances for the first time in twenty-three years. Said Spencer, immediately after the vote: "This is the best government meeting I've ever attended."

News of this progress both heartens and saddens Nay. From where she sits, John Spencer, her ally and friend, is succeeding where her husband could not. Nay is still the deputy city clerk of Yonkers. On the wall of her City Hall office she has hung a framed newspaper from the summer of contempt and a poster Nick gave her called "Love's First Kiss." Since his suicide she has mended her emotional fences with Vinni Restiano, and each woman describes the other as a close friend. A scholarship fund has been established in Nick's memory, and an east side park has been named after him.

Unable to sell the unfinished house on the hill, Nay abandoned it to the bank. She now lives in a one-bedroom apartment, only feet away from the northern border of the city. She took the WASICSKO LANE sign with her when she moved, but she left a pile of posters that said "Nick Wasicsko for City Council President" to rot in her damp garage. I salvaged one, and it hangs on my office wall, near my window, a reminder that heroes are rarely perfect.

The Department of Housing and Urban Development sees the townhouses of Yonkers as a success and a blueprint for the future. Sprinkling low-income families throughout middle-class neighborhoods is now department policy. Across the United States, in

Newark, in Cincinnati, in Boston, Chicago, and Houston, boxy brick towers, once filled with hundreds of public-housing units each, are being declared failures and dynamited down to dust. There will be no more monolithic housing projects, not because a judge has ordered it, but because such projects do not work. From now on there will be only townhouses, like the ones built after all those years of protest in Yonkers.

"The lesson of Yonkers," says Oscar Newman, who retired to create giant totem-pole-like sculptures in upstate New York, "is that it is coming soon to a town near you."

To that end, the agency demolished 30,000 high-rise units across the country in 1996, and a total of 100,000 will be torn down by the year 2000. HUD has a budget of $46 billion over that same period of time to produce scattered-site housing in the communities that surrounded those high-rises.

The private sector is embracing this approach, too. Over the past four years, groups like Habitat for Humanity International, the Enterprise Foundation, and the National Neighborworks Network have spent $8.9 billion building 136,300 units in 1,940 communities, many of them middle class. In March of 1997 they announced a campaign to spend $13 billion to build 193,800 units in 2,400 communities nationwide.

Each of these communities would do well to learn the lessons of Yonkers, to hear this story of an experiment that ultimately worked, but which nearly destroyed a city along the way. It is a story of two views of the world, of the most logical and intellectual of judges, and the most emotional and self-protective of towns. Of a man who had a weekend house on thirty-three acres, and a city that looked north with envy at its leafier, wealthier neighbors. Of a man who struggled and reached the top, and believed that others should be helped to do the same. And of people whose struggles did not bring them as much, and who were fighting to keep out others who had even less.

Yonkers is what happens when these views collide. When a judge tells a neighborhood to re-create itself from scratch. When he sparks a metaphorical explosion, then orders those who live in the rubble to rebuild. Yonkers is what happens to the people of that neighborhood, both those who were there before and those who, with all eyes upon them, are chosen to move in.

Some of the lessons of Yonkers are practical: demand townhouses instead of high-rises; spend resources on architects, not lawyers; accept the inevitable and move on. But other lessons are less tangible, and more difficult to master. To succeed where Yonkers failed means accepting that no neighborhood stays the same forever and that protecting our children might be better done by letting strangers in than by keeping them out.

Yonkers is what will happen—is happening—everywhere, the result not of a court case, but of a demolition ball. In time, the townhouses will find their way into nearly every community and every neighborhood. In some places it will happen quietly, in others the shouting will be deafening. But everywhere, it will happen. And one by one each of those neighborhoods will learn what that means for a nation whose people preach diversity, but who are most comfortable when surrounded by others like themselves.

Has Yonkers itself learned these lessons? Some moments make me think so. Shortly after John Spencer's election the new mayor paid a visit to Tony DiPopolo, who was housebound with ailments that would soon kill him. DiPopolo was so weak he could not speak above a whisper, and Spencer sat close so that DiPopolo might talk directly into the mayor's ear. "Those people," DiPopolo said, of the tenants in the townhouses, "they're nice. They aren't hurting nobody."

But other moments bring doubt.

Mary Dorman is now a member of the city's Civil Service commission, with her name painted in gold on the door of her office at City Hall. One morning, while out in her front yard, she was stopped by the driver of a passing car who was looking to buy a house in Mary's neighborhood. Were there any in the area? Mary did know of one house, an attractive Colonial with a big yard and, from the looks of it, three or four bedrooms. She told the woman those things, then surprised herself by adding that the home was "across the street from the public housing." She knew it shouldn't matter. But she also knew that it does.

Alma Febles knows it, too. Shortly after she moved into her hard-won home, she worried aloud at a rumor that more of the same were to be built—on her new street. "They should build more, but I hope not right near here," she said, with no hint of irony. "This is such a quiet, pretty block."

Acknowledgments

This book is the result of more than six years I spent in the neighborhoods, libraries, and archives of Yonkers. It is a work of nonfiction, and everything, to the best of my knowledge, is true. The historical events are taken from newspaper accounts, videotapes, hearing transcripts, and the descriptions of participants and eyewitnesses. More recent events and conversations I either observed firsthand or was told of in detail soon after. To ensure that my words matched their memories, I asked nearly all the main players to read the pages that told their stories before the book went to print.

Everyone in this book is real. There are no composites. Nearly every name is real, too, with two exceptions: Doreen James and her family; Billie Rowan and hers. In both cases the names were changed to protect the children. This book is about the right to a fresh start and a new beginning. Jaron, Johnny, and Shanda need not learn of any of their parents' past secrets and mistakes from me.

In saying thank you, I will start where I owe the most gratitude—to the people in this book. They invited me into their lives, gave me hours of their valuable time, shared their thoughts and memories—including ones they are not proud of and would have preferred to forget.

I am also indebted to the fellow journalists who wrote history's first draft. Having read practically every word they have written on this subject, I can say that the reporters at the *Herald Statesman,* particularly Dave Sheingold, Ed Tagliaferri, Bill Dentzer, Laurel Babcock, and columnist Maury Allen, are as thorough and sharp as they come. Thanks, too, to my colleagues who covered the contempt crisis for the *New York Times,* including James Feron, Lisa Foderaro, Alan Finder, Sara Rimer, James Barron, Wayne King, and Robert D. McFadden. I'm glad you were there first, so I could come along later.

A untold number of books, too many to list in an informal thank-you, were educational and inspiring, the first among these being *Common Ground,* by J. Anthony Lukas, the work that began it all. It sat on my desk, much thumbed and worn, for six years. I find myself missing a man I never had the good fortune to meet.

Also indispensable were the following: *The Promised Land,* by Nicholas Lemann; *There Are No Children Here,* by Alex Kotlowitz; *Race,* by Studs Terkel; *The Death and Life of Great American Cities,* by Jane Jacobs; *Two Nations,* by Andrew Hacker, and a number of books by Oscar Newman, including *Defensible Space.*

Countless people at the following offices spent hours explaining the fine points and finding me documents: the Department of Housing and Urban Development, the Yonkers Office of Municipal Housing, Yonkers Housing Court, the Westchester County Court, Mayor Spencer's office, Judge Sand's office, Judge LaCava's office. At the same time, Jeffrey Toobin and Jan Hoffman guided me through the foreign land of law.

Several people read the many versions of the manuscript—Todd Kessler, Sharon Hall, Mimi Swartz, Chuck Lesnick, and Esther Fein. They were kind enough not to be too kind, and the book is better because of them.

My other world is that of the *New York Times Magazine,* where I have had a front-row seat to the talents of Doreen Weisenhaus, Katherine Bouton, Adam Moss, Jack Rosenthal, Gerry Marzorati, Kathy Ryan, Sarah Harbutt, and Linda Magyar. A few floors below, the generosity and smarts of Joe Lelyveld, Soma Golden, Dean Baquet, and Bill Keller have often made me wonder why I ever left.

Gloria Glickman, everyone at Good Yarns in Hastings, Jeff Porter over at MailBoxes Etc., the librarians at the Grinton I. Will Library in Yonkers and the Ardsley Library—they were all responsible for the general maintenance of the book. Debbie Cronin and Noreen Mulholland—they took charge of the details of my daily life so that I could manage to write a book. Al and Cathy Cattabiani, Bob and Amy Sommer, Wendy Handler, Doreen Weisenhaus, Esther Fein, Sam Verhovek, Mimi Swartz, Todd Kessler, Debra Karl, Barbara Laing, Susan Chira, Lisa Wolfe — they were responsible for the general maintenance of *me,* a huge job, particularly on those days when I'm certain I don't know how to write. A belated thank-you to Diane Asadorian — because I promised.

And then there were those who somehow managed to take care of me and the book. Jim Silberman, whose insight and sharp intelligence kept me on course during the first five years of this marathon. Sarah Burnes, whose energy, friendship, and gift with an editing pencil got me through the final sprint. Mike Mattil, who is part copyeditor, part fact checker, and part poet, and who smoothed the words as he smoothed the way. And Kathy Robbins and her dynamic, dedicated crew, who were there to cheer and to advise at every point along the way.

Any six-year project takes a toll on those around you, and I hereby send an apology, a thank-you, and a lot of love to Mike and Janet Belkin, Noemi and Alan Gelb, Gary and Masha Belkin, Kira Belkin and Saul Fishman, and Dana and Alan Safran, all of whom became accustomed to my disappearing acts during family visits and vacations.

Most of all, I owe more than I can say to the three people to whom this book is dedicated. My husband, Bruce, and my sons, Evan and Alex, are the reason for everything. They are my heroes. They are my home.